PRAISE FOR THIS REMARKABLE BOOK!

"As a leader of a firm involved with the governance and strategic oversight of multi-billion dollar organizations and portfolios, we find the principles and techniques in this book incredibly valuable in advancing the thinking of executive teams and boards. It has a direct effect on the impact our organizations have. Leaders and managers of any organization can benefit from the wisdom and pragmatic advice which this book delivers so effectively."

—Mike Mohr,
founder and CEO, Comprehensive Financial Management LLC

"The brilliant and innovative tools in this book have had a profound effect on the way we in the Playfair organization run our meetings. Many of the Playfair facilitators who have been trained in the models presented here have achieved fabulous results with their clients, helping their interactions come alive with fun, originality and innovation. Highly recommended!"

—Matt Weinstein,
founder, Playfair Inc, and author, *Managing To Have Fun*

"In the field of international development, managing participatory decision-making among people from diverse backgrounds and cultures is a necessity not an option. Our organization employs a staff of several thousand who touch the lives of hundreds of millions of people living in poverty, in developing nations across the globe. As we build our capacity to convene and facilitate multi-stakeholder processes, we have found Sam Kaner's book and his teachings to be immensely beneficial. I strongly recommend *Facilitator's Guide to Participatory Decision-Making* to anyone who wants a deeper appreciation of the skills required to build sustainable agreements."

—Jamie Watts,
Institutional Learning and Change, Bioversity International,
Consultative Group for International Agricultural Research,
Rome, Italy

"Sam Kaner is one of the world's leading experts on collaboration. His grasp of the challenges and dilemmas of collaboration is superb, as are his models and methods for facilitating complex processes. The second edition of this widely-used book reflects his accumulated wisdom and teachings. Clearly written and wonderfully illlustrated, this book makes difficult issues understandable and provides sound, practical guidance."

—Sandy Schuman, editor, *Creating a Culture of Collaboration* and founding editor, *Group Facilitation: A Research and Applications Journal*

"Facilitator's Guide to Participatory Decision-Making is an outstanding resource for tackling complex community and business challenges. We have used it for strategic planning in our nationally recognized child welfare programs and in our innovative programs to end homelessness. The second edition adds many helpful process management tools, and the new material on difficult dynamics is brilliant. I keep a copy on my desk for easy reference."

—Roxane White, CEO, Denver Department of Human Services

"When I first heard about participatory decision-making, my reaction was that it sounded like a nice idea but I didn't see its relevance for my role as a leader and CEO. After seeing Sam Kaner and his colleagues facilitate so effectively in many different high-stake contexts, I have completely changed my mind. I now recognize that a highly participatory approach is often the most effective way to develop and drive strategy, particularly when dealing with complex problems with highly diverse participants.

Reading *Facilitator's Guide* was an 'aha' experience for me; it described the group dynamics that had previously been mysterious, and it showed me how to work with them effectively. Kaner's decision-making procedures are the best I've ever seen. At Goodwill, we use them all the time. The new edition gives us several more valuable tools to be effective at making decisions. For anyone who values collaboration and wants to put its guiding principles into practice, the book is a must-read!"

—Deborah Alvarez-Rodriguez, president and CEO, Goodwill Industries of San Francisco, San Mateo and Marin Counties

"In my opinion, *Facilitator's Guide to Participatory Decision-Making* is the best book on collaboration ever written. I say this as someone who has been a CEO or executive director for more than 20 years. During that time I have worked with countless facilitators and organization development consultants. For depth of impact and overall effectiveness, Sam Kaner and his colleagues are top-of-the-line. This book is loaded with the tools and guiding principles that make Sam's work so compelling."

—Diane Flannery, founding CEO, Juma Ventures, and director, Global Center for Children and Families, UCLA, Semel Institute

"Sam Kaner and his team have helped me create a culture of collaboration in science. This is no easy task! Twenty-five years ago I started with nothing. Now my organization has the potential to make a large impact by discovering causes of the most devastating diseases that affect children. Sam's superb skills in strategic thinking and group facilitation, and his deep expertise in organization design and systems change have been essential for our success. In *Facilitator's Guide to Participatory Decision-Making,* Sam and his team translate their own learnings from many different kinds of work environments into concrete techniques that will benefit business, government and non-profits alike."

— John Harris,
founder and CEO, California Birth Defects Monitoring Program, California Department of Health Services

"*Facilitator's Guide* gives readers tools and insights to enable effective participatory action and the potential to achieve strong principled results and positive social change."

— Michael Doyle, author, *How to Make Meetings Work*

"I am a longtime client and colleague of Community At Work. They are extraordinarily talented at facilitating effective teams and teaching others to do the same. Their consulting approach creates lasting solutions by promoting organizational health through collaborative working relationships. *Facilitator's Guide* reveals and explains many of their most compelling methods and practices."

—Ed Pierce, founder and CEO, Leadership Quality Inc.

"*Facilitator's Guide* takes the mystery and fear out of facilitating groups and provides useful tools for anyone working with groups. The materials are clear. The graphics are first rate. And complex issues are developed logically and with great care."

—Thomas Broitman, managing director,
Executive Education, PricewaterhouseCoopers, LLP

"This book is a must for anyone working with a team! It is loaded with new information, which will make your team facilitation and decision-making even better. It highlights key concepts underlying group process that are rarely defined in such a clear manner. And, at the same time, it provides easy-to-follow facilitation techniques to ensure group participation and convergence around decisions and ideas. This is a book that rarely stays on my shelf- I'm too busy using it as a reference. Truly a golden nugget in the vast pool of facilitation knowledge!"

—Tammy Adams, author, *Facilitating the Project Lifecycle*

"What a practical, sensible guide for helping groups work together in a realistic way! The graphics help you visualize how to manage many common – and puzzling – aspects of group behavior."

—Marvin Weisbord, consultant and author, *Productive Workplaces* and co-author, *Discovering Common Ground* and *Future Search*

"Marshall Medical Center is community based, and we have always valued a culture of participation. We frequently make inclusive decisions allowing buy-in to difficult actions we need to take as an organization. Using *Facilitator's Guide to Participatory Decision-Making* and working with Sarah Fisk has helped us to maintain and even increase participation while still making timely decisions. Rather than simply relying on Sarah, who is a true genius at facilitation, this book has allowed us to build our own capacity. We've learned how to convene multiple stakeholder teams, plan effectively, and make more sustainable decisions, thus maintaining our collaborative values as we grow to serve a wider community. I highly recommend this book."

—James Whipple, CEO,
Marshall Medical Center, El Dorado County, California

JB JOSSEY-BASS

Facilitator's Guide to Participatory Decision-Making

Second Edition

Sam Kaner
with
Lenny Lind, Catherine Toldi,
Sarah Fisk, and Duane Berger

Foreword by Michael Doyle

John Wiley & Sons, Inc.

Published by Jossey-Bass
A Wiley Imprint
989 Market Street, San Francisco, CA 94103-1741 www.josseybass.com

Jossey-Bass books and products are available through most bookstores. To contact Jossey-Bass directly call our Customer Care Department within the U.S. at 800-956-7739, outside the U.S. at 317-572-3986, or fax 317-572-4002.

Jossey-Bass also publishes its books in a variety of electronic formats. Some content that appears in print may not be available in electronic books.

Library of Congress Cataloging-in-Publication Data

Kaner, Sam.
    Facilitator's guide to participatory decision-making / Sam Kaner with Lenny Lind . . . [et.al.].
        p. cm.
    Includes bibliographical references and index.
    ISBN-13: 978-0-7879-8266-9 (cloth)
1. Group decision-making —Handbooks, manuals, etc. 2. Consensus (Social Sciences) —Handbooks, manuals, etc. 3. Management–Employee participation—Handbooks, manuals, etc. I. Lind, Lenny II. Title.
    HD30.23.K2753 2007
    658.4 ' 036–dc22

                                                                2006037961

Printed in the United States of America
SECOND EDITION
PB Printing   10 9 8 7

Cover art by Karen Kerney.
Book design by Lenny Lind/CoVision and Sam Kaner.

THE JOSSEY-BASS

BUSINESS & MANAGEMENT SERIES

DEDICATION

This book is dedicated to Michael Doyle and David Straus,

who found the language, the distinctions, and the methods to bring inclusive, participatory values into the mainstream of American management practices

and who, through their own continuing efforts and those of their students and grandstudents and great-grandstudents, may yet inspire humanity to use collaborative technology for finding sustainable, nonviolent solutions to the world's toughest problems.

CONTENTS

I see group facilitation as a whole constellation of ingredients: a deep belief in the wisdom and creativity of people; a search for synergy and overlapping goals; the ability to listen openly and actively; a working knowledge of group dynamics; a deep belief in the inherent power of groups and teams; a respect for individuals and their points of view; patience and a high tolerance for ambiguity to let a decision evolve and gel; strong interpersonal and collaborative problem-solving skills; an understanding of thinking processes; and a flexible versus a lock-step approach to resolving issues and making decisions.

Facilitative behaviors and skills are essential for anyone who wants to work collaboratively in groups and organizations today. Facilitative skills honor, enhance, and focus the wisdom and knowledge that lay dormant in most groups. These skills are essential to healthy organizations, esprit de corps, fair and lasting agreements, and to easily implement actions and plans.

Sam Kaner and the team from Community At Work have been developing and articulating these tools to further democratic action and to enable people from all walks of life to work together in more constructive and productive ways. The *Facilitator's Guide to Participatory Decision-Making* will give readers additional tools and insights to enable effective, participatory action and the potential to achieve strong, principled results and positive social change. Anyone wanting to increase their understanding of group dynamics and improve their skill at making groups work more effectively will benefit from this valuable book.

The Purpose of Group Facilitation

Those who work with and lead organizations today have learned two lasting lessons in the last twenty-five years of concerted action research in this field of organization development and change. Lesson one: if people don't participate in and "own" the solution to the problems or agree to the decision, implementation will be half-hearted at best, probably misunderstood, and, more likely than not, will fail.

The second lesson is that the key differentiating factor in the success of an organization is not just the products and services, not just its technology or market share, but the organization's ability to elicit, harness, and focus the vast intellectual capital and goodwill resident in their members, employees, and stakeholders. When that intellectual capital and goodwill get energized and focused, the organization becomes a powerful force for positive change in today's business and societal environments. Applying these two lessons has become a key element of what we have begun to think of as *the learning organization.*

How do leaders and their organizations apply these two lessons? By creating psychologically safe and involving group environments where people can identify and solve problems, plan together, make collaborative decisions, resolve their own conflicts, trouble-shoot, and self-manage as responsible adults. Facilitation enables the organization's teams, groups and meetings to be much more productive. And the side benefits of facilitated or self-facilitated groups are terrific: a sense of empowerment, a deepening of personal commitment to decisions and plans, increased organizational loyalty, and the building of esprit de corps.

Nowhere are these two lessons put more into practice than in groups. The world meets a lot. The statistics are staggering. There are over 25 million meetings every day in the United States and over 85 million worldwide. Making both our work groups and civic groups work much more effectively is a lifelong challenge as rich as the personalities that people them. Thus, what I call "group literacy" – an awareness of and strong skills in group dynamics, meeting facilitation and consensus building tools like the ones in this book – is essential to increasing the effectiveness of group meetings. They enable groups to work smarter, harder, deeper, and faster. These tools help build healthier groups, organizations, and communities.

Facilitative mind-sets, behaviors, and tools are some of the essential ingredients of high-commitment/high-performance organizations. They are critical to making real what we've come to think of as *the learning organization.* These skills and behaviors are aligned with people's higher selves. People naturally want to learn them in order to increase their own personal effectiveness in groups and in their families as well as to increase the effectiveness of groups themselves.

A Partial History of Group Facilitation

The concept of facilitation and facilitators is as old as the tribes. Alaskan natives report of this kind of role in ancient times. As a society we're starting to come full circle – from the circle of the tribe around the fire, to the pyramidal structures of the last 3,000 years, back to the ecology of the circle, flat pyramids, and networks of today's organizations. The philosophy, mind-set, and skills of facilitation have much in common with the approaches used by Quakers, Gandhi, Martin Luther King, Jr., and people in nonviolence movements over the centuries. More recently these include the civil rights movement, women's consciousness-raising groups, some parts of the environmental movement, and citizen involvement groups that started in the 1960s and 1970s.

Meeting facilitation started to appear as a formal process in the late 1960s and early 1970s and had become widespread by the late 1980s. Its proponents advocated it as a tool to assist people to become the architects of their own future. It evolved from the role of *learning facilitators* that emerged in the early 1960s. In learning or encounter groups, the facilitator's focus was on building awareness and enabling learning. These *learning/ awareness facilitators* played key roles in the nascent human potential movement and the women's consciousness-raising movement and continue to do so in today's version of lifelong learning situations where learning is seen as a dialogue rather than a rote process. Its pragmatic roots also include cognitive science, information processing theory, sociology, psychology, community organizing, arbitration and mediation principles, and experience.

Task-oriented group facilitation evolved out of the societal milieu of the last thirty years, especially in industrial and information-rich societies where time is a key factor. We needed to find methods for people to work together more effectively. Quality circle groups, cross-functional task forces, and civic groups were the early big users and advocates of this methodology. Facilitation was an informal, flexible alternative to the constricting format of parliamentary procedure and *Robert's Rules of Order*. Group facilitation was also an approach that was proactive, solving conflicts before they arose, as well as one that could handle multiple constituencies. It was a viable alternative to mediation-style approaches. Once participants in a learning group or consciousness-raising group raised their awareness, they wanted to take action. There was an expressed need to put their new insights and knowledge to work – to take actions, solve problems, plan, and make group decisions. Thus the role of the task-oriented facilitator evolved to serve these needs as well as the new approaches to organizational change and renewal that were developing in the early 1970s.

As two of the cofounders of meeting facilitation, David Straus and I were interested in giving people tools to architect their own more powerful futures. That meant giving them frameworks and tools to make the groups they worked and lived with much more effective, powerful, and productive. We saw group facilitation as both a social contract and a new, content neutral role – a more formalized third party role in groups. We articulated the difference and power between "content" and "process" neutrality. Content neutrality means not taking a position on the issues at hand; not having a position or a stake in the outcome. Process neutrality means not advocating for certain kinds of processes such as brainstorming. We found that the power in the role of the facilitator was in becoming content neutral and a process advocate – advocating for fair, inclusive, and open processes that would balance participation and improve productivity while establishing a safe psychological space in which all group members could fully participate.

The role of the facilitator was designed to help minimize wheel spinning and dysfunctional dynamics and to enable groups to work together much more effectively. Other key pioneers of facilitation in the 1970s were Geoff Ball and David Sibbet with their seminal work in graphic recording and graphic facilitation. The core concepts and tools of group facilitation seemed to grow out of the tight-knit organization development and training community in the San Francisco Bay Area in the 1970s and '80s. It is great to see Sam Kaner and his colleagues continuing this rich legacy of theory and skill building.

Researchers at the Institute for the Future postulate that it takes about thirty years for social inventions to become widespread. Group facilitation is one such social invention. Over these last twenty-five years, facilitation skills have spread widely in the United States and are being spread around the world. And now, organizations are coming full circle to where facilitators once again are being utilized in *learning organizations* to facilitate dialogue processes that surface deep assumptions and mental models about how we view our world. These existing mental models are often the underlying sources of our conflict and dysfunction. By surfacing, examining, and changing them, we are able to work together in new ways to build new systems thinking models that assist groups in articulating their core values and beliefs. These new mental models serve as the foundation for organizations as they evolve, grow, and transform themselves to meet the challenges of the next century.

Expanding Definitions of Facilitation

These skills have become so useful in organizations that they have spread beyond the role of facilitator: to facilitative leaders; to self-facilitative groups and teams; to facilitative individuals and even facilitative, user-friendly procedures. Facilitation has become part of our everyday language. The Latin root of *facilitate* means "to enable, to make easy." *Facilitation* has evolved to have a number of meanings today.

A facilitative individual is an individual who is easy to work with, a team player, a person aware of individual and group dynamics. He or she assists colleagues to work together more effectively. A facilitative individual is a person who is skilled and knowledgeable in the interpersonal skills of communication, collaborative problem solving and planning, consensus building, and conflict resolution.

A facilitator is an individual who enables groups and organizations to work more effectively; to collaborate and achieve synergy. She or he is a "content-neutral" party who by not taking sides or expressing or advocating a point of view during the meeting, can advocate for fair, open, and inclusive procedures to accomplish the group's work. A facilitator can also be a learning or a dialogue guide to assist a group in thinking deeply about its assumptions, beliefs, and values and about its systemic processes and context.

A facilitative leader is a leader who is aware of group and organizational dynamics; a leader who creates organization-wide involvement processes that enable members of the organization to more fully utilize their potential and gifts in order to help the organization articulate and achieve its vision and goals, while at the same time actualizing its spoken values.

Facilitative leaders often understand the inherent dynamics between facilitating and leading and frequently utilize facilitators in their organizations.

A facilitative group (team, task force, committee, or board) is one in which facilitative mind-sets and behaviors are widely distributed among the members; a group that is minimally dysfunctional and works very well together; a group that is easy to join and works well with other groups and individuals.

I think you, the reader, will find this book very useful for your work in groups, whether you are a leader, a group member, or a facilitator. I especially recommend to you the insightful chapters on understanding group dynamics, facilitative listening, and the importance of values. Where this book also makes a real contribution is in the chapters on reaching closure and the gradients of an agreement. I enjoyed the learnings and insights I received from this book, and I am sure you will too.

Michael Doyle
San Francisco, California
March 1996

INTRODUCTION

The benefits of group decision-making have been widely publicized: better thinking, better "buy-in," better decisions all around. Yet the promise often fails to materialize. Many decisions made in groups are neither thoughtful nor inclusive; they are unimaginative, watered-down mediocrities.

Why is this so?

To a large degree, the answer is deeply rooted in prevailing cultural values that make it difficult for people to actually think in groups. Without even realizing it, many people make value judgments that inhibit spontaneity and deter others from saying what is really on their minds. For example, ideas that are expressed in clumsy ways, or in tentative terms, are often treated as if they were decidedly inferior to ideas that are presented with eloquent rhetorical flourish. Efforts at exploring complexities are discouraged, in favor of pithy judgments and firm-sounding conclusions. Making action plans – no matter how unrealistic they might be – is called "getting something done," while analyzing the underlying causes of a problem is called "going off on a tangent." Mixed messages abound: speak your mind but don't ask too many questions; be passionate but don't show your feelings; be productive but hurry up – and get it right the first time. All in all, conventional values do not promote effective thinking in groups.

Yet, when it's done well, group decision-making remains the best hope for solving difficult problems. There is no substitute for the wisdom that results from a successful integration of divergent points of view. Successful group decision-making requires a group to take advantage of the full range of experience and skills that reside in its membership. This means encouraging people to speak up. It means *inviting* difference, not fearing it. It means struggling to understand one another, especially in the face of the pressures and contradictions that typically drive group members to shut down. In short, it means operating from *participatory* values.

Participatory and conventional approaches to group decision-making yield entirely different group norms. Some of the differences are presented in the table on the next page.

PARTICIPATORY GROUPS	CONVENTIONAL GROUPS
Everyone participates, not just the vocal few.	The fastest thinkers and most articulate speakers get more air time.
People give each other room to think and get their thoughts all the way out.	People interrupt each other on a regular basis.
Opposing viewpoints are allowed to co-exist in the room.	Differences of opinion are treated as *conflict* that must either be stifled or "solved."
People draw each other out with supportive questions. "Is *this* what you mean?"	Questions are often perceived as challenges, as if the person being questioned has done something wrong.
Each member makes the effort to pay attention to the person speaking.	Unless the speaker *captivates* their attention, people space out, doodle or check the clock.
People are able to listen to each other's ideas because they know *their own ideas will also be heard.*	People have difficulty listening to each other's ideas because they're busy rehearsing what *they* want to say.
Each member speaks up on matters of controversy. Everyone knows where everyone stands.	Some members remain quiet on controversial matters. No one really knows where everyone stands.
Members can accurately represent each other's points of view – even when they don't agree with them.	People rarely give accurate representations of the opinions and reasoning of those whose opinions are at odds with their own.
People refrain from talking behind each other's backs.	Because they don't feel permission to be direct *during* the meeting, people talk behind each other's backs outside the meeting.
Even in the face of opposition from the person-in-charge, people are encouraged to stand up for their beliefs.	People with discordant, minority perspectives are commonly discouraged from speaking out.
A problem is not considered solved until everyone who will be affected by the solution understands the reasoning.	A problem is considered solved as soon as the fastest thinkers have reached an answer. Everyone else is then expected to "get on board" regardless of whether s/he understands the logic of the decision.
When people make an agreement, it is assumed that the decision still reflects a wide range of perspectives.	When people make an agreement, it is assumed that they are all thinking the exact same thing.

As the table implies, a shift from conventional values to participatory values is not a simple matter of saying, "Let's become a thinking team." It requires a change of mindset – a committed effort from a group to swim against the tide of prevailing values and assumptions.

When a group undertakes this challenge, its participants often benefit from the services a competent facilitator can provide for them. Left to their own devices, many groups would slip back into conventional habits. A facilitator, however, has the skills to help a group outgrow their old familiar patterns. Specifically, the facilitator encourages full participation, s/he promotes mutual understanding, s/he fosters inclusive solutions and s/he cultivates shared responsibility. These four functions (discussed in depth in chapter 3) are derived from the core values of participatory decision-making.

Putting Participatory Values Into Practice

The facilitator is the keeper of the flame, the carrier of the vision of what Michael Doyle described, in his foreword, as "a fair, inclusive and open process." This is why many facilitators help their groups to understand the dynamics and values of group decision-making. They recognize that it is empowering for participants to acquire common language and shared points of reference about their decision-making processes.

When a facilitator helps group members acquire process skills, s/he is acting in congruence with one of the core values of participatory decision-making: shared responsibility. This value played a prominent role in the design of *The Facilitator's Guide to Participatory Decision-Making*. It was written as a series of stand-alone pages that facilitators can photocopy and distribute to the members of their groups. For example, newly forming groups often benefit from reading and discussing chapters 1 and 2. These pages take less than fifteen minutes to read; they are entertaining; and they provide the basis for meaningful conversations about the dynamics and values of participatory decision-making. Within the guidelines of the policy statement on photocopying (see page 313), feel free to reproduce any part of this book that will strengthen your group's capacity for reaching sustainable agreements.

Facilitating Sustainable Agreements

The process of building a sustainable agreement has four stages: gathering diverse points of view; building a shared framework of understanding; developing inclusive solutions; and reaching closure. A competent facilitator knows how to move a group from start to finish through those stages. To do so, s/he needs a conceptual understanding of the dynamics and values of participatory decision-making (as provided in Part I of this book). S/he also needs a standard set of process management skills (as provided in Part II). And s/he needs a repertoire of sophisticated thinking tools, to propose and conduct stage-specific interventions (as provided in Part III and Part IV).

Fulfilling The Promise of Group Decision-Making

Those who practice participatory methods often come to see that facilitating a meeting is more than merely an occasion for solving a problem or creating a plan. It is also an opportunity to support profound personal learning, and it is an opportunity to strengthen the capacity and effectiveness of the group as a whole. These opportunities are only realizable – the promise of group decision-making can only be fulfilled – through the struggle and the satisfaction of putting participatory values into practice.

Part One

GROUNDING PRINCIPLES

1

THE DYNAMICS OF GROUP DECISION-MAKING

IDEALIZED AND REALISTIC MODELS OF
COLLABORATION IN GROUPS

- ◗ Misunderstandings About the
  Process of Group Decision-Making

- ◗ The Struggle to Integrate Diverse
  Perspectives

- ◗ The Diamond of Participatory
  Decision-Making

DYNAMICS OF GROUP DECISION-MAKING

INTRODUCTION

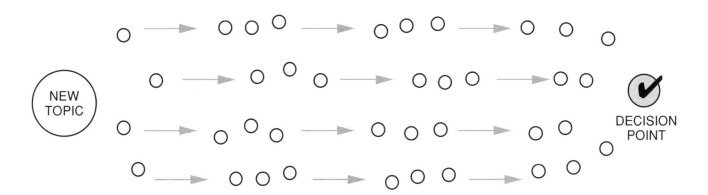

This picture portrays a hypothetical problem-solving discussion.

Each circle – O – represents one idea. Each line of circles-and-arrows represents one person's line of thought as it develops during the discussion.

As diagrammed, everyone appears to be tracking each other's ideas, everyone goes at the same pace, and everyone stays on board every step of the way.

A depressingly large percentage of people who work in groups believe this stuff. They think this picture realistically portrays a healthy, flowing decision-making process. And when their actual experience doesn't match up with this model, *they think it's because their own group is defective.*

If people actually behaved as the diagram suggests, group decision-making would be much less frustrating. Unfortunately, real-life groups don't operate this way.

DYNAMICS OF GROUP DECISION-MAKING

SAD BUT TRUE

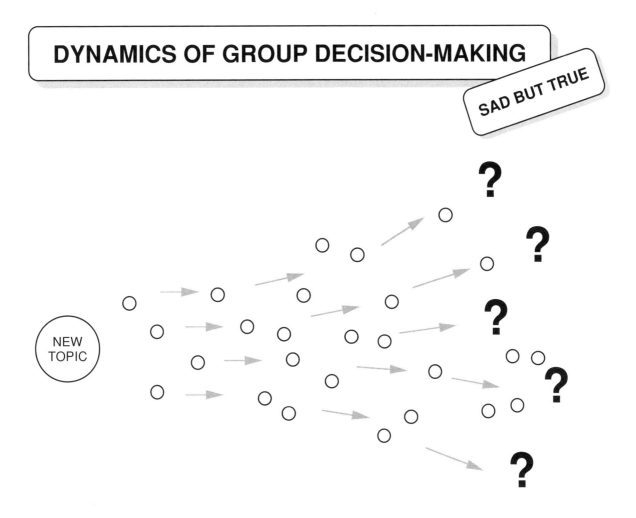

NEW TOPIC

Group members are humans. We *do* go on tangents. We *do* lose track of the central themes of a discussion. We *do* get attached to our ideas. Even when we're all making our best effort to "keep focused" and "stay on track," *we can't change the fact that we are individuals with diverging points of view.*

When a discussion loses focus or becomes confusing, it can appear to many people that the process is heading out of control. Yet this is not necessarily what's really going on. Sometimes what appears to be chaos is actually a prelude to creativity.

But how can we tell which is which? How do we recognize the difference between a degenerative, spinning-our-wheels version of group confusion and the dynamic, diversity-stretches-our-imagination version of group confusion?

DYNAMICS OF GROUP DECISION-MAKING

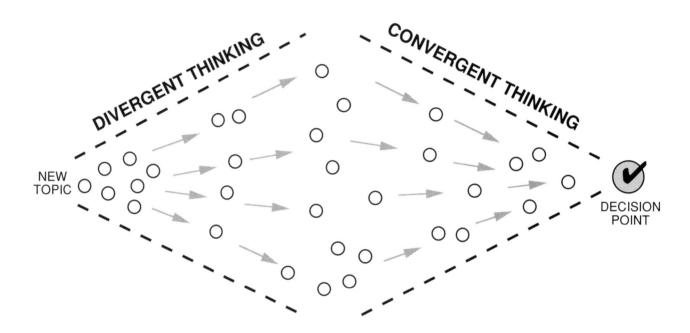

At times the individual members of a group need to express their own points of view. At other times, the same people want to narrow their differences and aim the discussion toward closure. These two sets of processes will be referred to as "divergent thinking" and "convergent thinking."

Here are four examples of the differences between the two thinking processes:

DIVERGENT THINKING		CONVERGENT THINKING
Generating a list of ideas	vs.	Sorting ideas into categories
Free-flowing open discussion	vs.	Summarizing key points
Seeking diverse points of view	vs.	Coming to agreement
Suspending judgment	vs.	Exercising judgment

DYNAMICS OF GROUP DECISION-MAKING

UNANSWERED QUESTIONS

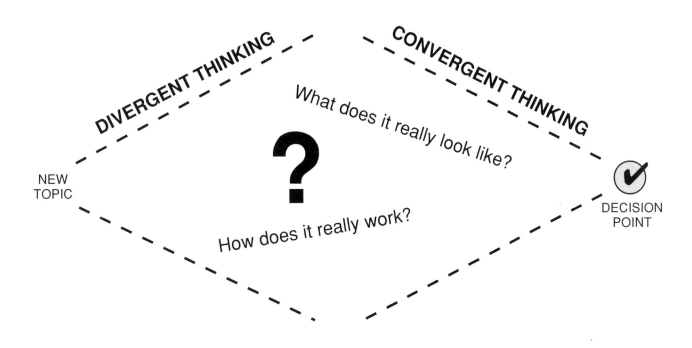

Some years ago, a large, well-known computer manufacturer developed a problem-solving model that was based on the principles of divergent thinking and convergent thinking.

This model was used by managers throughout the company. But it didn't always work so well. One project manager told us that it took their group *two years* to revise the travel expense-reimbursement forms.

Why would that happen? How does group decision-making *really* work?

To explore these questions in greater depth, the following pages present a series of stop-action snapshots of the process of group decision-making.

DYNAMICS OF GROUP DECISION-MAKING

DISCUSSION BEGINS

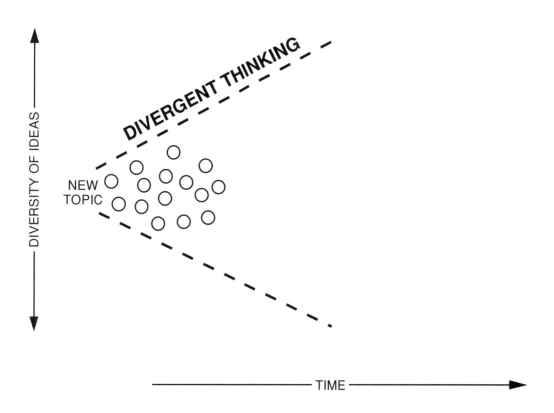

The early rounds of a discussion cover safe, familiar territory. People take positions that reflect conventional wisdom. They rehash well-worn disagreements, and they make proposals for obvious solutions. This is natural – the first ideas we express are the ones we've already thought about.

DYNAMICS OF GROUP DECISION-MAKING

QUICK DECISIONS

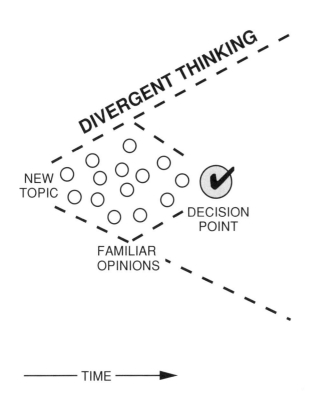

When a problem has an obvious solution, it makes sense to close the discussion quickly. Why waste time?

There's only one problem: most groups try to bring *every* discussion to closure this quickly.

DYNAMICS OF GROUP DECISION-MAKING

NO OBVIOUS SOLUTION

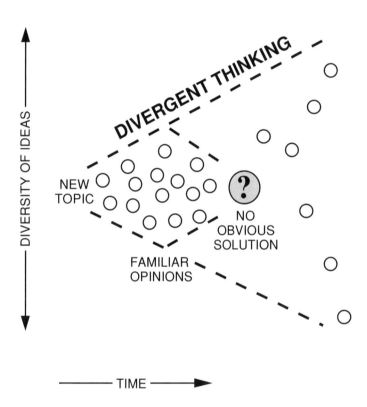

Some problems have *no* easy solutions. For example, how does an inner-city public school prevent campus violence? What steps should a business take to address the needs of an increasingly diverse workforce? Cases like these require a lot of thought; the issues are too complex to be solved with familiar opinions and conventional wisdom.

When a group of decision-makers has to wrestle with a difficult problem, they will not succeed in solving it until they *break out of the narrow band of familiar opinions* and explore a wider range of possibilities.

DYNAMICS OF GROUP DECISION-MAKING

THE CLASSIC DEAD END

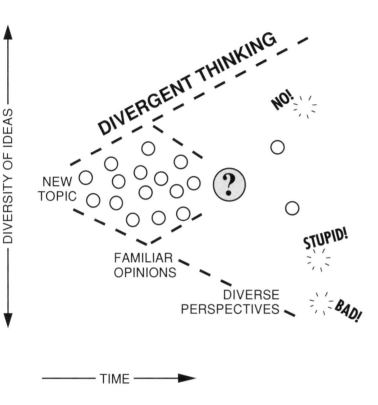

Unfortunately, most groups aren't very good at cultivating unfamiliar or unpopular opinions.

DYNAMICS OF GROUP DECISION-MAKING

EXPLORING POSSIBILITIES

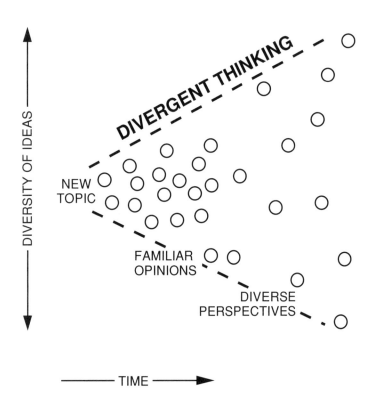

Now and then, when the stakes are sufficiently high and the stars are in proper alignment, a group can manage to overcome the tendency to criticize and inhibit its members. On such occasions, people tentatively begin to consider new perspectives. Some participants might take a risk and express controversial opinions. Others might offer ideas that aren't fully developed.

Since the goal is to find a new way of thinking about the problem, variety is obviously desirable . . . but the spread of opinions can become cumbersome and difficult to manage. Then what?

DYNAMICS OF GROUP DECISION-MAKING

IDEALIZED PROCESS

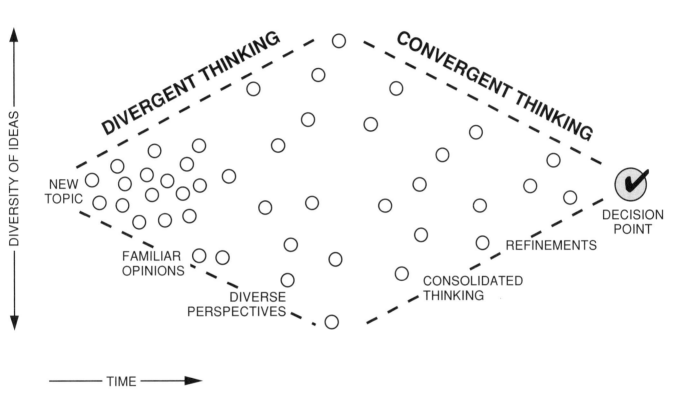

In theory, a group that has committed itself to thinking through a difficult problem would move forward in orderly, thoughtful steps. First, the group would generate and explore a diverse set of ideas. Next, they would consolidate the best thinking into a proposal. Then, they'd refine the proposal until they arrived at a final decision that nicely incorporated the breadth of their thinking.

Ah yes . . . if only *real life* worked that way.

DYNAMICS OF GROUP DECISION-MAKING

TYPICAL PROCESS

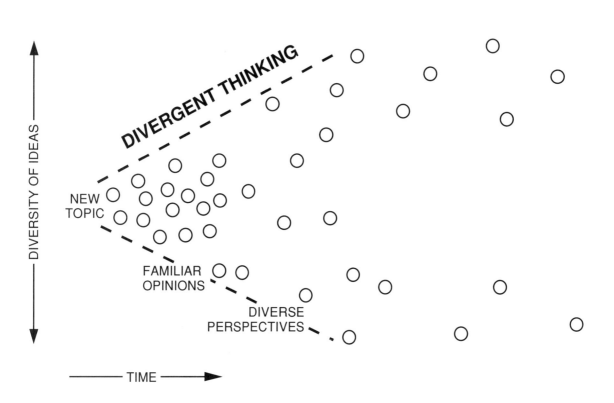

In practice, it's hard for people to shift from expressing their own opinions to understanding the opinions of others. And it's particularly challenging to do so when a wide diversity of perspectives are in play. In such cases people can get overloaded, disoriented, annoyed, impatient – or all of the above. Some people feel misunderstood and keep repeating themselves. Others push for closure. Sometimes several conversations develop; each occupies the attention of a few people but seems tangential or irrelevant to everyone else.

Thus, even the most sincere attempts to solve difficult problems can – and often do – dissipate into confusion.

DYNAMICS OF GROUP DECISION-MAKING

ATTEMPTED STEP-BACKS

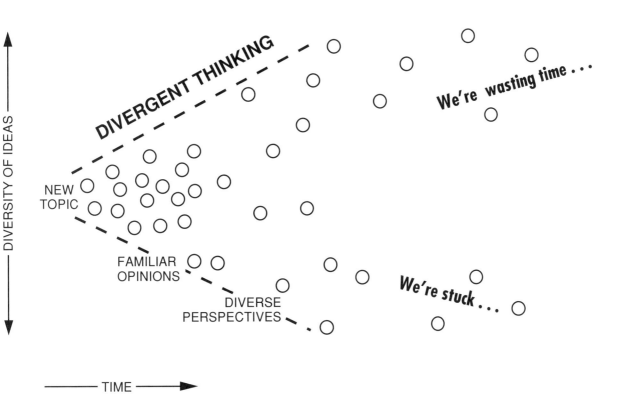

Sometimes one or more participants will attempt to step back from the content of the discussion and talk about the process. They might say things like, "I thought we all agreed to stick to the topic," or "We need better ground rules," or "Does anyone understand what's going on here?"

Groups rarely respond intelligently to this line of thought. More commonly, a process comment becomes merely one more voice in the wilderness – yet another poorly understood perspective that gets absorbed into the general confusion.

DYNAMICS OF GROUP DECISION-MAKING

POOR TIMING

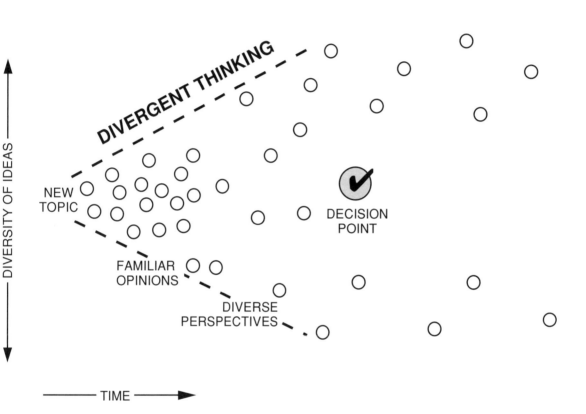

At this point in a process, the person in charge of a meeting can make the problem worse, if he or she attempts to alleviate frustration by announcing that s/he has made a decision. This is a common mistake.

The person-in-charge may believe that s/he has found a perfectly logical answer to the problem at hand, but this doesn't mean that everyone else will telepathically grasp the reasoning behind the decision. Some people may still be thinking along entirely different lines.

This is the exact situation in which the person-in-charge *appears* to have made the decision before the meeting began. This leads many people to feel deep distrust. *"Why did s/he tell me I'd have a say in this decision when s/he already knew what the outcome would be?"*

DYNAMICS OF GROUP DECISION-MAKING

WHAT'S MISSING?

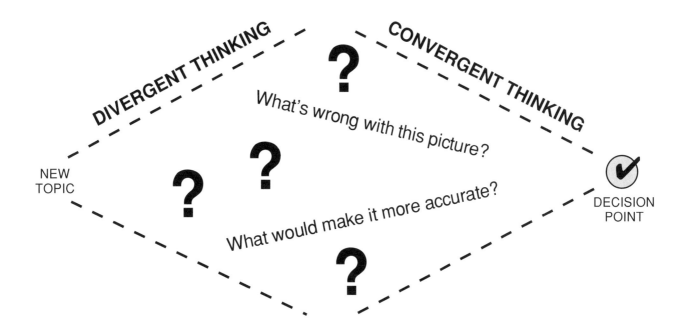

DIVERGENT THINKING

CONVERGENT THINKING

?

What's wrong with this picture?

? **?**

What would make it more accurate?

?

NEW TOPIC

DECISION POINT

Obviously, there's something wrong with the idealized model. Convergent thinking simply does not follow automatically from a divergent thinking process. What's missing?

DYNAMICS OF GROUP DECISION-MAKING

A REALISTIC MODEL

DIVERGENT THINKING

CONVERGENT THINKING

STRUGGLE
IN THE
SERVICE
OF
INTEGRATION

DECISION POINT

NEW TOPIC

FAMILIAR OPINIONS

DIVERSE PERSPECTIVES

TIME

A period of confusion and frustration is a natural part of group decision-making. Once a group crosses the line from airing familiar opinions to exploring diverse perspectives, group members have to struggle in order to integrate new and different ways of thinking with their own.

Community At Work © 2007

DYNAMICS OF GROUP DECISION-MAKING

INTRODUCING
THE GROAN ZONE

DIVERGENT THINKING

NEW
TOPIC

FAMILIAR
OPINIONS

DIVERSE
PERSPECTIVES

Groan Zone

CONVERGENT THINKING

DECISION
POINT

TIME

Struggling to understand a wide range of foreign or opposing ideas is not a pleasant experience. Group members can be repetitious, insensitive, defensive, short-tempered – and more! At such times most people don't have the slightest notion of what's happening. Sometimes the mere act of acknowledging the existence of the *Groan Zone* can be a significant step for a group to take.

Community At Work © 2007

DYNAMICS OF GROUP DECISION-MAKING

THE DIAMOND OF PARTICIPATORY DECISION-MAKING

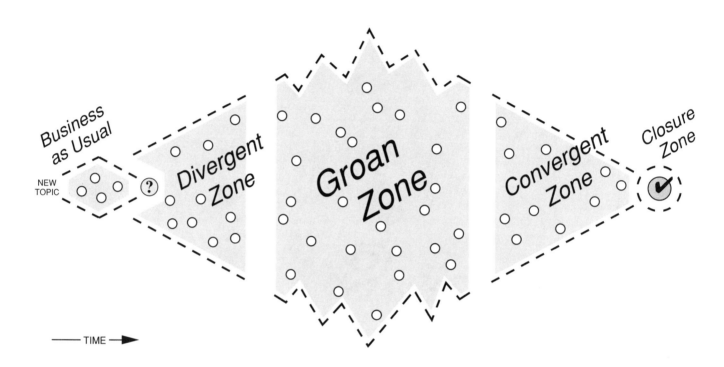

This is the *Diamond of Participatory Decision-Making*. It was developed by Sam Kaner with Lenny Lind, Catherine Toldi, Sarah Fisk and Duane Berger. Facilitators can use this model in many ways: as a diagnostic tool, a road map, or a teaching tool to provide their groups with shared language and shared points of reference.

Fundamentally, though, it was created to validate and legitimize the hidden aspects of everyday life in groups.

DYNAMICS OF GROUP DECISION-MAKING

THE POWER OF A REALISTIC MODEL

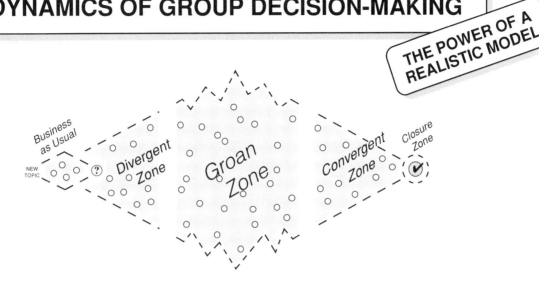

When people experience discomfort in the midst of a group decision-making process, they often take it as evidence that their group is dysfunctional. As their impatience increases, so does their disillusion with the process.

Many projects are abandoned prematurely for exactly this reason. In such cases, it's not that the goals were ill conceived; it's that the *Groan Zone* was perceived as an insurmountable impediment rather than as a normal part of the process.

This is truly a shame. Too many high-minded and well-funded efforts to resolve the world's toughest problems have foundered on the shoals of group dynamics.

So let's be clear-headed about this: misunderstanding and miscommunication are normal, natural aspects of participatory decision-making. The *Groan Zone* is a direct, inevitable consequence of the diversity that exists in any group.

Not only that, but the act of working through these misunderstandings is part of what must be done to lay the foundation for sustainable agreements. Without shared understanding, meaningful collaboration is impossible.

It is supremely important for people who work in groups to recognize this. Groups that can tolerate the stress of the *Groan Zone* are far more likely to discover common ground. And common ground, in turn, is the precondition for insightful, innovative co-thinking.

Understanding group dynamics is an indispensable core competency for anyone, whether facilitator, leader, or group member, who wants to help their group tap the enormous potential of participatory decision-making.

2

PARTICIPATORY VALUES

HOW FULL PARTICIPATION STRENGTHENS
INDIVIDUALS, DEVELOPS GROUPS AND
FOSTERS SUSTAINABLE AGREEMENTS

- ▶ The Four Participatory Values
- ▶ How Participatory Values Affect
  People and Their Work
- ▶ Full Participation
- ▶ Mutual Understanding
- ▶ Inclusive Solutions
- ▶ Shared Responsibility
- ▶ Benefits of Participatory Values

PARTICIPATORY DECISION-MAKING CORE VALUES

In a participatory group, all members are encouraged to speak up and say what's on their minds. This strengthens a group in several ways. Members become more courageous in raising difficult issues. They learn how to share their "first-draft" ideas. And they become more adept at discovering and acknowledging the diversity of opinions and backgrounds inherent in any group.

In order for a group to reach a sustainable agreement, the members need to understand and accept the legitimacy of one another's needs and goals. This basic recognition is what allows people to think from each other's point of view, which is the catalyst for developing innovative ideas that serve the interests of all parties.

Inclusive solutions are wise solutions. Their wisdom emerges from the integration of everybody's perspectives and needs. These are solutions whose range and vision are expanded to take advantage of the truth held not only by the quick, the articulate, the influential, and the powerful, but also of the truth held by those who are shy or disenfranchised or who think at a slower place. As the Quakers say, "Everybody has a piece of the truth."

In participatory groups, members recognize that they must be willing and able to implement the proposals they endorse, so they make every effort to give and receive input before final decisions are made. They also assume responsibility for designing and managing the thinking process that will result in a good decision. This contrasts sharply with the conventional assumption that everyone will be held accountable for the consequences of decisions made by a few key people.

HOW PARTICIPATORY VALUES CAN AFFECT GROUP DECISION-MAKING

FULL
PARTICIPATION

QUANTITY AND QUALITY OF PARTICIPATION DURING A BUSINESS-AS-USUAL DISCUSSION

In a typical business-as-usual discussion, self-expression is highly constrained. People tend to keep risky opinions to themselves. The most highly regarded comments are those that are the clearest, the smartest, the most well polished. In business-as-usual discussions, thinking out loud is treated with impatience; people get annoyed if the speaker's remarks are vague or poorly stated. This induces self-censorship, and reduces the quantity and quality of participation overall. A few people end up doing almost all the talking – and in many groups, those few people just keep repeating themselves and repeating themselves.

FULL PARTICIPATION DURING A PARTICIPATORY DECISION-MAKING PROCESS

Participatory decision-making groups go through a business-as-usual phase too. If familiar opinions lead to a workable solution, then the group can reach a decision quickly. But when a business-as-usual discussion does *not* produce a workable solution, a participatory group will open up the process and encourage more divergent thinking. What does this look like in action? It looks like people permitting themselves to state half-formed thoughts that express unconventional – but perhaps valuable – perspectives. It looks like people taking risks to surface controversial issues. It looks like people making suggestions "from left field" that stimulate their peers to think new thoughts. And it also looks like a roomful of people *encouraging each other* to do all these things.

HOW PARTICIPATORY VALUES
CAN AFFECT GROUP DECISION-MAKING

MUTUAL
UNDERSTANDING

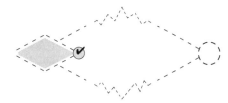

EXTENT OF MUTUAL UNDERSTANDING
DURING A BUSINESS-AS-USUAL DISCUSSION

In a business-as-usual discussion, persuasion is much more common than mutual understanding. The views of the "other side" are dissected point by point for the purpose of refuting them. Little effort, if any, is put into discovering the deeper reasons people believe what they do. Even when it appears unlikely that persuasion will change anyone's mind, participants continue to press home their points – making it appear as though the pleasures of rhetoric were the true purpose of continuing the discussion. Most participants tend to stop listening to each other, except to prepare for a rebuttal.

EXTENT OF MUTUAL UNDERSTANDING DURING
A PARTICIPATORY DECISION-MAKING PROCESS

Building a shared framework of understanding means taking the time to understand everyone's perspective in order to find the best idea. To build that framework, participants spend time and effort questioning each other, getting to know one another, learning from each other. They put themselves in each other's shoes. The process is laced with intermittent discomfort: some periods are tense, some are stifling. But participants keep plugging away. Over time, many people gain insight into their own positions. They may discover that their own thinking is out-of-date or misinformed or driven by inaccurate stereotypes. And by struggling to acquire such insights, members may discover something else about one another: that they truly do care about achieving a mutual goal.

HOW PARTICIPATORY VALUES CAN AFFECT GROUP DECISION-MAKING

INCLUSIVE SOLUTIONS

SOLUTIONS RESULTING FROM A BUSINESS-AS-USUAL DISCUSSION

Business-as-usual discussions seldom result in inclusive solutions. More commonly, people quickly form opinions and take sides. Everyone expects that one side will get what they want and the other side won't. Disputes, they assume, will be resolved by the person who has the most authority. Some groups settle their differences by majority vote, but the effect is the same. Expediency rather than innovation or sustainability is the driver of such solutions. When the implementation is easy, or when the stakes are low, expedient solutions are perfectly good – but not when the stakes are high, or creativity is required, or broad-based commitment is needed.

SOLUTIONS RESULTING FROM A PARTICIPATORY DECISION-MAKING PROCESS

Inclusive solutions are not compromises; they work for everyone who holds a stake in the outcome. Typically, an inclusive solution involves the discovery of an entirely new option. For instance, an unexpected partnership might be forged between former competitors. Or a group may invent a nontraditional alternative to a procedure that had previously "always been done that way." Several real-life case examples of inclusive solutions are presented in Chapter 16. Inclusive solutions are usually not obvious – they *emerge* in the course of the group's persistence. As participants learn more about each other's perspectives, they become progressively more able to integrate their own goals and needs with those of the other participants. This leads to innovative, original thinking.

HOW PARTICIPATORY VALUES CAN AFFECT GROUP DECISION-MAKING

SHARED RESPONSIBILITY

THE ENACTMENT OF RESPONSIBILITY DURING A BUSINESS-AS-USUAL DISCUSSION

In business-as-usual-discussions, groups rely on the authority of their leaders and their experts. The person-in-charge assumes responsibility for defining goals, setting priorities, defining problems, establishing success criteria, and arriving at conclusions. Participants with the most expertise are expected to distill relevant data, provide analysis, and make recommendations. Furthermore, the person-in-charge is expected to run the meeting, monitor the progress of each topic, enforce time boundaries, referee disputes, and generally take responsibility for all aspects of process management.

SHARED RESPONSIBILITY DURING A PARTICIPATORY DECISION-MAKING PROCESS

In order for an agreement to be sustainable, it needs everyone's support. Understanding this principle leads everyone to take personal responsibility for making sure they are satisfied with the proposed course of action. Every member of a group, in other words, recognizes that he or she is an owner of the outcome. Thus, people raise whatever issues they consider to be important. And everyone is expected to voice concerns if they have them, even when doing so could delay the group from reaching a decision. Moreover, the commitment to share responsibility is evident throughout the process: in the design of the agenda, in the willingness to discuss and co-create the procedures they will follow and in the overall expectation that everyone will accept and take responsibility for making their meetings work. In summary, participants are expected to take responsibility for both the content and the process of making decisions together.

THE BENEFITS OF PARTICIPATORY VALUES

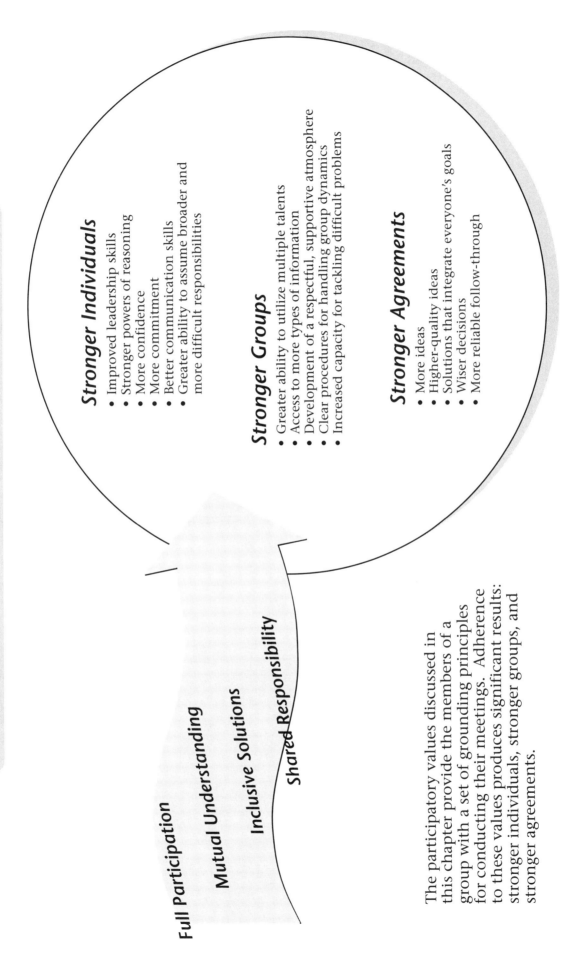

Full Participation

Mutual Understanding

Inclusive Solutions

Shared Responsibility

Stronger Individuals

- Improved leadership skills
- Stronger powers of reasoning
- More confidence
- More commitment
- Better communication skills
- Greater ability to assume broader and more difficult responsibilities

Stronger Groups

- Greater ability to utilize multiple talents
- Access to more types of information
- Development of a respectful, supportive atmosphere
- Clear procedures for handling group dynamics
- Increased capacity for tackling difficult problems

Stronger Agreements

- More ideas
- Higher-quality ideas
- Solutions that integrate everyone's goals
- Wiser decisions
- More reliable follow-through

The participatory values discussed in this chapter provide the members of a group with a set of grounding principles for conducting their meetings. Adherence to these values produces significant results: stronger individuals, stronger groups, and stronger agreements.

Community At Work © 2007

3

INTRODUCTION TO THE ROLE OF FACILITATOR

THE EXPERTISE THAT SUPPORTS
A GROUP TO DO ITS BEST THINKING

- ◗ **When Is a Facilitator Needed?**

- ◗ **First Function:**
  Encourage Full Participation

- ◗ **Second Function:**
  Promote Mutual Understanding

- ◗ **Third Function:**
  Foster Inclusive Solutions

- ◗ **Fourth Function:**
  Cultivate Shared Responsibilty

THE ROLE OF FACILITATOR

WHAT IS A FACILITATOR, AND WHY HAVE ONE?

The facilitator's job is to *support everyone to do their best thinking.* To do this, the facilitator encourages full participation, promotes mutual understanding and cultivates shared responsibility. By supporting everyone to do their best thinking, a facilitator enables group members to search for inclusive solutions and build sustainable agreements.

How much value does this have to a group? The answer depends on the group's goals. Suppose a group holds meetings specifically for the purpose of trading information through announcements and reports. Do the members of that group need much help to do their best thinking? Not really. Likewise, suppose another group has monthly business-as-usual meetings to make routine decisions about standard problems, like task assignments or scheduling. Those kinds of issues could be handled for years without any facilitation whatsoever.

But what about more difficult challenges? For example, suppose a group's goal is to reduce violence on a high school campus. The participants are parents, teachers, administrators, church leaders, and union officials. This group will quickly find out how difficult it is to conduct a sustained, thoughtful discussion. Despite a common goal, their frames of reference are very different. What seems to a parent like an obvious solution may seem simplistic to an administrator. What seems reasonable to an administrator may seem cowardly to a teacher. What seems responsible to a teacher may place too many demands on a parent. What is the chance that this group will survive the *Groan Zone?*

Groups face difficult challenges all the time. Long-term planning is hard to do well. So is restructuring or reengineering. Here are some other tough issues groups face: clarifying roles and responsibilities for individuals involved in projects that have not been done before; resolving high-stakes conflicts; introducing new technology into a workplace. In situations like these, a group is likely to make wiser, more lasting decisions if they enlist a facilitator who knows how to support them to do their best thinking.

Most individuals working in groups *do not know how* to solve tough problems on their own. They do not know how to build a shared framework of understanding – they seldom even recognize its significance. They dread conflict and discomfort, and they try hard to avoid it. Yet by avoiding the struggle to integrate one another's perspectives, the members of such groups greatly diminish their own potential to be effective. They *need* a facilitator.

THE ROLE OF FACILITATOR

FIRST FUNCTION

THE FACILITATOR ENCOURAGES FULL PARTICIPATION

A Fundamental Problem: Self-Censorship

Inherent in group decision-making is the basic problem that people don't say what they are really thinking. It's hard to take risks, and it's particularly hard to do so when the group's response is likely to be hostile or dismissive. Yet in so many groups, the norms are oppressive. Consider these comments:

- "Haven't we already covered that point?"
- "Let's keep it simple, please."
- "Hurry up – we're running out of time."
- "What does *that* have to do with anything?"
- "Impossible. Won't work. No way."

Statements like these are injunctions against thinking out loud in a group. They discourage people from saying what they're thinking. The message is: if you want to speak, be simple and polished, and be able to say something familiar enough or entertaining enough for the group to accept.

The injunctions against thinking in public run like an underground stream below the surface of a group's discussion. Without realizing it, most people constantly edit their thinking before they speak. Who wants his or her ideas criticized before they are fully formed? Who wants to be told, "We've already answered that question"? Who wants to make an effort to express a complex thought while others in the room are doodling or whispering? This type of treatment leaves many people feeling embarrassed or inadequate. *To protect themselves, people censor themselves.*

The Facilitator's Contribution

Imagine now that someone in the group understands this inherent difficulty and has taken responsibility for helping people overcome it. Imagine that this person has the skills and the temperament to draw people out and help everyone feel heard. Imagine this person knows how to make room for quiet members; how to reduce the incidence of premature criticism; how to support everyone to keep thinking instead of shutting down. If such a person is actually permitted to perform this role in a group, the quality of the group's participation will vastly improve.

THE ROLE OF FACILITATOR
SECOND FUNCTION

THE FACILITATOR PROMOTES MUTUAL UNDERSTANDING

A Fundamental Problem: Fixed Positions

A group cannot do its best thinking if the members don't understand one another. But most people find it difficult to detach from their fixed positions enough to actually listen to what others are saying. Instead, they get caught up in amplifying and defending their own perspectives.

Here's an example. A group of friends began exploring the possibility of forming a new business together. When the topic of money came up, biases emerged. One person wanted the profits divided equally. Another thought everyone should be paid on the basis of how much revenue they would generate. A third person believed the two visionaries should be paid more to make sure they would not leave. None of them were able to change their minds easily. Nor would it have been realistic to expect them to do so. Their opinions had been forming and developing for years.

And it gets worse! When people try to discuss their differences, they often misunderstand one another. Each person's life experiences are so individual, so singular; everyone has remarkably different views of the world. What people expect, what they assume, how they use language, and how they behave – all these are likely sources of mutual misunderstanding. What's more, when people attempt to clear up a misunderstanding, they usually want their *own* ideas understood *first*. They may not say so directly, but their behavior indicates, "I can't really focus on what you are saying until I feel that you have understood *my* point of view." This easily becomes a vicious cycle. No wonder it's hard for people to let go of fixed positions!

The Facilitator's Contribution

A facilitator helps the group realize that sustainable agreements are built on a foundation of mutual understanding. S/he helps members see that thinking from each other's points of view is invaluable.

Moreover, the facilitator accepts the *inevitability of misunderstanding*. S/he recognizes that misunderstandings are stressful for everyone involved. The facilitator knows that people in distress need support; they need to be treated respectfully. S/he knows it is essential to stay impartial, honor all points of view and keep listening, so that each and every group member has confidence that *someone* understands them.

THE ROLE OF FACILITATOR

THIRD FUNCTION

THE FACILITATOR FOSTERS INCLUSIVE SOLUTIONS

A Fundamental Problem: The Win/Lose Mentality

It's hard for most people to imagine that stakeholders with apparently irreconcilable differences might actually reach an agreement that benefits all parties. Most people are entrenched in a conventional mind-set for solving problems and resolving conflicts – namely: "It's either my way or your way." As a result, most problem-solving discussions degenerate into critiques, rationalizations, and sales jobs, as participants remain attached to their fixed positions and work to defend their own interests.

The Facilitator's Contribution

An experienced facilitator knows how to help a group search for innovative ideas that incorporate everyone's points of view. This can be a challenging task – the facilitator is often the only person in the room who has even considered the possibility that inclusive alternatives may exist.

To accomplish this goal, a facilitator draws from knowledge acquired by studying the theory and practice of collaborative problem solving. Thus s/he knows the steps it takes to build sustainable agreements:

- S/he knows how to help groups break free from restrictive business-as-usual discussions and engage in divergent thinking.

- S/he can help a group survive the *Groan Zone* as the members struggle to build a shared framework of understanding.

- S/he knows how to help a group formulate creative proposals that reflect the weaving together of several perspectives.

- S/he knows how to bring discussions to closure.

In short, the facilitator understands how to build sustainable agreements.

When a facilitator introduces a group to the values and methods that foster inclusive solutions, the impact is profound. Many people scoff at the very suggestion that a group can find meaningful solutions to difficult problems. As they discover the validity of this new way of thinking, they often become more hopeful about their group's potential effectiveness.

THE ROLE OF FACILITATOR

FOURTH FUNCTION

THE FACILITATOR CULTIVATES SHARED RESPONSIBILITY

A Fundamental Problem: Reliance on Authority

In group settings, many people defer to the group's leaders and experts – often without giving their deferential behavior a second thought.

It's easy to understand why. Leaders wield power. They control resources. They have access to privileged information. They are networked with others who hold power. Likewise, experts have the training, the knowledge, the connections, and the familiarity with key issues.

Furthermore, the choice to be passive often seems to make such good sense! For one thing, speaking truth to power can have adverse consequences. For another thing, it may not be worth the bother if "nothing I can say would matter anyway." And finally, if the expert knows more than the others, why not accept that person's judgment and follow his or her advice?

Terms like "empowerment," "enabling environment," and "self-managing teams" reflect a growing consensus that relying on authority is both costly and ineffectual. As Marvin Weisbord puts it, "People support what they help to create."* But even when a leader *wants* a group to take responsibility, the factors cited above can inhibit group members from breaking the pattern. In turn, this passivity induces the leaders and experts to do the work themselves. In this way, dependence on authority becomes a self-perpetuating cycle.

The Facilitator's Contribution

Creating a culture of shared responsibility requires serious effort. The group's leader has to endorse the value of shared responsibility, and both the leader and the members have to develop the procedures and acquire the skills to make participatory decision-making work.

The existence of a facilitator often makes the critical difference. This person is sometimes a coach, sometimes a teacher, sometimes a co-designer of systems and procedures, and sometimes a motivational speaker who inspires the group members to stand up and take risks.

In this sense a facilitator is the steward of a profound culture change. S/he helps the group evolve from business-as-usual deference and dependency to assertiveness, collaboration, and shared responsibility.

* M. Weisbord, *Productive Workplaces, Revisited* (San Francisco: Jossey-Bass/Pfiefer, 2004).

FACILITATOR'S GUIDE
TO PARTICIPATORY DECISION MAKING

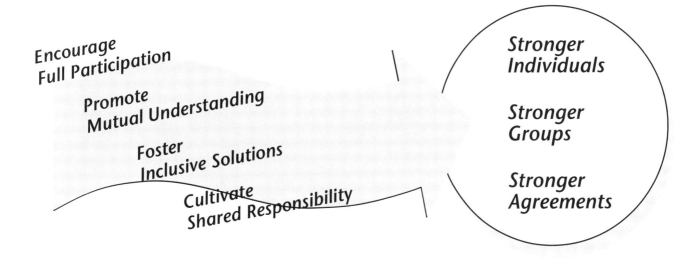

The facilitator's mission is to support everyone to do their best thinking.

This mission is enacted by the facilitator's four functions:

- encouraging full participation

- promoting mutual understanding

- fostering inclusive solutions

- cultivating shared responsibility

When a facilitator effectively performs these functions, the results are impressive. S/he strengthens the skills, awareness, and confidence of the individuals who work in that group; s/he strengthens the structure and capacity of the group as a whole; and s/he vastly increases the likelihood that the group will arrive at sustainable agreements.

Part Two

FACILITATOR FUNDAMENTALS

4

FACILITATIVE
LISTENING SKILLS

TECHNIQUES FOR HONORING
ALL POINTS OF VIEW

- ▶ Respecting Diverse Communication Styles
- ▶ Paraphrasing
- ▶ Drawing People Out
- ▶ Mirroring
- ▶ Gathering Ideas
- ▶ Stacking
- ▶ Tracking
- ▶ Encouraging
- ▶ Balancing
- ▶ Making Space for a Quiet Person
- ▶ Acknowledging Feelings
- ▶ Validating
- ▶ Empathizing
- ▶ Intentional Silence
- ▶ Linking
- ▶ Listening for Common Ground
- ▶ Listening with a Point of View
- ▶ Summarizing

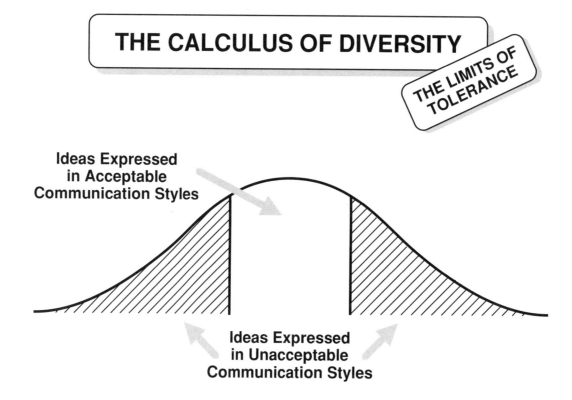

THE CALCULUS OF DIVERSITY

THE LIMITS OF TOLERANCE

Ideas Expressed in Acceptable Communication Styles

Ideas Expressed in Unacceptable Communication Styles

An idea that is expressed in an acceptable communication style will be taken more seriously by more people. Conversely, ideas that are presented poorly or offensively are harder for people to hear. Of the many ideas that are put forth in the course of a discussion, some gain quite a bit of attention while others disappear from awareness as if they had never been spoken. For example:

- Many people become antsy when a speaker is repetitious.

- Group members can be impatient with shy or nervous members who speak haltingly.

- Others may not want to listen to exaggerations, distortions, or unfounded pronouncements.

- Some people become overwhelmed when a speaker goes on a tangent and raises a point that seems unrelated to the subject.

- And some people are profoundly uncomfortable with anyone who shows too much emotion.

In any of these circumstances, some listeners will probably ignore the substance of the ideas being expressed, no matter how valuable those ideas might be.

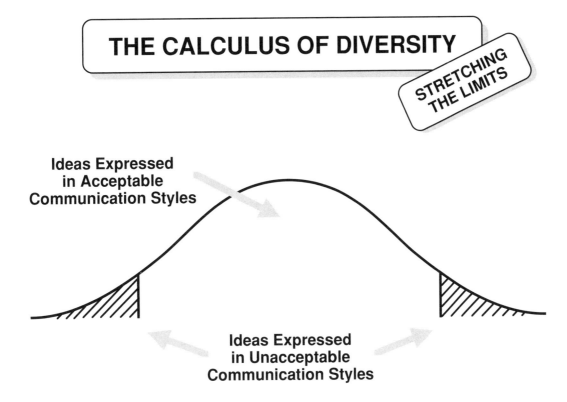

THE CALCULUS OF DIVERSITY

STRETCHING THE LIMITS

Ideas Expressed in Acceptable Communication Styles

Ideas Expressed in Unacceptable Communication Styles

Groups that tolerate diverse communication styles can utilize more of the ideas put forth by its members than groups who need those ideas to be expressed in an "acceptable fashion." By using good listening skills, a facilitator can be an excellent support to such groups. For example:

- When someone is being repetitious, a facilitator can use paraphrasing to help that person summarize his or her thinking.

- When someone is speaking haltingly, in awkward, broken sentences, a facilitator can help the speaker relax by drawing him or her out with open-ended, nondirective questions.

- When someone is exaggerating or distorting, a facilitator can validate the central point without quarreling over its accuracy.

- When someone goes off on a tangent, a facilitator can treat the speaker with full respect by asking the person to help everyone see how his or her point connects with the broader context.

- When someone expresses himself or herself with intense feeling, a facilitator can first acknowledge the emotion, then paraphrase the content of the thought to ensure that the speaker's point does not get lost amid the group's gut reactions to the feelings.

These situations demonstrate how important it is for a facilitator to listen skillfully and respectfully to *everyone*.

PARAPHRASING

WHY

- *Paraphrasing* is fundamental to active listening. It is the most straightforward way to demonstrate to a speaker that his or her thoughts were heard and understood.

- The power of *paraphrasing* is that it is nonjudgmental and, hence, validating. It enables people to feel that their ideas are respected and legitimate.

- *Paraphrasing* provides the speaker with a chance to hear how his or her ideas are being heard by others.

- *Paraphrasing* is especially useful on occasions when a speaker's statements are convoluted or confusing. At such times, it serves as a check for clarification, as in, "Is this what you mean?" followed by the paraphrase.

- In sum, *paraphrasing* is the tool of choice for supporting people to think out loud.

HOW

- In your own words, say what you think the speaker said.

- If the speaker's statement contains one or two sentences, use roughly the same number of words when you paraphrase.

- If the speaker's statement contains many sentences, summarize it.

- To strengthen the group's trust in your objectivity, occasionally preface your paraphrase with a comment like one of these:
  - "It sounds like you're saying . . ."
  - "Let me see if I'm understanding you . . ."
  - "Is this what you mean?"

- When you have completed the paraphrase, look for the speaker's reaction. Say something like, "Did I get it?" Verbally or nonverbally, the speaker will indicate whether s/he feels understood. If not, *keep asking for clarification until you understand what s/he meant.*

DRAWING PEOPLE OUT

WHY

- *Drawing people out* is the skill that supports people to clarify, develop, and refine their ideas.

- It sends the speaker this message: "I'm with you; I understand you so far. Now tell me a little more." This message allows people to express more of what they're thinking. It helps them go deeper into exploring what matters to them.

- *Drawing people out* is the tool of choice for handling two awkward circumstances:

  - When someone is having difficulty clarifying an idea.

  - When someone thinks s/he is being clear, but the thought is actually vague or confusing to the listeners.

- When deciding whether to draw someone out, ask yourself this question: "Do I think I understand the core of what s/he is trying to say?" If the answer is no, then draw the speaker out.

HOW

- The most basic technique of *drawing people out* is to paraphrase the speaker's statement, then ask open-ended, nondirective questions.

  Here are some examples:

  - "Can you say more about that?"

  - "What do you mean by . . .?"

  - "What's coming up for you now?"

  - "Can you give me an example?"

  - "How is that working for you?"

  - "What does this bring up for you?"

  - "What matters to you about that?"

  - "Tell me more."

  - "How so?"

- Here is a less common method that also works well. First, paraphrase the speaker's statement; then use *connectors* such as, "So . . ." or "And . . ." or "Because . . ." For example, "You're saying to wait six more weeks before we sign the contract, because . . ."

MIRRORING

WHY

- *Mirroring* is a highly structured, formal version of *paraphrasing,* in which the facilitator repeats the speaker's words verbatim.

- Some people experience *paraphrasing* as veiled criticism. For them, *mirroring* is evidence of the facilitator's neutrality.

- Newly formed groups and groups unfamiliar with using a facilitator often benefit from the trust-building effects of *mirroring.*

- *Mirroring* speeds up the tempo of a slow-moving discussion. Thus, it is the *tool of choice* when facilitating a brainstorming process.

- In general, the more a facilitator feels the need to establish neutrality, the more frequently he or she should *mirror* rather than paraphrase.

HOW

- If the speaker has said a single sentence, repeat it back verbatim.

- If the speaker has said more than one sentence, repeat back key words or phrases.

- In either case, *use the speaker's words, not your words.*

- The one exception is when the speaker says, "I." Then, change the pronoun to "you."

- Mirroring the speaker's words and mirroring the speaker's tone of voice are *two different things.* You want your tone of voice to remain warm and accepting, regardless of what the speaker's voice sounds like.

- Be yourself with your gestures and tone of voice; don't be wooden or phony. Remember, a key purpose of *mirroring* is building trust.

GATHERING IDEAS

WHY

- *Gathering* is the listening skill that helps participants build a list of ideas at a fast-moving pace.

- *Gathering* combines *mirroring* and *paraphrasing* – the reflective listening skills – with physical gestures. Taking a few steps to and fro, or making hand or arm motions, are physical gestures that serve as energy boosters. Such gestures help people stay engaged.

- When *gathering,* be sure to mirror more frequently than you paraphrase. This establishes a lively yet comfortable tempo that is easy for most participants to follow. Many people quickly move into a rhythm of expressing their ideas in short phrases – typically three to five words per idea. These phrases are much easier to record on flipcharts than long sentences.

HOW

- Effective *gathering* starts with a concise description of the task. For example, "For the next ten minutes, please evaluate this proposal by calling out pros and cons. First I'll ask for someone to call out a pro reaction. Then I'll ask for a con. And so on. We'll build both lists at the same time."

- If it's the group's first time listing ideas, spend a little time teaching them *suspended judgment*. Example: "For this next activity, I'd like everyone to feel free to express their ideas, even the offbeat or unpopular ones. So please let this be a time for generating ideas, not judging them. The discussion can come as soon as you finish making the list."

- Now have the group begin. As members call out their items, mirror or paraphrase whatever is said.

- Honor all points of view. If someone says something that sounds off the wall, just mirror it and keep moving.

STACKING

WHY	HOW

WHY

- *Stacking* is a procedure for helping people take turns when several people want to speak at once.

- *Stacking* lets everyone know that they are, in fact, going to have their turn to speak. So instead of competing for airtime, people are free to listen without distraction.

- In contrast, when people don't know when or even whether their turn will come, they can't help but vie for position. This leads to various expressions of impatience and disrespect, especially interruptions.

- Facilitators who do not stack have to pay attention to the waving of hands and other nonverbal messages that say, "I'd like to speak, please." Inevitably, some members are skipped or ignored. With *stacking,* a facilitator creates a sequence that includes all those who want to speak.

HOW

- *Stacking* is a four-step procedure. First, the facilitator asks those who want to speak to raise their hands. Second, s/he creates a speaking order by assigning a number to each person. Third, s/he calls on people when their turn to speak arrives. Fourth, after the final speaker, the facilitator asks if anyone else wants to speak. If so, the facilitator starts another stack. Here's a demonstration:

- Step 1. "Would all who want to speak, please raise your hands."

- Step 2. "Tyrone, you're first. Deb, you're second. James, you're third."

- Step 3. [*When Tyrone has finished*] "Who was second? Was it you, Deb? Okay, go ahead."

- Step 4. [*After the last person has spoken*] "Who'd like to speak now? Are there any more comments?" Then, start a new stack, and repeat Steps 2 through 4.

TRACKING

WHY

- *Tracking* means keeping track of the various lines of thought that are going on simultaneously within a single discussion.

- For example, suppose a group is discussing a plan to hire a new employee. Assume that two people are talking about roles and responsibilities. Two others are discussing financial implications. And two more are reviewing their experiences with the previous employee. In such cases, people need help keeping track of all that's going on, because they are focused primarily on clarifying their own ideas.

- People often act as though the particular issue that interests *them* is the one that *everyone* should focus on. *Tracking* makes it visible that several threads of the topic are being discussed. In so doing, it affirms that each thread is equally valid.

HOW

- *Tracking* is a four-step process. First, the facilitator indicates that s/he is going to step back and summarize the discussion so far. Second, s/he names the different conversations that have been in play. Third, s/he checks for accuracy with the group. Fourth, s/he now invites the group to resume discussion.

- Step 1. "It seems that there are three conversations going on right now. I want to make sure I'm tracking them."

- Step 2. "One conversation appears to be about roles and responsibilities. Another has to do with finances. And a third is about what you've learned by working with the last person who held this job."

- Step 3. "Am I getting it right?" Often someone will say, "No, you missed mine!" If so, don't argue or explain; just validate the comment and move on.

- Step 4. "Any more comments?" Now build a new stack.

ENCOURAGING

WHY

- *Encouraging* is the art of creating an opening for people to participate, without putting any one individual on the spot.

- There are times in a meeting when some folks may appear to be "sitting back" or "letting others do all the work." This doesn't necessarily mean that they are lazy or irresponsible. Instead, it may be that they are not feeling engaged by the discussion. With a little encouragement to participate, they often discover an aspect of the topic that holds meaning for them.

- *Encouraging* is especially helpful during the early stage of a discussion, while members are still warming up. As people get more engaged, they don't need as much encouragement to participate.

HOW

- Here are some examples of the technique of *encouraging:*

  - "Who else has an idea?"

  - "Is there a student's perspective on this issue?"

  - "Does anyone have a war story you're willing to share?"

  - "What do others think?"

  - "Jim just offered us an idea that he called a 'general principle.' Can anyone give us an example of this principle in action?"

  - "Are there comments from anyone who hasn't spoken for awhile?"

  - "What was said at table two?"

  - "Is this discussion raising questions for anyone?"

- A related technique is to begin by restating the objective of the discussion and then using *encouraging* to increase engagement:

  - "We've been looking for the root causes of this problem. Any other possibilities?"

BALANCING

WHY

- The direction of a discussion often follows the lead set by the first few people who speak on that topic. Using *balancing*, a facilitator helps a group broaden its discussion to include other perspectives that may not yet have been expressed.

- *Balancing* undercuts the common myth that silence indicates agreement. It provides welcome support to individuals who don't feel safe to express views that they perceive as minority positions.

- In addition to the support it provides to individuals, *balancing* also has a positive effect on the norms of the group. It sends the message, "It is acceptable for people to speak their mind, no matter what opinions they hold."

- When a group appears caught between two polizarized positions, *balancing* often reveals the presence of alternative positions.

HOW

- Here are some examples of *balancing* in action:

  - "Are there other ways of looking at this issue?"

  - "Does everyone else agree with this perspective?"

  - "Okay, we have heard where three people stand on this matter. Does anyone else have a different position?"

  - "Can anyone play devil's advocate for a few minutes?"

  - "Let's see how many people stand on each side of this issue. We're not making a decision, and I'm not asking you to vote. This is just an opinion poll to find out how much controversy we have in the room. Ready? How many people think it would be good if . . .?"

  - "So, we've heard the X point of view and the Y point of view. Is there a third way of looking at this?"

MAKING SPACE FOR A QUIET PERSON

WHY

- *Making space* sends the quiet person this message: "If you don't wish to talk now, that's fine. But if you *would* like to speak, here's an opportunity."

- Every group has some members who are highly verbal and others who speak less frequently. When a group has a fast-paced discussion style, quiet members and slower thinkers may have trouble getting a word in edgewise.

- Some people habitually keep out of the limelight because they are afraid of being perceived as rude or competitive. Others might hold back when they're new to a group and unsure of what's acceptable and what's not. Still others keep their thoughts to themselves because they're convinced their ideas aren't "as good as" those of others. In all of these cases, people benefit from a facilitator who makes space for them to participate.

HOW

- Keep an eye on the quiet members. Be on the lookout for body language or facial expressions that may indicate their desire to speak.

- Invite them to speak. For example, "Was there a thought you wanted to express?" or "Did you want to add anything?" or "You look as if you might be about to say something . . ."

- If they decline, be gracious and move on. No one likes being put on the spot, and everyone is entitled to choose whether and when to participate.

- If necessary, hold others off. For example, if a quiet member makes a move to speak but someone jumps in ahead, say, "Let's go one at a time. Terry, why don't you go first?"

- If participation is *very* uneven, consider suggesting a structured go-around to give each person a chance to speak.

ACKNOWLEDGING FEELINGS

WHY

- People communicate their feelings through their conduct, their language, their tones of voice, their facial expressions, and so on. These communications have a direct impact on anyone who receives them.

- That impact is much easier to manage when feelings are communicated directly rather than indirectly, and intentionally rather than unconsciously.

- Yet the fact remains that human beings are frequently unaware of what they're feeling. In other words, our communications are often driven or shaped by information that we aren't even aware of sending.

- By identifying a feeling and naming it, a facilitator raises everyone's awareness. By then *paraphrasing* and *drawing people out,* the facilitator assists the group to recognize and accept the feelings of its members.

HOW

- *Acknowledging feelings* is a three-step process:

- First, when a group is engaging in a difficult conversation, pay attention to the emotional tone. Look for cues that might indicate the presence of feelings.

- Second, pose a question that names the feelings you see.

- Third, use facilitative listening to support people to respond to the feelings you named.

- Here are some examples of the second step in action. As the examples suggest, be sure to pose any observations as a question.

  - "Sounds as though you might be feeling worried. Am I right?"

  - "Seems like this discussion is bringing up something for you. Are you feeling disappointed?"

  - "From the tone of your voice, I wonder if you're feeling . . . ?"

  - "Looks like you have some feelings about that. Are you at all frustrated?"

  - "Is this what you're feeling . . . ?"

VALIDATING

WHY

- *Validating* is the skill that legitimizes and accepts a speaker's opinion or feeling, without agreeing that the opinion is "correct."

- Many facilitators wonder whether it is possible to support the expression of a controversial opinion without appearing to take sides. Can we acknowledge someone's feelings without implying we agree with the speaker's rationale for feeling that way?

- The answer is yes. *Validating* means *recognizing* a group's divergent opinions, not taking sides with any one of them.

- Just as you don't have to agree with an opinion to paraphrase it, you do not have to agree that a feeling is justified in order to accept and validate it.

- The basic message of *validating* is, "Yes, clearly that's one way to look at it. Others may see it differently; even so, your point of view is entirely legitimate."

HOW

- *Validating* has three steps. First, paraphrase. Second, assess whether the speaker needs added support. Third, offer the support.

- Step 1. Paraphrase or draw out a person's opinion or feeling.

- Step 2. Ask yourself, "Does this person need extra support? Has he or she just said something that takes a risk?"

- Step 3. Offer that support by acknowledging the legitimacy of what the person just said. For example:
  - "I see what you're saying."
  - "I know just how that feels."
  - "I get why this matters to you."
  - "I can see how you got there."
  - "Now I see where you're coming from."

- *Validating* often induces the affected individual to open up and say more. If this happens, be respectful. You're not agreeing; you're supporting someone to express their truth.

EMPATHIZING

WHY	HOW

WHY

- *Empathizing* is commonly defined as the ability to understand and share the feelings of another.

- This involves putting oneself in another person's shoes and looking out on the world through that person's eyes. The listener then imagines what the person might be feeling, and why – and forms this insight into a statement of acceptance and support.

- *Empathizing* and *validating* both serve to identify and legitimize feelings. *Empathizing* goes one step further: the listener attempts to *identify with and share the actual feeling*. For example, "If it were me I'd be worried!" "That must be really hard." "I'd be feeling very, very sad."

- Moreover, *empathizing* benefits the entire group, providing everyone with a fuller, compassionate understanding of a person's subjective reality.

HOW

- *Empathizing* can be performed using different techniques.

- The most basic technique is to name what you think a person is experiencing. For example, "I imagine this news might be quite upsetting to you."

- Another technique is to mention the factors that led up to the person's experience: "After all the effort you made to keep this project alive, I imagine this news might be quite upsetting."

- A third technique is to speculate on future impacts. "I can see how this news could also play havoc with your other commitments. Has that brought up any feelings yet?"

- A fourth option is to identify concerns about communicating these feelings to others. "I can imagine it might be hard to talk about this topic in this group."

- Always ask for confirmation. If the speaker says, "That's not my experience," encourage him or her to correct your perception.

INTENTIONAL SILENCE

WHY	HOW

WHY

- *Intentional silence* is highly underrated. It consists of a pause, usually lasting no more than a few seconds, and it is done to give a speaker that brief extra "quiet time" to discover what s/he wants to say.

- Some people need brief silence in order to organize a complex thought and turn it into a coherent statement. Others need a bit of time to consider whether to take a risk and make a controversial statement. Still others need the silence to digest what has already been said, in order to understand their own reactions better.

- *Intentional silence* can also be used to honor moments of exceptional poignancy. After a statement of passion or vulnerability, intentional silence allows the group to pause, reflect, and make sense of the experience.

HOW

- Ten seconds of silence can seem a lot longer than it really is. The crucial element of this listening skill is the facilitator's ability to tolerate the awkwardness most people feel during even brief silences. If the facilitator can survive it, everyone else will too.

- With eye contact and body language, stay focused on the speaker.

- Say nothing, not even, "Hmm" or "Uh-huh." Do not even nod or shake your head. Just stay relaxed and pay attention.

- If necessary, hold up a hand to keep others from breaking the silence.

- Sometimes everyone in the group is confused or agitated or having trouble focusing. At such times, silence may be very helpful. Say, "Let's take a few moments of silence to think what this means to each of us."

LINKING

WHY

- *Linking* is a listening skill that invites a speaker to explain the relevance of a statement he or she just made.

- In conversations about complex subjects, it is hard for everyone to stay focused on the same thing at the same time. People often raise issues that seem tangential – in other words, irrelevant – to everyone else.

- When this occurs, it's not uncommon to hear a group member say something like, "Let's get back on track." Or, "Can we put this in the parking lot?" Remarks like those are hard to argue with. Unless a facilitator intervenes, *the speaker is likely to simply stop talking.*

- Yet ideas that seem unrelated to the main topic can actually be connected with it, often in unexpected ways. *The thought that comes from left field is often the one that triggers the breakthrough.*

HOW

- *Linking* is a four-step process. First, paraphrase the statement. Second, ask the speaker to link the idea with the main topic. Third, paraphrase and validate the speaker's explanation. Fourth, follow with an action from the list below.

- Step 1. Paraphrase. A speaker who fears getting off track needs the support and reassurance of *paraphrasing.*

- Step 2. Ask for the linkage: "How does your idea link up with . . . [our topic]? Can you help us make the connection?"

- Step 3. Paraphrase, then validate the explanation: "Are you saying . . . [paraphrase]?" Then say, "I see what you mean."

- Step 4. Follow with one of these:
  - *Draw out* the speaker's idea.
  - Use *balancing* or *encouraging* to pull for other reactions.
  - Return to *stacking.* ("Okay, we have Jim's idea. Whose turn is it to go next?")
  - Use a *parking lot* flipchart.

LISTENING FOR COMMON GROUND

WHY

- *Listening for common ground* is a powerful intervention when group members are polarized. It validates the group's areas of disagreement and focuses the group on their areas of agreement.

- Many disputes contain elements of agreement. For example, civil rights activists often argue vehemently over priorities and tactics, even while they agree on broad goals. When disagreements cause the members of a group to take polarized positions, it becomes hard for people to recognize that they have *anything* in common. This isolation can sometimes be overcome when the facilitator validates *both* the differences in the group *and* the areas of common ground.

- *Listening for common ground* is also a tool for instilling hope. People who believe they are opposed on every front may discover that they share a value, a belief, or a goal.

HOW

- *Listening for common ground* is a four-step process. First, indicate that you are going to summarize the group's differences and similarities. Second, summarize differences. Third, note areas of common ground. Fourth, check for accuracy. Here's an example:

- Step 1. "Let me summarize what I'm hearing from each of you. I'm hearing a lot of differences but also some similarities."

- Step 2. "It sounds as if one group wants to leave work early during the holiday season, and the other group would prefer to take a few days of vacation."

- Step 3. "Even so, you all seem to agree that you want *some* time off before New Year's."

- Step 4. "Have I got it right?"

- Caution: To use this technique effectively, make sure to use it with all parties. People who do not feel validated are likely to continue advocating for their position regardless of the quality of their thinking.

LISTENING WITH A POINT OF VIEW

WHY

- On occasion a group's facilitator is also the group's leader (or expert, or staff person) – in other words, a person who is not a neutral third party. This creates a dilemma: How does this person promote his or her own point of view effectively, while still making room for all other opinions to be voiced?

- The resolution – first and foremost – involves *the mind-set* of the person who is playing the dual role.

- On the one hand, s/he has to retain the leader's mind-set, and *be responsible for clarifying his or her own thinking and communicating it effectively.*

- On the other hand, s/he has to adopt the facilitator's mind-set, and *care about helping the group do its best thinking.* This means wanting to support others to develop *their* lines of thought.

- *Listening with a point of view* supports this person to keep both roles in balance.

HOW

- *Listening with a point of view* is a five-step process:

- Step 1. As the leader (or expert or staff person), raise the issue about which you have an opinion. State your position.

- Step 2. Ask for reactions.

- Step 3. Respond to participants' comments as a facilitator would, by *paraphrasing* and *drawing people out.* Err on the side of more drawing out rather than less. (Many people find it hard to challenge authority; they may need extra support to risk voicing a differing opinion.)

- Step 4. After *at least two* moves of facilitative listening, give yourself the floor to speak. Now make statements that reflect your own perspective. Answer questions, provide information, explain, advocate, and so forth.

- Step 5. Repeat Steps 2 through 4 as needed, remembering to balance expressing your own point of view with at least twice as much facilitative listening.

SUMMARIZING

WHY

- Good facilitators know the value of encouraging participants to engage in thoughtful discussion. But the most interesting conversations can also be the hardest ones to close.

- If the facilitator does an effective job of *summarizing,* people will feel ready to move on to a new topic. However, if the facilitator does a poor job of it, some of the participants will push back and attempt to keep the discussion going. This places the facilitator in an awkward position, which probably could have been avoided with better technique.

- Making a deliberate effort to summarize a discussion also helps participants consolidate their thinking. The restatement of key themes and main points provides people with mental categories. These internal categories serve as both memory aids and devices for improving understanding.

HOW

- *Summarizing* is a five-step process:

- Step 1. Restate the question that began the discussion: "We've been discussing the success of your program."

- Step 2. Indicate the number of key themes you heard: "I think people raised three themes."

- Step 3. Name the first theme, and mention one or two key points related to that theme: "The first theme was about your strategy. You explored its effectiveness and suggested some improvements."

- Step 4. Repeat this sequence for each theme: "Another theme was the validity of your main goal. You questioned whether it was feasible and realistic. Finally, you examined some personnel issues and you created a new staff role."

- Step 5. Make a statement that bridges to the next topic: "We've done some thinking about the effectiveness of the program. Now let's discuss specific changes that you might want to propose."

5

CHARTWRITING TECHNIQUE

USING MARKERS AND FLIPCHARTS
TO SUPPORT FULL PARTICIPATION

- The Power of a Group Memory

- The Role of ChartWriter

- Lettering

- Colors

- Symbols

- Formats

- Spacing

- Tips and Technique

- After the Meeting

THE POWER OF A GROUP MEMORY

In many groups, participation is not balanced. A few people do most of the talking, while others sit and listen. This pattern shifts dramatically when people's ideas are written on flipcharts that everyone can see.

Writing a group's ideas on flipcharts and displaying them on the wall provides participants with a *group memory.** This strengthens full participation in several ways.

First, *it validates.* Recording people's words sends the message, "This is a valuable idea." And when their *ideas* are valued, *people* feel valued. That's the central benefit of group memory.

Second, *having a group memory extends the limits of the human brain.* A vast amount of scientific research has shown that most people can retain roughly seven chunks of information in their short-term memory. Once someone's short-term memory is full, the person simply cannot absorb another idea without forgetting something. (For example, you can probably remember a new friend's seven-digit phone number by repeating it over and over. But try remembering two new phone numbers at once!)

In a meeting this can pose a real problem. Typically, people hang onto the ideas they care about, and let the rest float in one ear and out the other. The group memory solves this problem. Participants know that if they forget something, they can look at it on the chart. This frees the mind and supports people to keep thinking. **

It is important to recognize that the group memory is not merely a tool for keeping the record of a meeting. Primarily it is a vehicle for encouraging full participation. It equalizes and balances. It enlivens the discussion. It helps people work toward understanding and integrating each other's points of view. In summary, *group memory is one of the facilitator's most fundamental tools for supporting groups to do their best thinking.*

---

* The term "group memory" was coined by Geoff Ball, a California specialist in multi-party conflict resolution. He is the founder of RESOLVE, one of the nation's first consulting firms to promote collaborative problem-solving as an alternative to litigation.

** For a detailed discussion on the benefits of using a group memory, see "The Case for a Group Memory" by M. Doyle and D. Straus in *How to Make Meetings Work* (pp. 38–48). New York: Jove Press, 1982.

THE ROLE OF CHARTWRITER

The chartwriter is the person who records the group's thinking on flipcharts. This role is also referred to as "the recorder" or "the scribe." The reason to have a chartwriter is to capture ideas and build a group memory.

The purpose of having a group memory has already been discussed: it supports good thinking and strengthens participation. But in order for the group memory to fulfill that purpose it has to be used by the participants – and that's where the role of the chartwriter makes all the difference. Sloppy, crowded, illegible charts are not much better than no charts at all. By learning the simple techniques discussed in this chapter, a chartwriter can make the group memory inviting, helpful, and easy to read.

Even more important than visual effects, the chartwriter's neutrality is essential. The chartwriter should record the group members' exact words whenever possible. People want to see their own ideas written down. Sometimes, of course, a person's statement is too long or complex to be recorded verbatim. In those cases, the facilitator often assists the speaker by paraphrasing and summarizing the speaker's key themes. It is permissible for the chartwriter to record the facilitator's paraphrase as long as the chartwriter believes the speaker has assented to the rewording.

Moreover, it is imperative that the chartwriter treat each person's contributions with equal respect. It is up to the group, not the chartwriter, to determine which ideas are valuable and which are not.

Many facilitators tend to perform the role of chartwriter themselves. Other facilitators bring a chartwriter with them whenever a meeting is larger than five or six participants. In general the latter aproach is superior to the former. To be optimally effective, facilitators should face forward, with their attention focused on their groups. By looking people in the eyes, a facilitator can pay close attention to group dynamics, and stay connected with the individuals and the process. In contrast, chartwriters stand with their backs to the group. Their attention is consumed by the meanings of people's words and keeping up with the flow of the discussion.

Some groups might not want an outside chartwriter. The facilitator can then ask the group to provide a chartwriter, either by assigning someone the role in advance or by providing volunteers at key points in the meeting.

LETTERING

1. PRINT IN CAPITAL LETTERS

Most group members have an easier time reading UNIFORM, CAPITAL LETTERS. Writing in cursive may be slightly faster, but taking a few extra seconds to print will make your text more legible.

2. MAKE **THICK-LINED** LETTERS

Use the *wide end* of the marker tip. Press firmly against the paper. Firm, thick-lined lettering is much easier to read from a distance than soft, thin-lined lettering.

3. WRITE STRAIGHT UP AND DOWN

Straight lettering is easier to read than *slanted* lettering.

4. CLOSE YOUR LETTERS

Don't leave gaps in letters like B and P. Letters without gaps are easier to read and less confusing. In contrast, letters with gaps require more concentration from the reader.

5. USE PLAIN, BLOCK LETTERS

Letters without curlicues are easier on the eyes. *Fancy script slows down reading time,* so it should be saved for occasional special effects.

6. PRACTICE MAKES PERFECT

If your printing isn't perfect, don't panic – practice!

A painless way to improve lettering is to practice whenever you might otherwise be doodling or taking notes, or writing grocery lists, memos, love letters – whatever. *Habits you develop with pen and paper will transfer to the flipchart.* *

* Thanks to Jennifer Hammond-Landau, noted San Francisco graphic facilitator, who gave us this tip in 1982.

COLORS

1. ALTERNATE COLORS

People read faster, retain more, and have a longer concentration span when the text is written in two or three colors. Therefore, switch colors each time a group member states a new idea. It's not necessary to follow a pattern in your alternation. The goal is simply to break up the monotony.

2. USE *EARTH TONES* FOR TEXT

The earth tones, also called the "soft colors," are blue, brown, purple, and green. They are easy on the eyes.

3. USE HOT COLORS FOR HIGHLIGHTING

The "hot colors" are orange, red, yellow, and pink. They are harder on the eyes and should be reserved for borders, shading and underlining, and for special symbols like arrows or stars. Note also that yellow is very difficult to see at a distance.

4. AVOID **BLACK**

Reserve black for numbering pages. It's too heavy and dense for much else.

5. BEWARE OF COLOR CODING

Beginners often try to organize their work by color coding – one color for headings, a second color for key points, a third for sub-points, and so on. This usually turns into a mixed-up mess. A group's thinking process is generative and dynamic – the categories keep shifting as people build on each other's ideas. *"Rough-draft thinking" is not the time for color coding*. By contrast, color coding is very effective with documents like agendas that are created before the meeting begins or whenever the content of the document is known in advance.

6. USE THE *ChartWriter's Grip* TO HOLD FOUR MARKERS AT ONCE

The *chartwriter's grip* involves sticking a marker between each finger on the hand you don't write with. Keep the tops off and point the ink-tips outward. This way, you are ready for action with any color!

SYMBOLS

1. BULLETS

Bullets are big dots that make items stand apart from one another. Use them often – especially when listing ideas.

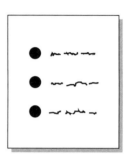

2. STARS

A star indicates that something is especially noteworthy.

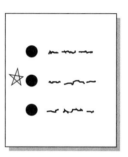

3. BORDERS

Borders have a pleasant visual impact. They can be used to frame a whole page or to highlight certain blocks of text or a title. Pink or orange borders work beautifully.

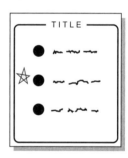

4. CIRCLES

Circles can do many things, such as:
- Lasso one idea and connect it with another.
- Draw attention to a decision that has been made.
- Highlight the most important issue on the page.
- Separate and categorize information on the page.
- Break up the visual monotony of a page full of text.

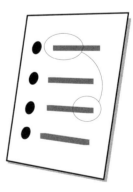

SYMBOLS

5. ARROWS

An arrow is a very powerful symbol, because it grapically represents a connection between two items. The nature of that connection might be causal, sequential, logical, or even cyclical. Usually the meaning of the arrow is self-evident from the context. For example:

- Ideas A and B (above right) form a vicious cycle.
- Idea 1 comes first; Idea 2 comes second.
- Ideas X, Y and Z all belong to Topic Q.

Because an arrow is so powerful, it is imperative that the chartwriter take extra care not to draw an arrow unless the connection has been explicitly suggested by a participant. In other words, remain neutral. Let the group do its own thinking.

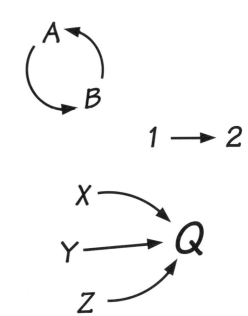

6. OTHER SYMBOLS

Many ideas can be expressed with simple drawings.

* The "Star-Person" was created by David Sibbet, who has developed a large family of easy-to-draw Star-People. See his *Fundamentals of Graphic Language Practice Book* (San Francisco: Grove Consultants, 1991).

FORMATS

1. THE LIST

The list is the most common format. It consists of a title, or heading, followed by a series of items, each demarked by an oversized dot, often called a "bullet."

Some lists contain subdivisions of items organized into categories, as shown in the right-hand diagram. For lists of this type, the category titles are numbered or underlined. Bullets are used to demark the items within each category.

TITLE
- ITEM
- ITEM
- ITEM
- ITEM
- ITEM

TITLE
1. SUB-TITLE
   - ITEM
   - ITEM
2. SUB-TITLE
   - ITEM
   - ITEM

2. THE MATRIX

A matrix is a grid with headings placed both horizontally (across the top) and vertically (along the left side). A matrix can be used to help a group discuss relationships between two or more variables.

	PRO	CON
IDEA 1		
IDEA 2		
IDEA 3		

3. THE FLOWCHART

A flowchart can describe how something works, or it can show a sequence of events.

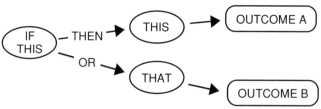

MORE FORMATS

 THE ORBIT DIAGRAM

An orbit diagram can highlight a key point and describe others in a less linear way.

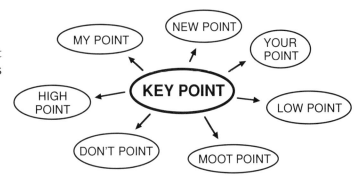

5. FORMATS FOR OPEN DISCUSSION

Open discussions are unstructured. During a period of open discussion, expect the group's ideas to flow in many different directions. The chartwriter's job is to use a recording format that preserves maximum flexibility .

The safest approach is to *skip three or four lines* after each new thought. As the discussion unfolds, go back to fill in the blank spaces if relevant ideas emerge.

If the writing surface is wide, hang sheets of flipchart paper side-by-side on a large wall and proceed as follows.

- Mentally divide the sheet of paper into five sections. Do not actually draw the sections on the paper. (The illustration below is meant only to show you, the reader, the arrangement of the sections.)

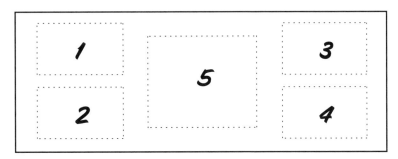

- As you record the discussion, put each completely new theme in a different section. Within each section, record using the list format. *Leave the center section blank.*

- As the discussion moves along, group members often discover that they can use the center space to list central themes of the discussion.

SPACING

1. LETTER SIZE

One inch is a good height for letters. You may have to write larger if the group is large – say, more than 30 – because some people will be sitting too far away to read one-inch letters.

2. MARGINS

Margins should be at least two inches on all four sides of the page. Having a wide margin beside each line of text encourages members to edit or add to their previous ideas. This space is also useful for tallying votes – as, for example, when group members prioritize a long list of ideas.

3. BETWEEN LINES

Leave roughly one inch between lines of text, and one and a half inches between lines when switching color.

4. INDENTING

Indenting is confusing because charts don't follow a "friendly letter paragraph format." Furthermore, using indentation to demark subcategories will create the same potential difficulty as color-coding: people's categories shift as their discussion unfolds.

5. UNDERLINING

Underline titles and subtitles only, and leave two inches below the line.

6. WHITE SPACE

White space is your friend. Especially at the margins – top, bottom and sides – an open, spacious page looks inviting and gives the group a breezy feeling about its work. Too much space is not advisable, yet even that is preferable to overcrowded pages. Dense text discourages readers from staying attentive to all that is being recorded.

7. DON'T CROWD THE BOTTOM OF THE PAGE

Start a new page before you really need to, because a group will lower its output at the end of a page. Participants often behave as if the task is finished once the page is full. If you start a new page, it is amazing how frequently people catch a second wind and start generating new material.

TIPS AND TECHNIQUES

WHAT TO LISTEN FOR	HOW TO WRITE IT

Suggestions

Example: "Let's check in with each other once a day until we actually hold the conference."

CHECK IN DAILY
TILL CONFERENCE

Logical Connections

Example: "In this organization, it's clear to me that absences and low morale are related to one another."

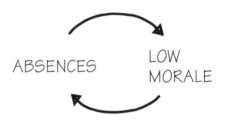

ABSENCES   LOW MORALE

Summary Statements

Example: "So what we're saying is that we want this program to target both teachers and parents."

TARGET GROUPS:
TEACHERS AND PARENTS

Open Questions

Example: "I know this is off the subject, but I'm still confused about whether we're ever going to hire a new financial assistant."

☆ HIRE FINANCIAL ASS'T?

 ☆ OPEN QUESTION

Don't worry about capturing every word a speaker says. Just be sure to preserve the meaning of what has been said.

TIPS AND TECHNIQUES

1. SENTENCES ARE EASY TO READ

"Send thank-you note to Bill" is much easier to understand than "note to Bill" because it includes a noun and a verb. Here's the guideline: *Will it be understandable in a week?*

2. DON'T BE SHY – WRITE "WE" AND "I"

Some beginners feel awkward using these pronouns. For example, instead of writing, "We want a meeting," a beginner might write, "They want a meeting" or "You want a meeting." Remember: it's the group's record – write with their voice.

3. VERBS AND NOUNS ARE HIGH PRIORITY

Example: If you hear "I hope we remember to write a warm thank-you note to that great caterer," get the key verbs and nouns first: "Send note to caterer."

4. ADJECTIVES AND ADVERBS ARE LOW PRIORITY

It's fine to write the adjectives and adverbs – like "warm" and "great" in the example above – but only if you have the time.

5. USE ONLY STANDARD ABBREVIATIONS

Do not invent abbreviations in order to write faster. For example, do not write "defnt" for "definite" or "expl" for "explain." Here's the guideline: *Will this be understandable to someone who did not attend the meeting?*

6. TITLE EVERY PAGE

Every page needs a title, even if it says "[title of previous page] page 2."

7. ENCOURAGE PROOFREADING

Invite people to read over your work. Accept corrections gladly. Even if it messes up your beautiful chart, remember that's how it becomes *their* chart.

AFTER THE MEETING

1. CHECK TITLES AND PAGE NUMBERS

Make sure all pages are titled, numbered, and arranged in a way that will be understandable at a later date.

2. ROLL UP THE PAGES TOGETHER, AND LABEL THEM

Flipcharts are often brought back to the next meeting. It is difficult to hang pages that have fold creases in them. It's also difficult to read them. Therefore, when you're taking charts off the wall, roll rather than fold.

Label the outside of the rolled-up paper with three items of information:
- Name of the meeting
- Date of the meeting
- Topics

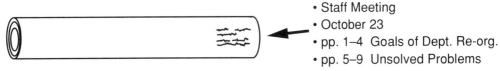

- Staff Meeting
- October 23
- pp. 1–4 Goals of Dept. Re-org.
- pp. 5–9 Unsolved Problems

3. SECURE THE PAGES WITH TWO RUBBER BANDS

Most people instinctively reach for cellophane tape or masking tape to secure the pages once they're rolled. Don't. The adhesive often sticks to the pages so well that the pages rip when you peel them apart. Instead, use paper clips or rubber bands.

4. CLARIFY YOUR ROLE IN RELATION TO DOCUMENTATION

- Will you be responsible for organizing and distributing copies of the flipcharts, or will you be handing off the charts "as is" to someone in the group?

- If you are responsible for creating the documents, consider photographing the charts with a digital camera. Copies can be downloaded and printed inexpensively. Letter-size documents are much easier to copy, store, and distribute than flipcharts, and photos are more effective as a memory jog than typed minutes of a meeting.

5. THESE STEPS DEMONSTRATE PROFESSIONALISM

Each of the previous four steps is an excellent opportunity to demonstrate thoroughness and efficiency. Group members will notice it. They may not acknowledge it verbally, but they will recognize that they are working with a professional.

FACILITATING
OPEN DISCUSSION

TECHNIQUES FOR SUPPORTING A FREE-FLOWING EXCHANGE OF IDEAS

- ▶ Facilitator's Two Central Questions

- ▶ Organizing the Flow of a Discussion

- ▶ Informal Techniques for Broadening Participation

- ▶ Helping Individuals Make Their Points

- ▶ Managing Divergent Perspectives

- ▶ Techniques for Focusing a Discussion

- ▶ Further Process Considerations

FACILITATING OPEN DISCUSSION

INTRODUCTION

Open discussion is the unstructured, conversational, familiar way of talking in groups. People speak up when they want to, and talk for as long as they choose. It is absolutely essential to know how to facilitate an open discussion; it is by far the most common approach to thinking in groups.

Open discussion serves many purposes. If someone raises an important issue, the entire group can discuss it. And if the issue does *not* engage the group, someone else can switch topics simply by voicing a new line of thought. Points of dispute can be clarified. Analyses can be deepened. Proposals can be sharpened. Stakeholders can express diverse perspectives.

At its best, open discussion can be very effective. But in reality, most open discussions are hard to sit through. Sometimes the conversation meanders or drifts. Sometimes a few individuals dominate. Sometimes people talk past one another without even attempting to link their ideas to the previous speaker's statements. All in all, the term "open discussion" is often a synonym for *"Groan Zone."*

THE FACILITATOR'S TWO CENTRAL QUESTIONS

When facilitating an open discussion, a facilitator is making decisions constantly. ("How much should I say? When should I say it?") In most cases, these decisions are simply judgment calls. But underlying such judgments are two central questions. The first question involves deciding *who talks when.* The second involves deciding *what content* to support.

DETERMINING WHO TALKS WHEN   Should the facilitator keep attention focused on the person currently speaking? Or should the facilitator move the focus away from that speaker and call on others? The theory and technique of making this choice are discussed in the sections "Organizing the Flow of a Discussion," "Informal Techniques for Broadening Participation," and "Helping Individuals Make Their Points."

FOCUSING THE DISCUSSION   Should the facilitator keep the focus on the specific points being made by the current speaker? Or should the facilitator help the group move away from those specific points and move on to an entirely different line of thought?   The theory and technique of making this choice is discussed in the "Managing Divergent Perspectives" section.

FACILITATING OPEN DISCUSSION

ORGANIZING THE FLOW OF A DISCUSSION

A BASIC PROBLEM   When an open discussion is underway, many groups have trouble determining whose turn it is to speak next. Usually the decision is left to individual members via the unspoken principle, "Speak up whenever you have something you want to say." This principle may seem reasonable, but in practice it often creates confusion and inequity. Those who think it is polite to wait for a lull in the conversation usually end up waiting much longer than those who start talking whenever the current speaker takes a breath. Furthermore, those who are more assertive may be seen by some as rude or domineering, while those who are more tentative may be perceived as having fewer ideas to contribute.

STACKING   The technique of *stacking* is a highly effective yet easy-to-master method for directing traffic. To stack, a facilitator simply asks the group, "Would you please raise your hand if you'd like to speak." Then, before anyone actually begins speaking, the facilitator assigns a number to each person. "You'll be first . . . You're second . . . You'll go third . . . " and so on. Whenever someone finishes speaking, the facilitator calls on the person next in line: "Who was third? Was it you, Maria? Okay, your turn – go ahead." After the stack is complete, the facilitator begins the next stack by asking, "Does anyone else want to speak? If so, please raise your hand now."

INTERRUPTING THE STACK   The problem with stacking is that it impedes spontaneity – no one has the opportunity to make an immediate response to someone else's remarks. No matter how provocative those remarks might be, one must wait until the end of the current stack in order to raise one's hand and respond. Many minutes could elapse, during which time other comments might take the discussion down an entirely different path. If the facilitator observes a sudden flurry of hand waving or agitated body language, these are indicators that people may feel more-than-usual pressure to respond quickly to an important remark. To handle this problem, the facilitator can adopt a technique called *interrupting the stack.* S/he can say, "I'm going to interrupt the stack for a couple of minutes and let two or three people respond to this last comment. For those of you who are already in line to speak, don't worry. I won't forget about you. I will definitely return to the designated speaking order soon."

Interrupting the stack allows a group to spontaneously intensify a discussion. But it can also create the appearance of a facilitator who plays favorites. To prevent this a facilitator should, *when first asking for raised hands*, state that s/he might interrupt the stack to permit a few responses to a hot topic.

FACILITATING OPEN DISCUSSION

ADVANTAGES AND LIMITATIONS OF STACKING   Facilitators who rely too heavily on stacking often receive comments like these: "I felt you were being very fair and even-handed with us, but I wish you had done more to help us stay focused. There were too many different topics on the floor – I couldn't follow the discussion." Or, "I wanted us to be able to get deeper into the meat of the controversy, and I felt you were too intent on having everyone participate. I would have liked it if two or three people could have just debated each other for awhile."

As these statements illustrate, *stacking* alone is not sufficient. If overdone, it can become tiresome. But it is nonetheless a very important intervention. Often it is *stacking* that enables a group to break habitual patterns of deference and favoritism. For example, *stacking* is sometimes the simplest way to help a rigidly hierarchical group make room for participation from low-status members. In the final analysis, *stacking* is the clearest and the most explicit – and therefore the most accessible – technique for organizing the flow of an open discussion.

INFORMAL TECHNIQUES FOR BROADENING PARTICIPATION

THE PROBLEM   Not all groups benefit from *stacking*. For example, some groups have a fast-paced, almost competitive style of interacting. For them, *stacking* would seem artificial and forced. As another example, *stacking* is too structured for very small groups consisting of, say, three or four members. Yet members of such groups may still need help knowing when they can speak. This problem becomes acute whenever the flow of discussion falls under the spell of two or three high-participating speakers who are allowed to dominate the proceedings. At those times, a facilitator can use informal methods to shift the focus away from the frequent contributors and create opportunities for less frequent contributors to speak. Four such methods – *encouraging, balancing, making space,* and *using the clock* – are discussed next.

ENCOURAGING   When using the technique of *encouraging,* a facilitator says, "Who else wants to say something?" or "Could we hear from someone who hasn't talked for awhile?" The assumption that underlies this technique is that some people may need a nudge to speak up. *Encouraging* is thus a means of providing extra support to those who need it. The entire group can benefit from this intervention because it takes pressure off everyone. Frequent participators are freed to speak without fear that their contributions will overpower the others; infrequent participators feel invited to offer their ideas without fear of appearing rude or aggressive.

FACILITATING OPEN DISCUSSION

BALANCING   The technique of *balancing* is useful when most members of a group appear reticent to disagree with the opinion of the person who has just spoken. For example, suppose a member of the group's senior management says, "Internal politics is not a problem here. If your work has merit, you will be rewarded appropriately." Using *balancing*, a facilitator could say, "As we all know, there are many times when different people have entirely different perspectives on the same situation. In this case, there has been a statement that internal politics is not a problem. Does *everyone* see it that way, or are there other points of view?" Under less threatening circumstances a facilitator can ask, simply, "What are some other ways of looking at this?" Or, "Does anyone have a different point of view?" All of these accomplish the same goal: they lend some support to people who do not agree with the mainstream point of view.

MAKING SPACE   The technique of *making space* involves questions or supportive statements that are aimed at specific individuals. For example, a facilitator may say, "Frankie, you look as if you want to speak. Do you?" Or, "Leticia, did you have something you wanted to say?"

Of course, it's always a bit dicey to call on people by name. Many people do not want to be singled out. Thus, a facilitator should use this technique sparingly – only when s/he sees a gesture that appears to mean, "May I talk?" or "I have an opinion too."

For example, some people lift their index finger without raising their hand. Others raise their chin in a sort of reverse nod. On occasion someone might look directly at a facilitator and crinkle his nose or purse her lips, as if to say, "No, I don't agree with what was just said." These are nonverbal cues that give a facilitator permission to invite a quiet member to speak.

USING THE CLOCK   The technique of *using the clock* involves statements like these: "We have five minutes left. I want to make sure we've heard from everyone who wants to speak, particularly those who haven't had a chance yet. Who wants to speak?" Or, "We have time for only one or two more comments – perhaps we should hear from someone who hasn't spoken for awhile." These interventions communicate that the stakes have gone up a little: if you want to speak, now is your chance.

Another way of *using the clock* is aimed at situations when a few people have become highly engaged in a conversation. To give other members an opportunity to participate, a facilitator can say, "We still have more than fifteen minutes left in this discussion. How about if we hear from someone who hasn't spoken for awhile?"

FACILITATING OPEN DISCUSSION

HELPING INDIVIDUALS MAKE THEIR POINTS

PARAPHRASING AND MIRRORING Through the use of reflective listening techniques, a facilitator can help a speaker feel understood. This keeps the focus of attention on the individual who was just speaking, but the facilitator does not push the speaker for any particular behavior. The speaker is left to his or her own judgment to decide whether to continue talking or stop.

When a facilitator engages in *paraphrasing* and *mirroring*, it is important to do it for as many participants as possible. Otherwise, some people will wonder why the facilitator seems to be playing favorites.

But continual reflective listening during an open discussion can become tiresome and annoying. It slows down the pace and interferes with spontaneity. Therefore, many facilitators reserve the use of *paraphrasing* and *mirroring* during an open discussion primarily for times when the need for support is obvious – for example, when a speaker is having difficulty being clear, or when two people are talking past one another. Since the reflective listening is being done during moments of obvious stress, participants are not likely to perceive the intervention as indicating preferential treatment.

DRAWING PEOPLE OUT By asking questions or even by saying, simply, "Can you say more about that?" the facilitator helps a speaker develop a line of thought. This supports the speaker to advance his or her own thinking – for example, by making explicit an unstated assumption or hunch.

When a facilitator decides to draw someone out, he or she is in effect making a judgment that it would benefit the group to hear more from the person who has just been speaking. In this way, the facilitator has a subtle but very real influence over who gets how much airtime and whose ideas will develop more, become better organized, better articulated, and ultimately more accessible to other members.

Therefore, it is imperative that facilitators *resist the temptation to draw out the people whose ideas sound the most promising.* This would violate the cardinal rule of impartiality; soon group members would suspect that the facilitator had a hidden agenda. Instead, a good rule of thumb is to draw someone out only when that person's ideas are hard to understand, regardless of whether the ideas are interesting or realistic.

FACILITATING OPEN DISCUSSION

MANAGING DIVERGENT PERSPECTIVES

THE PROBLEM: MULTIPLE FRAMES OF REFERENCE   Broad participation in a discussion usually produces a divergence of perspectives. This diversity can cause serious misunderstandings.

EXAMPLE   The owner of several large parking garages met with his nine managers to discuss a reorganization of duties that would take place in another month, after automated ticket-payment machines were installed in each garage. Partway through the meeting, the owner raised the problem of customers who lose their tickets. He asked for suggestions. Someone quickly responded with an idea. Someone else explained why that idea wouldn't work. A third person then wondered if the cashiers would cooperate. He pointed out that many of the cashiers would realize that their jobs were in jeopardy. This speaker concluded by proposing that the whole idea of payment by machine be reconsidered – perhaps even abandoned. A fourth person said she wasn't in favor of abandoning the project, but she did have some concerns about the reliability of the equipment. She said, "Maybe we could test the new equipment in one or two smaller locations and get the bugs out of the system before the major installation." At this point, the owner became impatient and scolded everyone for failing to stay on topic.

What the owner did not understand is that in a discussion like this one, each person must approach the topic from his or her own individual frame of reference. The person who suggested considering the question from the cashiers' perspective was thinking out loud. As he did so, he realized for the first time that a layoff, with all its unpleasant consequences, might well be forthcoming. The person who suggested testing the equipment was remembering her last job, where a computer system had been installed without adequate preparation – causing a plunge in her company's efficiency and morale.

The owner clearly felt that his employees were doing something wrong. Notwithstanding his feelings, however, the employees were not misbehaving. *In fact, the opposite was true. The employees were doing their best to formulate their ideas.* Each person was working hard to answer the question the owner had posed – but they were all working from their own frames of reference. They could not respond to the exhortation to stay on topic; they felt they *were* on topic.   This is a perfect example of the confusions that arise from the inevitable presence of divergent perspectives.

FACILITATING OPEN DISCUSSION

THE FACILITATOR'S CHALLENGE   The parking garage discussion is an example of a common challenge that many facilitators do not handle well. It's tempting to say something like, "It seems as if we're getting off track," or "I think we should return to the topic of lost tickets." These interventions sound good, but they are usually ineffective. They tell participants, in effect, "Don't think from your own frame of reference."

Everyone approaches a discussion from his or her own individual frame of reference. The meaning, the significance, and the priority of any given point of view are all matters of interpretation. And each participant arrives with different instincts about such matters. *It's essential for a facilitator to recognize that this is not unhealthy.*

The *goal* of a good discussion is to produce more harmony among individually different perspectives – to reconcile the diversity through a process of mutual understanding. But many people seem to think that participants in a discussion should *start out* with a shared framework. When they hear statements they consider to be tangential, they seek to solve the problem of divergent perspectives through a process of persuasion or control. "That's a side issue." "Let's get back to the point." "Would everyone please get focused?" These statements may cause a speaker to stop talking, but they certainly don't help the speaker to feel understood.

The point is that people of goodwill can and do differ on such matters as what's important and what's not; what's on track and what's off track; what's useful and what's useless. When these differences occur, discomfort arises. This is normal and healthy. It means people are participating. But the discomfort can deepen – even to the point of ruining a group's ability to think together – when participants don't realize that their individual frames of reference are biasing their assessment of the value of one another's contributions. At such times, people become impatient with one another: they say things they regret, they stop listening, or they act childishly.

TECHNIQUES FOR FOCUSING A DISCUSSION

What can a facilitator do to prevent this deterioration? Here are several techniques that can be used effectively when a discussion has branched into multiple lines of thought.

Pertinent skills are *sequencing, calling for responses, deliberate refocusing, tracking, asking for themes,* and *framing.*

FACILITATING OPEN DISCUSSION

SEQUENCING IN ACTION   A group of teachers met monthly to discuss the school's curriculum. Carter, a second-year teacher, made a controversial statement. Toni, the librarian, had a private reaction to that statement. "I hope Carter stops talking soon," thought Toni. "He's going on a tangent, and it's wasting our time." But the next person to speak responded to Carter's points in earnest. After a few minutes, Toni said, "Okay, folks, we need to get this discussion back on track." Someone else then said, "Thanks, Toni. I, too, thought we'd drifted away from our topic." This was a critical juncture. Carter felt he had been put down. Toni felt irritated and guilty. Both stopped participating, and the meeting ended on a sour note.

If a facilitator had been present, a simple *sequencing* intervention might have produced an entirely different result. The facilitator could have intervened at the critical juncture and said, "We appear to have two conversations going on simultaneously. Some of you want to respond to Carter's statement. At the same time, others of you would prefer to return to the previous topic. So here's what I'm going to do. I'm going to take two or three more comments on Carter's statements, and then I'm going to ask Toni to reintroduce the other line of thought. We'll spend at least a few minutes on *that* topic area. Then, if necessary, we can take stock and see what seems most important to focus on at that point."

This example demonstrates how *sequencing* works: (1) validate both perspectives, (2) help the group pay attention to one line of thought for a few minutes, and (3) help the group pay attention to a *different* line of thought for the next few minutes.

ADVANTAGES AND LIMITATIONS OF SEQUENCING   When a facilitator sequences two conversations that are underway simultaneously, s/he is keeping a discussion focused without taking sides. This intervention usually earns a group's appreciation. By validating both perspectives, the facilitator establishes a greater sense of safety for everyone. By identifying and labeling two separate lines of thought, the facilitator helps members keep track of what is going on. And by organizing the group's participation – first a few minutes on one idea, then a few minutes on the other – the facilitator demonstrates that s/he can guide the group through the *Groan Zone*.

But *sequencing* works only when there are two perspectives.   When a discussion heads down three or four different tracks, as in the example of the parking garage – the chances are great that the group *would not* appreciate hearing the facilitator say, "First, we'll spend a few minutes on idea A, then we'll shift to idea B, then we'll go to idea C, and then to idea D." That sequence would seem *too* controlled and too tedious to sit through.

FACILITATING OPEN DISCUSSION

CALLING FOR RESPONSES At times a facilitator may say something like, "Does anyone have a reaction to what Erin just said?" Or, "After listening to the previous three speakers, does anyone have any questions for them?" Questions like these guide whoever speaks next to remain on the same track as the person who has just spoken. *Calling for responses* is thus a method for preserving the focus of the discussion, even though it also encourages participation from new speakers.

This technique has the same effect as drawing someone out: the ideas that receive a facilitator's support are likely to be more fully discussed. Yet since the facilitator is asking for broader participation, this move is rarely opposed or even distrusted. Participants tend to view *calling for responses* as a neutral effort to keep the discussion moving. This tends to be true even when it is apparent that the facilitator has made a choice between two or more topics. So long as a facilitator makes the choice in good faith – not for the sake of favoring certain ideas but rather to keep the discussion balanced – most group members will give the facilitator the benefit of the doubt.

DELIBERATE REFOCUSING A facilitator deliberately refocuses the conversation by saying things like, "For the past ten minutes, you have been discussing topic ABC. But some of you indicated that you wanted the group to discuss topic DEF too. Is now a good time to switch?" Or, "A while ago Robin raised an issue, but no one responded. Before we lose that thought altogether, I just want to check: Does *anyone* have a comment for Robin?" As these examples illustrate, *deliberate refocusing* is another method for keeping the discussion balanced. Rather than permit one content area to dominate, the facilitator refocuses the conversation in order to provide fair opportunities for other issues. One of the most effective, and least offensive, occasions for *deliberate refocusing* is when a group has allowed two or three speakers to monopolize the discussion for several minutes or longer.

Of all the techniques described here, *deliberate refocusing* is the most directive. It pushes people to move away from one track of discussion and move onto another track, at the same time as it encourages everyone to move their attention away from one set of speakers and give their attention to a different set of speakers. Accordingly, the bias that is built into this technique is more noticeable. When a facilitator refocuses a discussion s/he runs the risk of being perceived as non-neutral – as choosing to cut off discussion perhaps before the group has completed a train of thought. Therefore, it is recommended that this technique be used sparingly.

FACILITATING OPEN DISCUSSION

TRACKING   As illustrated by the case of the parking garage managers, open discussions often branch into several distinct subconversations. *Tracking* means keeping track of those various lines of thought. A facilitator *tracks* by saying things like, "I think you are discussing several issues at the same time. Here they are. . . " Then s/he identifies each track. Thus, a facilitator might have said to the parking garage managers, "I think you are discussing four issues. First: How to deal with customers who lose tickets. Second: Will cashiers cooperate? Third: Should you reconsider the *very idea* of payment by machines? Fourth: Concern about the reliability of the equipment."

Tracking is valuable when a discussion is at its most competitive and its most unruly – when people are least likely to be listening to each other. These are precisely the times when directive methods like *sequencing* don't work. When everyone is intent on pushing individual agendas, suggestions by the facilitator are hard to hear and respond to. At such times, a facilitator must refrain from prioritizing or structuring the discussion. Instead, he or she remains neutral and alert to the necessity for supporting every speaker. *Tracking* reassures everyone that at least *someone* is listening.

COMPLETING A TRACKING INTERVENTION   After showing a group the themes they have been discussing, how should a facilitator complete the intervention? The most effective method is to ask for accuracy and then do no more. Ask, "Have I captured all the themes?" Someone may answer, "No! You missed *my* ideas." If so, correct the omission, and finish with a summary. "So there you are – discussing five topics all at once." Then stop.

A COMMON MISTAKE OF TECHNIQUE   Many facilitators are tempted to complete a *tracking* intervention by asking, "Which topic would you like to focus on now?" But it is nearly impossible for a group to *answer* that question. Typically, the members then go into a tailspin as they dicker over the most suitable focus, becoming mired in talking about what to talk about.

If a facilitator refrains from asking what people want to focus on, a group generally responds to a tracking intervention in one of two ways. The most common response is an *integrative* one. Someone combines a few of the tracks named by the facilitator and makes a clever proposal or offers an insightful analysis or raises a provocative question. In other words, someone integrates and advances the group's thinking. The other response is a *persistent* one: someone returns to his or her pet theme. At times the members will follow that person's lead, in which case the group has created its new focus – at least temporarily. At other times a quarrel ensues: "I don't *want* to talk about that issue now." In those cases the facilitator can be an honest broker and propose a simple *sequence*. "Can we spend a few minutes on this issue, then shift to some of the other themes?"

FACILITATING OPEN DISCUSSION

ASKING FOR THEMES   This technique is quite similar to *tracking,* with one major difference: the lines of thought are identified by group members, not by the facilitator. To *ask for themes,* a facilitator first says, "You are now discussing several issues, all at the same time," and then asks, "Can anyone identify any of the themes or topic areas currently being discussed?" As people call out their responses, the facilitator writes them on a flipchart.

When people have finished listing themes, the facilitator can say, "Now let's return to open discussion and see what happens in the next few minutes. If necessary, we'll come back to this list and structure it more. But we might be able to skip that step altogether. Let's find out. Does anyone have any comments about *any* of these themes?" As with *tracking,* the next response will probably be either an integrative response or a persistent one.

FRAMING   As with the two preceding interventions, the facilitator begins by pointing out that several subconversations are underway. The facilitator then says, "Let's remember how this discussion began." S/he then restates the discussion's original purpose. For example, "Originally, Susan asked for input into next month's agenda. The conversation has now branched out in several directions. Some might be important to pursue right now; perhaps others can be deferred. Which ones do *you* think are relevant?" The remaining steps are the same ones taken when a facilitator *asks for themes.* Record the group's answers, then return the group to open discussion.

FURTHER PROCESS MANAGEMENT CONSIDERATIONS

TOLERATING SILENCES   A typical silence during an open discussion lasts about three to five seconds. A painfully long silence lasts ten or fifteen seconds. Those silences mean that *people are thinking.* For example, people may need a few seconds to form an analysis of a complex problem. Or in a tense meeting, participants might become quiet while they search for tactful ways to express difficult feelings. Silence is not dysfunctional; it occurs when participants turn inward. Yet some facilitators find it exceedingly hard to tolerate silences of those lengths. This has little to do with the needs of the group. Rather, it reflects the facilitator's *own* discomfort with silence.

To discern *your* level of discomfort, ask a friend to help with this experiment. During a conversation, say, "Okay, let's be quiet now." Allow five seconds to elapse. Now discuss how that felt. Repeat the experiment with a lapse time of fifteen seconds. *Tolerating silence* is like any other skill – it is acquired through practice. Let *someone else* break the silences in your conversations.

FACILITATING OPEN DISCUSSION

SWITCHING FROM OPEN DISCUSSION TO A DIFFERENT FORMAT   When a discussion becomes tedious and people appear to be restless or bored, the wisest choice might be to end the open discussion and switch to another format. Alternative formats include working in small groups, individual writing, listing ideas without discussion, structured go-arounds, and many more. These are discussed in great detail in Chapter 7.

INTRODUCING AN OPEN DISCUSSION   When a facilitator works with a group for the first time, s/he should briefly explain his or her approach so they can cooperate with it. Unusual interventions like *stacking* and *interrupting the stack* require more explanation than self-evident ones like *sequencing*.

Here is a sample of an effective introduction: "We're about to spend half an hour in open discussion. Since we haven't done this before, I want to tell you how I work. I see an open discussion as a free-flowing opportunity for an interchange of ideas between each participant and the entire group. My basic plan, therefore, is to stay out of your way so you can talk to each other.

"If more than one person wants to talk at the same time, I'll ask you to raise hands and I'll number you off. That way, you'll know when your turn is coming and you won't have to keep waving your hand to get my attention. Once in a while, if someone makes a statement that produces immediate reactions, I might take a few comments from people who weren't in line to speak. But I'll do that only when it's an obvious choice. And if I *do* let anyone take a cut, I will *definitely* return to those who were in line."

That introduction takes roughly a minute to deliver – perhaps even a minute and a half. That's a long time for a facilitator to be speaking. But unless s/he explains the approach, the group may not be capable of cooperating.

CONCLUSION

Open discussion is the most common of all the formats for thinking in groups. But without strong facilitation, an open discussion can become tedious, frustrating, and ultimately nonproductive. Harnessing a group's potential to work productively in this format depends to a large degree on the facilitator's mastery of the participatory techniques described in this chapter.

7

ALTERNATIVES TO OPEN DISCUSSION

BUILDING GROUP MOMENTUM,
BY VARYING PARTICIPATION FORMATS

- Process Management
- Types of Participation Formats
- Listing Ideas: Uses and Procedure
- Listing Ideas: Variations
- Structured Go-Arounds: Uses and Procedure
- Structured Go-Arounds: Variations
- Small Groups: Uses and Procedure
- Small Groups: Variations
- Using Small Groups for Multi-Tasking
- Individual Writing: Uses and Procedure
- Improving Presentations and Reports
- Tradeshow
- Roleplays
- Fishbowls
- Scrambler
- Jigsaw
- Setting the Frame for a Structured Activity
- Debriefing a Structured Activity

COMMON VIEW OF MEETING "PROCESS"

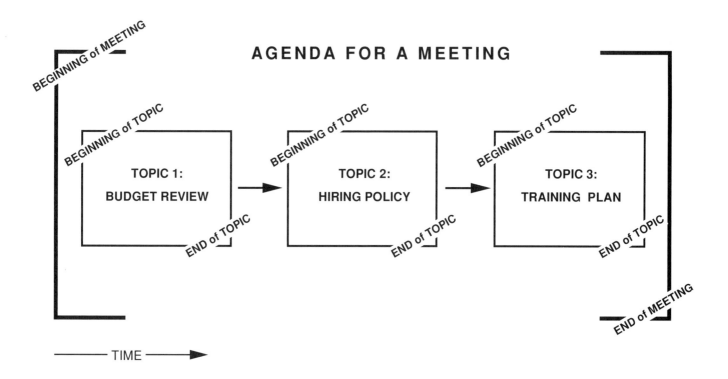

When most people think about what will happen in a meeting, they think about the topics to be covered. For example: "First, we should talk about the budget. Then we should focus on our hiring policy. After that, we can resume work on next year's training plan."

This illustrates a prevalent mind-set about *process:* that the process of a meeting is the same thing as the *sequence of topics* that will be covered at that meeting. "We'll begin with Topic 1 and we'll work on it until we finish with that topic. Then we'll move to Topic 2 and work on *that* until we're done with it. Then we'll go on to Topic 3."

PROCESS DESIGN, BY DEFAULT

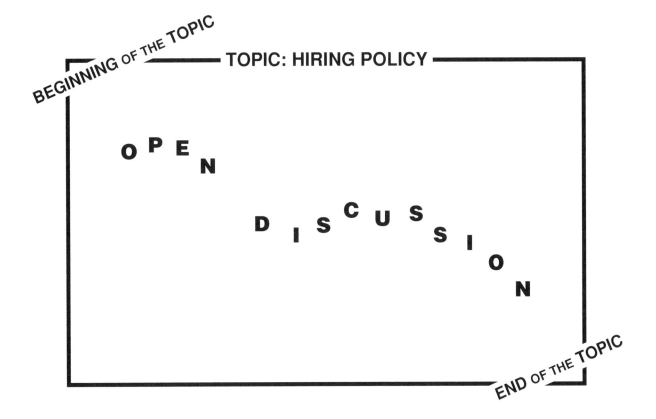

When a topic is introduced at a meeting, most groups automatically slip into a discussion. And they typically continue having the discussion until they come to the end of that topic – at which point they move to the next topic and begin another discussion.

Although there are many valid reasons for engaging in a discussion, it is also important to recognize the limitations. As a process, *open discussion* puts a lot of performance pressure on participants. One might think that it would encourage spontaneity and interaction. But in reality, it encourages participation from the fastest, the smartest, and the most confident members, while inhibiting participation from everyone else.

VARYING THE PARTICIPATION FORMAT

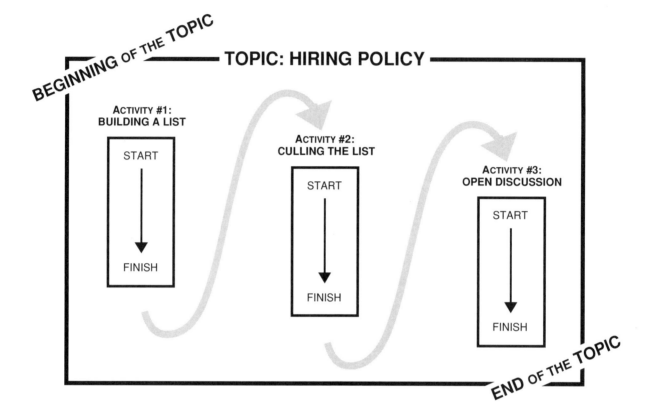

Many people don't realize it is possible to subdivide the thinking time on any topic into different styles of activity. As the diagram makes clear, *open discussion* is one approach to structuring participation in a group, and there are many others. Taken as a set, the various approaches are called *participation formats*.

Note that the topic – our hiring policy – stays the same from one activity to the next. It is the *participation format* that keeps changing.

Each *participation format* has its own distinctive ground rules. For example, when building a list, a group must suspend judgment and call out items with no discussion. (The ground rules of most common participation formats are described in this chapter and in Chapter 9.) Obviously, different ground rules encourage different group behavior. Therefore, a facilitator can shift a group's behavior (and by extension, the group's energy) every time s/he shifts the *participation format*.

BOOSTING THE ENERGY IN A MEETING

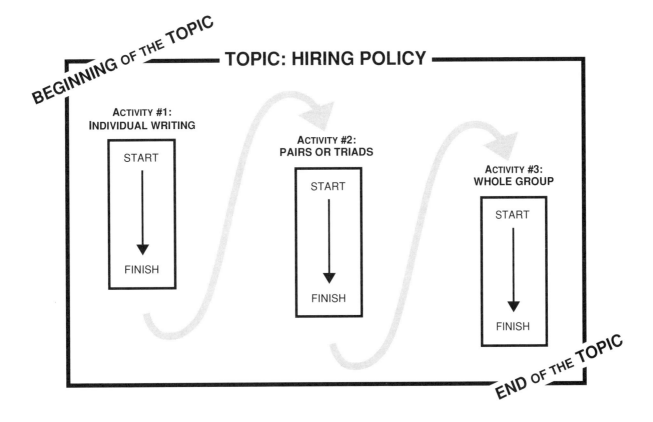

The simplest way to boost energy in a meeting is to give participants frequent opportunities to work individually, in pairs, and in triads. These subgroup formats are crucial for keeping everyone's battery charged.

Shifting back and forth – sometimes working in the whole group and sometimes working in subgroups of various size – is truly a "best practice" for facilitators to utilize. Although it seems almost too basic to take seriously, the fact is that this underlying structure will significantly improve the perceived quality of a meeting.

EFFECTIVE PROCESS MANAGEMENT

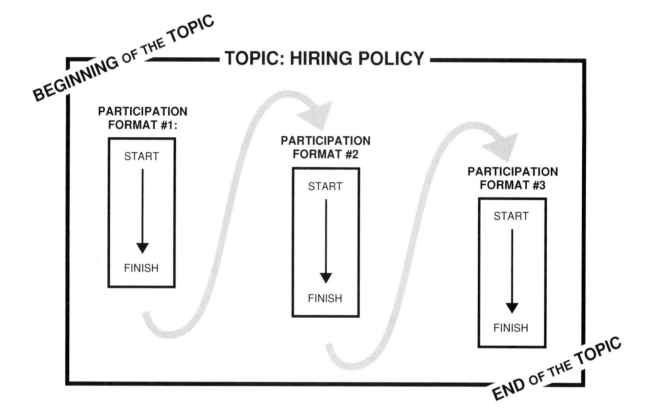

Varying the *participation formats* during a meeting strengthens participation in many ways. The tight structure of the activities assists people in preserving their focus and staying clear about the short-term objectives of their participation. And the variety supports people to maintain their energy.

Furthermore, your group will have a continuing experience of starting something and finishing it: starting and finishing; starting and finishing; starting and finishing. As the group accomplishes one step and moves on to the next, *this is how momentum builds.*

Learning when and how to use a variety of *participation formats* is the focus of this chapter.

Most groups rely heavily on *open discussion* and *presentations and reports,* seldom using the other formats shown above. Ironically, *open discussion* and *presentations and reports* are the two formats that place the most pressure on people to appear polished and conclusive when they speak. By contrast, the other formats give people latitude to do rough-draft thinking.

LISTING IDEAS

RECOMMENDED USES

1. *Jump-starting a discussion.* Listing ideas will help a group to rapidly identify many aspects of the subject, even when they're just beginning to think about it.

2. *Showing the members of a polarized group that there are actually more than two competing opinions in the room.* Listing ideas will draw out a wide range of thoughts on a given topic. This tends to happen even when there is a polarized, us-versus-them atmosphere in the group.

3. *Searching for a better understanding of the causes or elements of a problem.* When a problem is more complicated than it originally appeared, use idea-listing to explore questions like, "What's really going on here?" or "What are some influences we have not yet considered?"

4. *Generating a list of innovative or unconventional solutions to a difficult problem.*

5. *Bringing a large group back together after people have been working in small groups.* Listing ideas is the fastest way to collect the fruits of their various discussions. The group then has more time to go into depth on topics of interest.

6. *Providing structure when a topic feels overwhelming, unwieldy, or out of control.* By listing ideas, participants can see the breadth of the whole group's thinking. The list creates a basis for sorting and prioritizing the elements they want to tackle first. Thus, listing ideas is often an important first step in reducing the complexity of a difficult task.

LISTING IDEAS

PROCEDURE

1. *Hang large sheets of paper on the wall.*

2. *Ask for a volunteer to serve as the chartwriter.*
The job of the chartwriter is to write down everyone's ideas without censoring or improving anything.

3. *Explain the ground rules for suspending judgment:*

- Anyone may put anything on the list that seems relevant.

- Suspend judgment. No arguing or criticizing permitted.

- No discussion while the listing is underway. Ideas can be discussed later, after the list has been built.

4. *State the group's task in the form of a question.* For example, "What are our options for reducing our budget?"

5. *Give a time estimate for the activity, and have the group begin.*

6. *Have people call out ideas one at a time.*

- Honor everything everyone says.

- Use mirroring as often as possible.

- Summarize complex sentences for the chartwriter.

- If anyone begins arguing or discussing an item, politely remind the whole group of the ground rules.

7. *Don't panic when the pace slows down.* It usually means people are *thinking,* now that the obvious ideas have been said. Tolerate silences. If you push for more ideas, many people will feel pressured and stop thinking altogether.

8. *Toward the end of the allotted time, announce, "Two more minutes."* This often produces one final burst of ideas.

Listing Ideas: Standard Approach

A group generates answers to a question. Ideas are recorded on flipcharts. All ideas are acceptable.

Brainstorming

Creative ideas – particularly those that are silly, oddball, or impossible – are eagerly encouraged. Quantity is more important than quality.

Using Sticky Notes

Members write ideas on stickies, one idea per sheet. All stickies are posted on a wall. Later, ideas can be categorized.

LISTING IDEAS: VARIATIONS

Small Group Jump-Start

Have members form pairs and discuss a question. Then reconvene the group to build a list of good ideas.

Brainwriting

Members write ideas on individual sheets of paper. Every few minutes, people trade sheets, read them, and add fresh ideas.

Multi-Topic, Multi-Station

Flipcharts on different topics are posted around the room. Members may begin at any station. They move to new ones every few minutes.

Listing ideas can be done in various ways, all of which elicit divergent thinking. Using these variations keeps the process fresh and interesting.

Note that although there are clear differences in the specific procedures associated with each approach, *suspended judgment* remains the enduring grounding principle.

STRUCTURED GO-AROUNDS

RECOMMENDED USES

1. *Opening a meeting.* A structured go-around (also known as a "round robin") is an excellent way to begin a meeting of ninety minutes or longer. It breaks the ice and affirms the value that everyone's participation is welcome and expected.

2. *Structuring a complex discussion.* During open discussion, there are often several subconversations going on simultaneously. A structured go-around acknowledges this fact, and allows each person's pet topic to become the focus of group attention for a brief period of time.

3. *Making room for quiet members.* A go-around supports those who have trouble breaking into conversations.

4. *Gathering diverse perspectives when the membership consists of varied interest groups.* Go-arounds restrain members from arguing about the validity of each other's frames of reference.

5. *Compensating for differences in status and rank.* A go-around provides equal time to all participants, regardless of the degree of their authority in the group.

6. *Returning from a break after a heated disagreement.* After any disturbing episode, a break followed by a go-around is an ideal method for allowing everyone to voice reactions to what occurred before the break.

7. *Closing a meeting.* This gives each member a final chance to express thoughts and feelings that might otherwise not be spoken – at least, not in front of everyone.

STRUCTURED GO-AROUNDS

PROCEDURE

1. *Have group members pull their chairs together to form a circle or a semicircle.* It is important in a go-around that every member see every other member's face.

2. *Give a one-sentence overview of the topic to be addressed.* Example: "In a moment, we'll each have a chance to give our reactions to the presentation we just heard."

3. *Explain the process.* Example: "We'll go clockwise from whoever speaks first. While someone is talking, no one may interrupt. When you're through speaking, say 'pass' or 'I'm done,' so the person next to you knows when to begin his or her turn."

4. *If there are specific variations in the ground rules, go over them now.* For example, a facilitator might sometimes decide to give participants explicit permission to pass without speaking when it is their turn.

5. *After clarifying the ground rules, restate the topic.* People often forget the topic when they are focusing on your review of the ground rules. Now is the time to remind them and provide a more detailed explanation, if necessary.

6. *Give people an idea of how much time to take.* Example 1: "This will work best if each of you spends about a minute sharing your reactions." Example 2: "Take as much time as you like to give your impressions of why this problem keeps reappearing."

The Standard Structured Go-Around

Go clockwise – or counterclockwise – from whoever speaks first.

Toss the Beanbag

When the speaker is done, s/he tosses an object (an eraser, for example) to someone else, who speaks next.

Seven Words or Less

People end a meeting with no more than seven words. Incomplete sentences are fine.

GO-AROUND VARIATIONS

Two or Three Feeling Words

People end a meeting with two or three *feeling words* that describe the mood. (Example: "I'm tired but happy.")

Talking Stick

A member picks up the *talking stick,* then speaks from the heart. No one else may speak until the stick has been set down.

Popcorn

Everyone takes a turn whenever they choose. When most have spoken, the facilitator asks, "Who still hasn't had a turn?"

These are all variations of the basic go-around. They all have two ground rules in common: (1) one person speaks at a time, and (2) the speaker indicates when s/he's done speaking – for example, by saying "pass." All of the variations encourage and equalize participation.

WORKING IN SMALL GROUPS

RECOMMENDED USES

1. *Breaking the ice — making it feel safer to participate.* People feel less reticent in small groups, which seem less public.

2. *Keeping the energy up.* It's physically energizing to get out of a chair and move around. Furthermore, working in small groups allows everyone to talk. Active involvement energizes people.

3. *Deepening everyone's understanding of a topic.* In small groups, people have more time to explore and develop their own ideas.

4. *Exploring different aspects of an issue quickly.* Small groups can work on several components of a single problem simultaneously. This use of small groups is efficient, effective, and quite common.

5. *Building relationships.* Small groups provide more opportunity for people to get to know one another personally.

6. *Greater commitment to the outcome.* Small groups support more participation. More participation means more opportunity to influence the outcome. When the outcome incorporates *everyone's* thinking, participants have a deeper understanding of its logic and nuance, and they are more likely to feel committed to its effective implementation. This is what is meant by "ownership" of the outcome.

BREAKING INTO SMALL GROUPS

PROCEDURE

1. *Give a one sentence overview of the purpose of the next task.* Example: "Now we're going to discuss our reactions to Dr. Stone's last lecture." Leave the instructions vague for now. (Clarify them in Step 4.)

2. *Tell the participants how to find partners for their small groups.* Examples: "Turn to the person next to you," or "Find two people you don't know very well."

3. *Wait until everyone has formed their small groups before giving further instructions.*

4. *After everyone has settled down, clarify the task at hand.* State the topic people will be discussing; then state the expected outcome. Example: "Dr. Stone claimed that married managers and single managers are treated very differently. Do you agree? What has *your* experience been? See if each of you can come up with two or three examples that have arisen at your place of work."

5. *If you have any instructions about specific ground rules or procedures, give them now.* Example: "One person should be 'the speaker' while the other person is 'the listener.' Then reverse roles when I give the signal."

6. *Tell people how much time has been allotted for this activity.*

7. *As the process unfolds, announce the time remaining.* Example: "Three more minutes!" When time is almost up, give a final warning: "Just a few more seconds."

8. *Reconvene the large group by asking a few people to share their thoughts and learnings.*

Casual Conversation

- Two or more participants.
- Informality prevails.
- Usually brief: 3 to 7 minutes.

2 – 4 – 8

- Eight participants.
- Round one: four pairs.
- Round two: two foursomes.
- Round three: group of eight.
- Typically 20 to 30 minutes.

2 – 4 – 2

- Four participants.
- Round one: two pairs.
- Round two: all four people.
- Round three: two new pairs.
- Typically 15 to 20 minutes.

SMALL GROUP VARIATIONS

Talk, Then Switch

- Two participants.
- One talker, one listener.
- Switch roles at a set time.
- Often brief: 5 to 8 minutes.

Two Rounds or More

- Two participants.
- Round one: talk, then switch.
- Round two: repeat sequence.
- Typically 10 to15 minutes.

Cocktail Party

- Temporary groupings.
- Objective: informal discussion of key themes.
- Participants mill about.
- Typically 20 to 30 minutes.

Breakout Groups

- Any number of participants.
- Objective: make significant headway on a task.
- Chartwriting adds value.
- Often 30 to 45 minutes.

Buddy System

- Two or three participants.
- Partners remain together while activities change.
- Can last all day.

MORE SMALL GROUP VARIATIONS

Activity with Feedback

- Three or more participants.
- Objective: skillbuilding.
- One person observes silently while others do an activity.
- Observer gives feedback when activity concludes.

Speed Dating

- Two participants.
- Objective: explore diversity.
- Casual conversation.
- Switch partners at a set time.
- Typically 15 to 30 minutes.

There are many more ways to work in small groups than most facilitators realize. Variety prevents boredom and keeps people wondering what will come next.

USING SMALL GROUPS FOR MULTI-TASKING

BREAKOUT GROUPS

1. Divide the group into *breakout groups* (i.e., committees) and assign a different task to each. For example, suppose the group is planning a conference. They might divide into three *breakout groups*. One makes a list of people to invite; a second group lists topics to discuss; and a third identifies logistics to handle.

2. Have each *breakout group* select people to play needed roles, such as presenter, discussion leader, and recorder.

3. Specify the time limit for working in committee. Then begin. Give a 10-minute warning before ending.

4. Reconvene the large group. Ask for a report from each *breakout group*. Allow 5 to 10 minutes for questions.

THE GALLERY TOUR

1. Divide the group into *breakout groups*.

2. Give flipcharts and markers to each *breakout group* and send them to their "stations." These could be in separate rooms, or in different corners of the same room. Have every *breakout group* record their work on flipcharts and post the charts on nearby walls.

3. When time is up, reconvene the large group. Now form "tour groups." Each tour group should have at least one member from every *breakout group*.

4. Tell the groups to take a 7 to 10 minute tour of each station. Have someone from each *breakout group* explain the charts from that group.

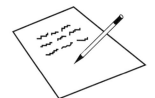

INDIVIDUAL WRITING

RECOMMENDED USES

1. *Giving members a chance to collect their thoughts in preparation for open discussion.*

2. *Reflecting privately on something unusual or noteworthy that happened recently in the group.*

3. *Preserving anonymity.* People may hesitate to speak freely when their superiors or subordinates are present, or when they fear other group members will disapprove of their comments. Sometimes members are more willing to share their thoughts when they can submit them anonymously.

4. *Helping people remain engaged when the discussion has bogged down.* Individual writing gives participants a break from the interpersonal intensity of group dynamics, while allowing them to keep working on the issues at hand.

5. *Allowing group members to collect their thoughts and feelings after tempers have flared.* When emotions go out of control, people can benefit from taking five minutes to write about the hurt and anger they may be feeling.

6. *Producing a first draft of a written product, such as a letter or a mission statement.* In this use of individual writing, each person writes a rough-draft version of the product. Then, those who like what they've written can share their drafts with the group.

7. *Providing input to a sponsor or decision-maker who does not attend the meeting.*

8. *Evaluating a meeting when time is scarce but constructive criticism is needed.*

INDIVIDUAL WRITING

PROCEDURE

1. *Give an overview of the task.* For example, "We're going to take five minutes writing our thoughts about the problems with our performance review process."

2. *Ask everyone to take out a pen and paper.* (Note: Bring extra pens and paper. It's surprising how many people don't bring writing materials to meetings.)

3. *Wait until everyone has settled in.*

4. *Give detailed instructions about the task.* For example, "Many people are not satisfied with our performance review process. Your task is to clarify specifically what you don't like about it. First, write two or three problems with the policy as it now stands. Then, write about the ways you have been adversely affected by that policy."

5. *Let people know whether they will be expected to show their work to someone else.* It is reassuring to say, "You won't have to show this to anyone. This is intended solely to help you clarify your own thinking."

6. *Let people know how much time has been allotted for individual writing. Then begin.*

7. *Give a one-minute warning when time is almost up.*

8. *When time runs out, reconvene the group.* Allow ample time for discussion of the material that was generated during the writing period.

IMPROVING PRESENTATIONS AND REPORTS

PROBLEM	SOLUTION
Disorganized, complicated reports that group members cannot follow.	Encourage the presenter to take a few minutes ahead of time to think through the logic of his or her report.
Tedious, rambling, repetitive reports.	Have the presenter jot down key points on paper before speaking.
Group members do not appear to understand the report's central point.	Encourage the presenter to state the most important point in the first few sentences, then restate it as summary.
People sit passively through a PowerPoint slide presentation, with no indication of reactions.	Break up the presentation with periods of high-engagement activitiy, such as small group discussions.
People react to a report with a dazed and uncomprehending look, as though it made no sense.	Ask the presenter to set aside time for questions and answers. Then facilitate an actual Q&A session.
Confusion about what the listeners are expected to do with information presented.	Encourage the presenter to tell people what s/he expects them to do with the information afterward.
Reports that barrage the listeners with details, causing people to get overloaded and shut down.	Encourage the presenter to use simple visual aids and replace details with diagrams. Hand-drawn flipcharts often work better than PowerPoint slides.
Presenters keep talking while handing out written materials. Participants stop listening in order to look over the handouts.	Advise the presenter to pause while people look over the material being distributed. Or wait until the report is done before distributing handouts.

TRADESHOW

DESCRIPTION

- *Tradeshow* is an audience-friendly method of presenting information to a group. It is useful whenever at least three speakers are expected to make consecutive presentations that will each run 15 minutes or longer.

- Normally multiple speakers give their presentations to the entire audience, sequentially. With *Tradeshow*, speakers present to subgroups simultaneously.

- In this format, audience members rotate to a new speaker's station after a set time has elapsed. Speakers then repeat their talk to the new arrivals.

- *Tradeshow* has several benefits. The smaller group size enables more participation and deeper discussion. And walking from station to station is energizing; it counteracts the mind-numbing effect of "presentation overload."

INSTRUCTIONS

1. In advance, identify locations where different speakers can create stations for their presentations. Each speaker should have his or her own station.

2. At the scheduled time, send presenters to their stations. Then send group members to stations. Send an equal number of participants to each station.

3. Have speakers give their presentations for a set time, followed by questions and/or discussion, also for a set time.

4. When time runs out, have everyone leave their stations and go to new ones. (Clockwise rotations work well.)

5. Have speakers repeat the same presentation to their new audiences.

6. Repeat steps 3 to 5 as often as necessary, so that all participants have heard all presentations.

7. Reconvene the whole group to debrief.

ROLEPLAYS

DESCRIPTION

- A roleplay starts with a fabricated scenario, which then unfolds over the course of 15 to 20 minutes. Among its beneficial uses are these: participants can test "what if" ideas; they can try out new skills; or they can put themselves in the shoes of characters they're roleplaying, thus gaining insight and compassion.

- Roleplays should not be designed too elaborately. They are effective only when everyone has a shared understanding of how the activity is going to work, and why. Clear role definitions and a clear explanation of the plot line are essential to success.

- On the other hand, rigid roles set up participants to run out of ideas, and become goofy or overly aggressive. To prevent this common problem, give everyone permission to change their minds as the roleplay unfolds.

INSTRUCTIONS

1. Start by explaining the purpose of the roleplay. For example, "This activity will help us gain insight into some communication problems between managers and employees."

2. Break into small groups.

3. Assign a role to each participant, and provide some background to bring that role to life. For example, "Your boss gave you an impossible task and you were afraid to challenge him."

4. Give any specific instructions that might be needed. For example, "In this roleplay, you must explain why you did not finish the task, to a boss who may react defensively."

4. Clarify the time limits. Then begin.

5. When finished, reconvene the large group, and debrief the activity.

FISHBOWLS

DESCRIPTION

- *Fishbowls* are done to help build mutual understanding among people whose backgrounds or jobs are significantly different. For example, a fishbowl might help doctors, nurses, and managers to understand each other's viewpoints.

- For a set amount of time, one group (for example, the nurses) sits together in the center of the room and talks among themselves, while others listen in on the discussion. When time is up, a brief whole-group conversation ensues. Then a new group moves into the fishbowl.

- In this way, like-minded participants are afforded a time-limited opportunity to publicly discuss an issue without needing to defend their thoughts against competing perspectives.

INSTRUCTIONS

1. Introduce the activity by explaining its purpose. For example (to a group of government officials, service providers, and community activists), "This activity will help you better understand each other's priorities and challenges without getting tangled up in debate."

2. Invite one stakeholder group to be "in the fishbowl." Seat them in a circle in the center of the room.

3. Ask those in the fishbowl to discuss a given issue. Set a time limit. Ask all others to remain quiet and listen.

4. When time is up, allow everyone to make comments and ask questions. Optional: Ask those who were in the fishbowl to report on how it felt.

5. Bring the next stakeholder group into the fishbowl, and repeat the process.

SCRAMBLER

DESCRIPTION

- *Scrambler* is a way to organize a small-group activity so that participants can work with many different partners within the frame of that single activity.

- The key is to break the activity into rounds. Upon completion of each round, the members of each subgroup separate from one another and form new subgroups.

- To avoid chaos, the instructions should give participants a clear way to find new partners. Best practice is to send one person clockwise to the next station, while another goes counterclockwise. Have the third person remain seated. If the activity is designed for more than three participants per subgroup, send people two stations to the left, two to the right, and so on.

INSTRUCTIONS

1. Form groups of three. Then have eveyone number off (#1... #2... #3...) within their small groups.

2. Assign roles, describe the activity in suitable detail, and let the action begin.

3. When time is up, ask everyone who is a #1 to stand up. Send them clockwise to the next group.

4. Now ask the #2s to stand. Send them *counterclockwise* to the next group.

5. All #3s remain in place.

6. Repeat Step 2, reassigning new roles to each individual. For example, if the #1s were listeners before, this time the #2s would be listeners.

7. Repeat Steps 4 to 7 once more.

8. Reconvene the group, and debrief.

JIGSAW

DESCRIPTION

- *Jigsaw* is a small-group procedure that allows multiple stakeholders to spend time first with members who share their interests, and then with members who may have different priorities – thus influencing and being influenced by all points of view.

- The activity begins with the whole group identifying key themes that are relevant to the topic at hand.

- Participants then break up into *interest groups* with others who share their interest.

- After time has elapsed, everyone reorganizes into *jigsaw groups,* which are composed of representatives from the various *interest groups.*

- In *jigsaw groups* they report and discuss key ideas that arose during the work done in the *interest groups.*

INSTRUCTIONS

1. Define the topic to be worked on.

2. Have participants distill the topic into themes that interest them.

3. Have everyone form small groups based on their interest areas. Give these *interest groups* a relevant task, such as, "Discuss the issues you find most challenging."

4. When a set time runs out, have everyone form *jigsaw groups.* Each *jigsaw group* should contain one representative from each *interest group.* For example, if there were five *interest groups*, each *jigsaw group* would have five members.

6. In *jigsaw groups,* report on discussions that took place in the *interest groups.* Further discussion is optional.

7. Reconvene the whole group, and debrief the activity.

– COMMUNITY AT WORK –

SETTING THE FRAME

1. The Task:
    "Here's what we're going to do..."

2. The Outcome:
    "This is what we'll have when we're done..."

3. The Process:
    "Here's how we'll do it..."

4. The Rationale:
    "Here's why we're using this process ..."

5. The Expected Time:
    "Here's how long this will take ..."

When a facilitator introduces a new activity, some group members may not fully understand what they're being asked to do, or why. To help participants see the whole picture, a facilitator can effectively set the frame by following the five steps shown above.

DEBRIEFING A STRUCTURED ACTIVITY

WHY

Structured activities, like *listing ideas* or *breaking into small groups,* usually produce a wide range of perspectives. At the completion of a structured activity, it is usually worthwhile to provide time for reflecting on the discussion as a whole. For example, people might make observations like, "I never realized that there were so many different ways of looking at this issue!" or, "Now I'm starting to understand why this is such a problem."

This step is particularly important when people have been working in separate groups. It creates an immediate context for resuming work together, thus restoring the group's integrity as a single entity.

HOW

1. Before starting, select a question from the following list. All such questions work equally well.

   Now that [the given activity] is complete,
   - How did this go for you?
   - What have you learned?
   - What concerns has this raised for you?
   - What feelings did this bring up for you?
   - What are you noticing about this group?
   - What do you think of our prospects for success?
   - Have you heard anything fresh and new?
   - How do you react to hearing so many different points of view?

2. Ask for a few participants to respond to the chosen question. Alternatively, have a *go-around* so everyone can respond.

3. Upon completion of Step 2, proceed to the next item on the agenda. Alternatively, have the group discuss, "Where do we go from here?"

8

BRAINSTORMING

THE THEORY AND TECHNIQUE
OF SUSPENDED JUDGMENT

- ▶ **The Cost of Premature Criticism**

- ▶ **Suspended Judgment**

- ▶ **Ground Rules for Brainstorming**

- ▶ **Facilitator's Do's and Don'ts
  for Brainstorming**

- ▶ **The Many Uses of Brainstorming**

THE COST OF PREMATURE CRITICISM

Rough-draft thinking is just like rough-draft writing: it needs encouragement, not evaluation. Many people don't understand this. If they notice a flaw in someone's thinking, they point it out. They think they've been helpful. But rough-draft ideas need to be clarified, researched, and modified before being subjected to critical evaluation. The timing of critical evaluation can make the difference between the life and death of a new idea.

EXAMPLE

A small but growing law firm was looking for office space. The firm's administrator researched the possibilities, then offered a proposal: "I found 8,000 square feet on the north side of town for $10,000 per month for a one-year lease. The owner will lower the rent to $8,000 if we sign a five-year lease. We could offset our rent by subletting to the current tenant. The north side isn't great at night, but it's near public transportation and has plenty of parking. I think we should seriously consider this location." This was a fully developed proposal, ready to be critiqued. If it contained any flaws, now was the time to find them.

However, several months earlier, the group had shot down the administrator's initial proposal. "Since larger spaces are cheaper," the administrator had said, "what if we rented a big office and sublet some of it?" Someone responded, "Forget it. We don't have time or energy to find people to sublet." Someone else said, "I don't want to be responsible for too much space. After all, every landlord in town will make us sign a five-year lease. We could really get stuck."

Note that these quick reactions were based on erroneous assumptions. It did not require much effort to find a sublet, and the firm did not have to sign a five-year lease. Nonetheless, some participants were so quick to criticize the administrator's thinking that they killed the idea before the group had a chance to develop it. After the first discussion, the administrator stopped looking for places that required sublets. But six months later, after looking and looking for a smaller office at a good rent, he remembered his original idea and pursued it.

Premature criticism is often inaccurate. And stifling. When ideas are criticized before they are fully formed, many people feel discouraged and stop trying. Furthermore, they may become unwilling to volunteer their rough-draft thinking at future meetings. They anticipate objections and keep quiet unless they can invent a counterargument. Thus, people learn to practice self-censorship. A group is then deprived of access to its most valuable natural resource: the creative thinking of its members.

SUSPENDED JUDGMENT
COMMON QUESTIONS AND ANSWERS

1. **How can I suspend my judgment if I truly do not agree with what someone else is saying?**

Suspended judgment does not imply agreement; it implies tolerance. You don't have to let go of *anything*. You're just making room for other people to express *their* ideas.

2. **What if I know that an idea won't work?**

Suspended judgment encourages people to use their creative imagination. This often produces impossible ideas. For example, "If we were all 20 feet tall, we could save lots of gasoline by walking more." Ideas like these can be the starting point for a new line of thought. You don't have to believe an idea is true; just let yourself try it on and see what your imagination produces. After all, "if humans could fly" was a crazy idea until the twentieth century.

3. **Isn't collecting silly ideas a waste of time? Wouldn't it be more efficient for us to focus on the realistic options?**

Suspended judgment comes into play precisely when the so-called "realistic" options have all been found lacking. In other words, creative thinking is the most efficient use of a group's time when nothing else works! Besides, what seems silly to one person may seem *innovative* to another.

4. **Doesn't suspended judgment produce chaotic discussions that go off in a dozen directions?**

Only if the process is handled poorly. To use suspended judgment effectively, the group should establish clear ground rules and a clear time limit. To paraphrase de Bono, informality in the content of a group's thinking requires formality in the structure of a group's approach to its thinking.*

5. **If I suspend judgment of an idea I think is wrong, how will I get a chance to critique that idea?**

Suspended judgment is *temporary*, not permanent. Most processes that call for suspended judgment are designed to last no more than thirty minutes. *Suspended* does not mean *abandoned*.

* Source: E. de Bono, *Lateral Thinking* (New York: Harper & Row, 1970), p. 151.

– COMMUNITY AT WORK –

GROUND RULES FOR BRAINSTORMING*

1. Every contribution is worthwhile.
    - Even weird, way-out ideas
    - Even confusing ideas
    - *Especially* silly ideas

2. Suspend judgment.
    - We won't evaluate each other's ideas.
    - We won't censor our own ideas.
    - We'll save these ideas for later discussion.

3. We can modify this process
    before it starts or after it ends,
    but not while it's underway.

* The inventor of brainstorming as a technique for stimulating
creativity was Alex Osborn. His classic, *Applied Imagination*
(New York: Charles Scribner & Sons, 1953), has spawned
more than one hundred variations of brainstorming.

When introducing the technique of formal brainstorming to a group, spend a little time discussing the value of *suspended judgment*. Then ask each participant if s/he is willing to follow these ground rules. If one or more members are not, encourage the group to modify the ground rules to fit the needs of all members.

FACILITATOR TIPS FOR BRAINSTORMING

DO

- Do a lot of *mirroring* to keep the pace brisk and lively.

- Do remind people to suspend judgment. No critiquing allowed.

- Do treat silly ideas the same as serious ideas.

- Do move around to hold people's attention and boost the group's energy.

- Do encourage full participation: "Let's hear from someone who hasn't spoken for a while."

- Do repeat the purpose often: "Who else can explain why our office systems are so inefficient?"

- Do start a new flipchart page before the previous one is full.

- Do give a warning that the end is approaching.

- Do expect a second wind of creative ideas after the obvious ones are exhausted.

DON'T

- Don't interrupt.

- Don't say, "We've already got that one."

- Don't say, "Ooh, good one!"

- Don't say, "Hey, you don't really want me to write that one, do you?"

- Don't favor the "best" thinkers.

- Don't use frowns, raised eyebrows, or other nonverbal gestures that signal disapproval.

- Don't give up the first time the group seems stuck.

- Don't simultaneously be the leader, the facilitator, and the chartwriter.

- Don't start the process without clearly setting the time limit.

- Don't rush or pressure the group. Silence usually means that people are thinking.

THE WIDE WORLD OF BRAINSTORMING

Most groups use brainstorming for very limited purposes: generating solutions to a problem or creating new products. But brainstorming can be put to a much greater variety of uses. It can be used to help build lists of such things as:

- New goals

- Underlying causes of a problem

- Points of view held by persons not in the room

- Unexpressed concerns

- Helpful people or resources

- Ways to build teamwork

- New directions of inquiry

- Lessons from the past

- Obstacles to meeting a goal

- Ways to improve how a meeting is run

- Hidden beliefs or assumptions

- Sources of inspiration

Groups members' willingness to *suspend judgment* will probably free them to list ideas or perspectives they would not otherwise consider.

9

TOOLS FOR MANAGING LONG LISTS

ORGANIZING DIVERGENT STRANDS
OF THOUGHT

- ▶ What to Do After the Brainstorm

- ▶ Theory of Categorizing

- ▶ Creating Categories from Scratch

- ▶ Creating Categories Based on
  Predefined Criteria

- ▶ Categorizing with Sticky Notes

- ▶ Methods for Selecting High-Priority
  Items

- ▶ Formats for Selecting High-Priority
  Items

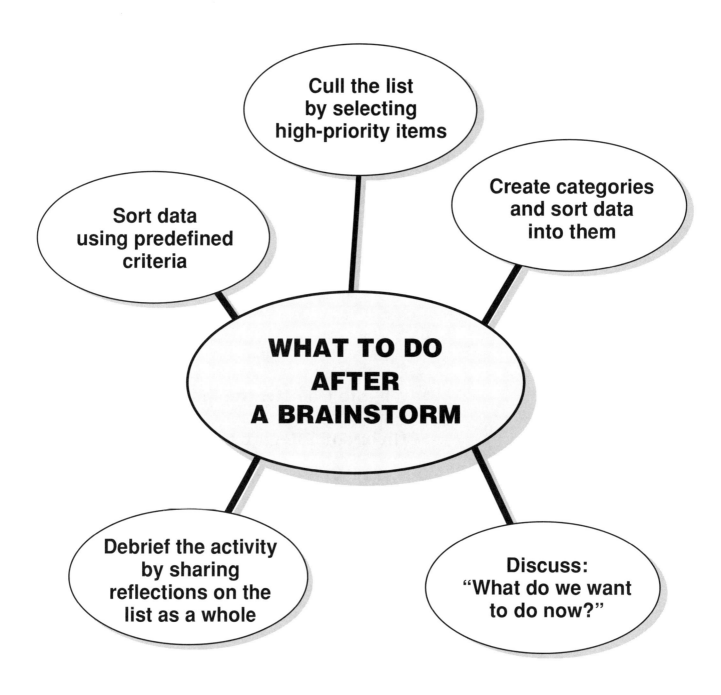

It's easy to get overwhelmed by the sheer volume of ideas that are generated by a divergent-thinking process. Many people respond to this dilemma by glomming onto one idea and pushing the group to focus on it. This knee-jerk reaction almost always plunges a group into the *Groan Zone*, because different people usually want to focus on different items. Several better options are indicated above. Techniques for culling, sorting, and categorizing are discussed in detail on the following pages.

CATEGORIZING IN THE REAL WORLD

INTRODUCTION

When a group has finished a brainstorming process, they often want to categorize the resulting list of items. This is natural. Most people cannot hold long lists in their head; they get overwhelmed. The group has to find some way of reducing the list to a manageable number of items. Many people think categorizing is the simplest way to organize the data. But categorizing involves two separate mental tasks – *creating categories* and *sorting items into categories* – and groups easily confuse these two tasks.

Creating categories is a relatively challenging task for a group, because people don't easily reach agreement on the meaning or the importance of a given category. Therefore, this task takes time. *Sorting,* on the other hand, is comparatively straightforward once the categories are well defined. The problem is that most groups want to *do* the task of creating categories, but they want it to *feel* as simple and easy as the task of sorting items into categories. This problem is illustrated by the following case study.

CASE STUDY

A group of front-line supervisors brainstormed a list of "Ways to Get More Training." They decided to categorize the list. First they created four categories: *Workshops, Apprenticeships, Readings,* and *Finding Mentors.* Then they began to sort each item into the four categories.

Soon someone suggested that some of the items might better fit into a new category, *Going Back to School.* This elicited a debate on whether *Going Back to School* was the same as *Workshops.* The discussion ended with an agreement to add the new category. Then the group immediately got caught in a disagreement over where to place the item "take classes on computer skills." Should it be placed in *Workshops* or in *Going Back to*

School? After a brief squabble, the members decided to put it in both places. But people were starting to get that feeling of, "Hey I don't care, let's just get on with it."

Then someone pointed out that many of their ideas for apprenticeships involved mentors. "Don't all apprenticeships," he asked, "require mentoring? I don't know if mentoring should even be a separate category." Several participants now got involved in a spirited discussion about the role of a mentor. They found this issue to be interesting on its own merits. Unfortunately, not everyone felt this way. A few members got very antsy. One person, irritation in her voice, asked, "What difference does it make? Come on, *please.*"

This led someone to say, "Let's get focused. What's our purpose here? What are we trying to accomplish by doing this categorizing?" And sure enough, the next three speakers had three different answers to that question.

At this point, forty minutes into what was expected to be a quick-and-easy sorting task, someone said, "Hey folks, we're making this way too hard. Let's just do it and get it over with." And many heads nodded, desperately. From that point on, everyone agreed to anything; the experience had gone sour, and people wanted just to be done with it. Five minutes later it was over.

And the finished product? It was typed up and promptly forgotten.

CATEGORIZING IN THE REAL WORLD

INSIGHTS

THE NATURE OF THE PROBLEM

Why is categorizing harder than people expect it to be? First of all, many people tend to assume that crucial terms mean the same thing to everyone. ("Why are we wasting time over the meaning of *workshops?* Let's just use common sense.") But, in fact, people *don't* share common meanings for the terms they're using, and this causes group members to feel pulled in two opposing directions. (Should we slow down and make an effort to define our terms? Or would that just be a waste of precious time?) This tension between the desire to clarify meaning and the desire to complete the task creates an uncomfortable undercurrent of ambiguity.

In addition, individuals vary greatly in the *number* of categories they use to organize their perceptions. Some people are detail-oriented. Their minds make a lot of distinctions between things, and as a result they tend to subdivide a list into many categories. Others are global thinkers; they make fewer distinctions because their minds operate at a more general, more abstract level of analysis. Accordingly, they tend to subdivide a list into fewer categories. Neither approach is right or wrong. But when people with differing cognitive styles try to create categories together, they are destined to disagree on such issues as whether *workshops* is a separate category from *go back to school.* And since disagreements like these are derived from individual cognitive styles, logical reasoning cannot help to resolve them.

USING PREDEFINED CRITERIA TO SORT A LIST

In the case study, it would have been much easier for the group if they had used predefined criteria to sort their list. For example, *cost* is a predefined criterion, as is *desirability.* If the group had employed categories like those, the sorting would have proceeded smoothly and produced useful results. After identifying some inexpensive training opportunities and some expensive ones, the group would have been able to discuss next steps.

Sorting the list into categories using predefined categories can usually be done quite adequately by two or three people. When this is done, they show their work to everyone else for revision. While the small group sorts the list, the large group can take a break. Or the large group could divide into teams that sort the same list into additional categories, using other predefined criteria. For example, one team could sort the list by *desirability* while another team sorted by *importance.*

CATEGORIZING IN THE REAL WORLD

OPTIONS

CREATING CATEGORIES FROM SCRATCH

Creating categories as a group means having a philosophical discussion. This is both the value and the cost of creating categories from scratch. A philosophical discussion puts a group into the *Groan Zone*, where they will have to struggle to integrate one another's beliefs and definitions. The process is uncomfortable and frustrating, and people will resist it. Sometimes the result is worth the struggle; often it is not.

When people present and define their own categories, they are essentially presenting their own worldview. Sometimes this is worth doing, such as when group members have not yet discussed their values or goals. Consider, for example, a community planning group made up of teachers, parents, and elected officials. The members of this type of group have diverse frames of reference. It may be well worth their time to use a discussion of categories as a way to develop mutual understanding. A similar example in a business setting would be a product-development group consisting of members from marketing, manufacturing, and research and development. In cases like these, the opportunity to define categories can prove very useful.

SUMMARY

Creating categories is a difficult task. It takes a lot of time and can produce a lot of frustration. It should be done when people want to gain a deeper understanding of one another's values and goals. *Sorting items into predefined categories* is a fairly simple task. It should be done whenever the primary reason for categorizing a list is to reduce the list to a mentally manageable number of items. A list of thirty or forty items can be sorted in roughly 10 minutes by two or three people. The results can then be reviewed by the whole group and revised as needed.

Because the opportunity to categorize a list arises so frequently in meetings, facilitators must understand the differences between *creating categories* and *sorting*. Those who do can make a real contribution to the development of a group's thinking skills.

TWO METHODS OF CATEGORIZING

CREATING CATEGORIES FROM SCRATCH

1. Each person in turn proposes his or her own set of categories. It is acceptable to propose one category or many on each turn.

2. Everyone takes as many turns as they want. Combinations and variations are encouraged.

3. After all sets of categories have been listed, discuss them.

4. Sometimes the group's thinking converges easily into one set of categories. If so, the task is done. If not, be prepared for a lengthy discussion.

CREATING CATEGORIES BASED ON PREDEFINED CRITERIA

1. As a group, select one or more predefined criteria to use as categories (e.g., "How urgent is each item: high, medium or low?" See page 129.)

2. Recruit two or three people to sort the list into the selected categories.

3. The sorters review the list item by item, making sure to place every item in a category.

4. Clarify that it is perfectly fine to place one item in more than one category, especially if there is disagreement about which category is "right."

5. When the list is sorted, reconvene the large group, and revise as needed.

CREATING CATEGORIES BASED ON PREDEFINED CRITERIA

CRITERIA ———————— **CATEGORIES** ————————

IMPORTANCE	Very high	High	Important to some; not to all	Moderate to low
TIME NEEDED	A lot	Some	Not much	Unknown
COST	Expensive	Mid-range	Cheap	Unknown
FEASIBILITY	Probably will work	Fifty-fifty chance	Probably won't work	Uncertain
DESIRABILITY	Highly desirable	Worth a try	Undesirable	Unknown
URGENCY	High	Medium	Low	Unknown
NEXT STEPS	Collect more info	Talk to boss	Meet with someone	Analyze further

There is nothing sacred about these categories; they are simply useful in many situations. Some situations may call for a category that is not listed on this page. For example, at times it might be useful to sort a list by "likelihood of provoking intense emotions." Everyone should feel free to create a category to fit the circumstances.

CATEGORIZING WITH STICKY NOTES

DESCRIPTION

- Participants write their ideas on stickies, then post them on a wall.

- Once all ideas have been posted, participants approach the wall and begin to move the stickies around, grouping related ideas into themes.

- The entire process is done silently.

- Anyone may relocate a sticky from one cluster to another. Thus, ideas move back and forth until everyone accepts the categorization. The titles of the themes emerge from the group as well.

- In this way, participants develop a common understanding of the themes as they are built.

INSTRUCTIONS

1. Hand out large sticky notes, and have people write their ideas, one per sticky.

3. Ask everyone to post their stickies on the front wall.

4. Next, have participants physically cluster the stickies into common themes. No talking is permitted.

5. Each time a new cluster is created, a participant should title that cluster with a different colored sticky note.

6. Over the next several minutes, expect the clusters to change as new participants rethink the groupings.

7. The process ends when everyone sits, indicating acceptance of the categories.

SELECTING HIGH-PRIORITY ITEMS FROM A LONG LIST

STRAW VOTE

1. Each member gets three, four or five straw votes to distribute however s/he wants.

2. It is permissible to cast all votes for a single item.

3. Half-votes are permitted, but not encouraged.

4. The top few items become the group's high-priority list.

   Advantages:
   • Fast and dirty.
   • Obvious items are clear.

DIVIDE THE LIST BY THREE

1. Divide the number of items on the brainstormed list by three.

2. Each person receives that number of choices.

3. Everyone may distribute his or her choices any way s/he wants.

4. The top third of the list – the items chosen most often – becomes the high-priority list.

Advantages:
• Preserves creative ideas.
• Protects minority voice.

ALL YOU GENUINELY LIKE

1. Each person casts one vote for every item s/he wants the group to treat as a high priority.

2. Only one vote per item per person.

3. All items that receive unanimous or nearly unanimous support become the group's high-priority list.
   (Note: Most groups accept "near unanimity" – i.e, unanimity minus one or minus two.)

Advantages:
• Reflects what people actually feel.
• Identifies unanimous preferences.

SELECTING HIGH-PRIORITY ITEMS FROM A LONG LIST

FORMATS

METHOD	HOW TO DO IT	MAJOR ADVANTAGE	MAJOR DRAWBACK
ITEM BY ITEM	The facilitator reads down the list one item at a time, noting how many people raise their hands for each item. For example: "How many people like *item 3?* How many like *item 4?*"	The procedure is intuitive to participants and needs no explanation. Reduces awareness of the preferences of influential members.	With lengthy lists of options, this is usually a tedious, draining experience.
PERSON BY PERSON	Each person takes a turn to state his or her preferences. Often a go-around is the simplest way to get this done.	Builds shared understanding of everyone's reasoning. Supports people in attempting to influence the group, regardless of the status of their role.	Those who go last have an unfair advantage: they can revise their preferences based on what others have said.
EVERYONE AT THE WALL	Everyone stands up, takes a colored marker, and puts dots beside his or her preferences.	People get out of their chair and move around. This is energizing.	With short lists, this method is often overkill.
SECRET BALLOT	All items on the list are numbered. Participants indicate their preference by writing their chosen numbers privately on paper. Results are tabulated by two or more people.	Useful in highly controversial situations, especially when someone might make a different choice if his or her vote were going to be made public.	Reinforces the perception that it is not safe for people to reveal their preferences openly.

TEN COMMON TACTICS
FOR MISHANDLING A LENGTHY LIST

☐ 1. Roll up the flipcharts and put them under your desk.

☐ 2. Take a break, and never come back.

☐ 3. Say, "Let's categorize these quickly, then move on."
And then, two hours later . . .

☐ 4. Publish the list in the next newsletter, to show everyone that your group is making progress.

☐ 5. Vaguely recall a similar list that was generated at a meeting last year; then postpone further consideration of the current list until the old one can be found. "After all, we don't want to do the same work all over again."

☐ 6. Have someone go away and sort the list. Then at the next meeting, forget to put that person on the agenda.

☐ 7. Give the flipcharts to the administrative assistant.

☐ 8. Assume that every item is now taking care of itself. Later, complain bitterly about the problems that still exist: "I thought we decided . . ."

☐ 9. Try to shorten the list by combining items. Then argue over the meaning of each new item.

☐ 10. Congratulate yourself on a very productive meeting.

10

DEALING WITH DIFFICULT DYNAMICS

SUPPORTIVE INTERVENTIONS
THAT DON'T MAKE ANYONE WRONG

- ▶ Injunctions Against Thinking in Public

- ▶ Developing a Supportive Attitude

- ▶ Difficult Dynamics Cause Difficult People

- ▶ Communication Styles That Bug People

- ▶ Whole Group Interventions for Difficult Communication Styles

- ▶ Stepping Out of the Content and Talking About the Process

- ▶ Handling Out-of-Context Distractions

- ▶ Teaching a Group About Group Dynamics

- ▶ Using a Check-In to Build Community

- ▶ Reducing Deference to a Person-in-Charge

- ▶ Classic Facilitator Challenges

- ▶ Continuous Improvement of Meetings

"Impossible!!"

"Stop wasting our time."

"That has nothing to do with what we're talking about."

"Your idea doesn't make sense."

"Getting pretty intellectual here, aren't we?"

"Hurry up – we're running out of time."

"Where'd *that* come from?"

INJUNCTIONS AGAINST THINKING IN PUBLIC

"You're not being clear."

"You're confusing people."

"You're making me think too hard."

"That's crazy!"

"Don't ramble."

"You keep going off on tangents."

"Haven't we already been around that block?"

"Enough joking around – let's get back to business."

"Please, no sermons."

"You're repeating yourself."

"Please wrap it up – you're taking too long."

"Get to the point!"

"Don't confuse me with the facts."

"Let's keep it simple."

"That's ridiculous."

"If you'd been listening, you wouldn't have to ask that question."

"Stop beating around the bush."

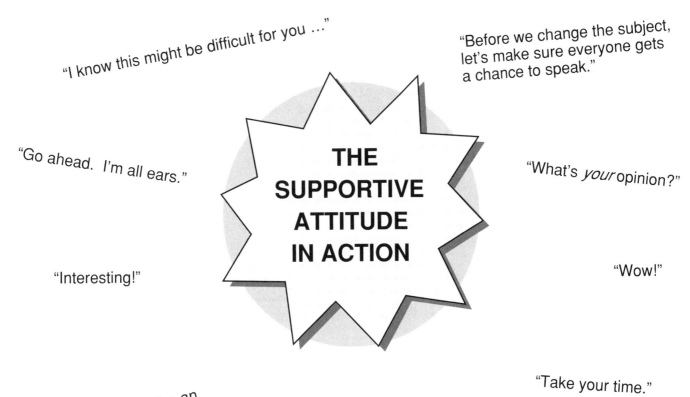

"Can you say more about that?"

"I know exactly what you're talking about."

"I'm not quite sure I followed you. Could you repeat what you said?"

"Hold on! I think she has a point here."

"I know this might be difficult for you ..."

"Before we change the subject, let's make sure everyone gets a chance to speak."

THE SUPPORTIVE ATTITUDE IN ACTION

"Go ahead. I'm all ears."

"What's *your* opinion?"

"Interesting!"

"Wow!"

"Take your time."

"What would be an example of that?"

"Go for it!"

"Does anyone have more to add?"

"Is *this* what you're saying?"

"I heard *that.*"

"I can see you're having a hard time putting this into words. Keep trying."

"That must have felt *bad.*"

"Even though we don't see eye to eye on this issue, I'm glad you keep standing up for your point of view."

———— *PRACTICE EXERCISE* ————

DEVELOPING A SUPPORTIVE ATTITUDE

WHY

Many groups have not developed respectful, supportive group norms. Their members do not talk to each other in the responsive, encouraging style shown on the preceding page, *The Supportive Attitude in Action*.

Instead these groups develop norms that stifle spontaneity and discourage first-draft thinking. Members make statements like those found on the page 136, *Injunctions Against Thinking in Public*.

Such groups have very little capacity to overcome difficult dynamics. Instead they become trapped in recurring patterns of frustration, conflict, and withdrawal. To overcome their patterns, it is essential for these groups to change their norms and develop cultures that are more supportive. This exercise is a strong first step in that direction.

HOW

1. Form groups of three.

2. Have everyone look over *Injunctions Against Thinking in Public* (p. 136) and privately identify one or two messages that would be particularly upsetting or intimidating for them.

3. Have each person pick an injunction that might cause him or her to shut down, and describe its impact. Then have each person speculate on how s/he might be affected if, instead, the words were said to *someone else*.

4. Now have everyone read *The Supportive Attitude in Action* (p. 137).

5. Have each person describe how it feels to be on the receiving end of the supportive attitude and how it feels to be on the giving end.

6. Invite everyone to jot down answers to this question: "What changes would I be willing to make in my own communication style, to help the group develop a more supportive atmosphere?"

7. Reconvene the large group and invite people to share their reflections.

DIFFICULT DYNAMICS PRODUCE DIFFICULT PEOPLE

Each member of a group has his or her own style of communicating. Some people talk in long, detailed paragraphs, while others say one sentence and quickly withdraw. In a simple discussion – for example, during Q&A sessions – people can generally tolerate diverse communication styles without too much difficulty.

However, when a group has to wrestle with a tough problem, people have a harder time communicating. Periods of misunderstanding and confusion are common, leading to feelings of impatience and frustration.

Staying focused at such times is an enormous challenge. Clear-headed thinking deteriorates as emotional urgency intensifies. Some people get so exasperated and overwhelmed they can barely pay attention. Others feel compelled to take over the leadership of the discussion, whether or not they know how to do it effectively. Some people just want to withdraw and get away. And others, feeling their anger rise, struggle privately to stay cool when what they *really* want to do is pick a fight.

Despite the rise in tension, many people continue making efforts to stay present and committed to the task. They keep trying – but they're trying under pressure. This can't help but affect their moods, their communication styles, and their thinking abilities. Their behavior toward others may be less than sensitive. They might blurt out their ideas with less tact than usual. They might go on and on – oblivious to the effect they're having on their audience – because they feel they're on the verge of an important line of thought. These are a few of the countless examples of the symptoms people exhibit when trying to contribute their best thinking under stress.

The expression of these symptoms makes many people uncomfortable. If there is a facilitator, people usually look to the facilitator to "save them" from their anguish. For example, many people expect a facilitator to interrupt those who talk to long and silence them. Alternatively, some facilitators think it is appropriate to talk to "the difficult person" during a break to request that s/he tone it down. So-called solutions like these are based on a faulty line of analysis – namely, that eliminating a symptom will somehow remove the cause of the distress.

This chapter offers the reader a different perspective. Difficult dynamics are treated as group situations that can be handled supportively rather than as individual personalities that need to be fixed.

COMMUNICATION STYLES THAT BUG PEOPLE

Many Groups Have Someone Who . . .

❏ Repeats ideas that someone else has already expressed

❏ Quibbles over minor details

❏ Openly expresses strong emotion

❏ Takes the discussion to a very abstract level

❏ Uses jargon that is difficult to understand

❏ Continually raises a pet issue no matter what topic is being discussed

❏ Criticizes without offering constructive suggestions

❏ Complains about how little progress the group is making

❏ Repeats his or her own point over and over again

❏ Argues as a way of clarifying an idea

❏ Goes off on tangents

❏ Makes long-winded speeches

❏ Cloaks disagreements with insincere sugar-coating

❏ Talks loudly

❏ Apologizes for everything s/he says

❏ Blames other people without acknowledging his or her own part

❏ Nitpicks whenever someone uses an analogy to make a point

❏ Just sits silently and rarely contributes

❏ Acts smug and self-assured, as if s/he knows everything

❏ Whispers to someone sitting nearby, while someone else is talking

Which of these Styles Bug You?

SUPPORTING DIVERSE COMMUNICATION STYLES

Instructions:

1. Read the handout titled "Communication Styles That Bug People." Identify any styles that might irritate *you*. (It's okay to include styles that are not listed on the handout.)

2. Form small groups. With your partners, discuss your personal reactions to the communication styles that annoy you.

3. In the space provided below, write down anything about your own communication style that might bother someone else.

4. At your discretion, share your reflections with your partners.

5. Discuss: When group members send one another subtle messages of disapproval and annoyance because of their diversity of communication styles, what consequences are created?

6. Return to the large group for discussion. When individuals are suppressed because their styles are "unacceptable," what are the costs to the group as a whole? How can group members become more tolerant of diverse communication styles?

Bothersome Aspects of My Communication Style:

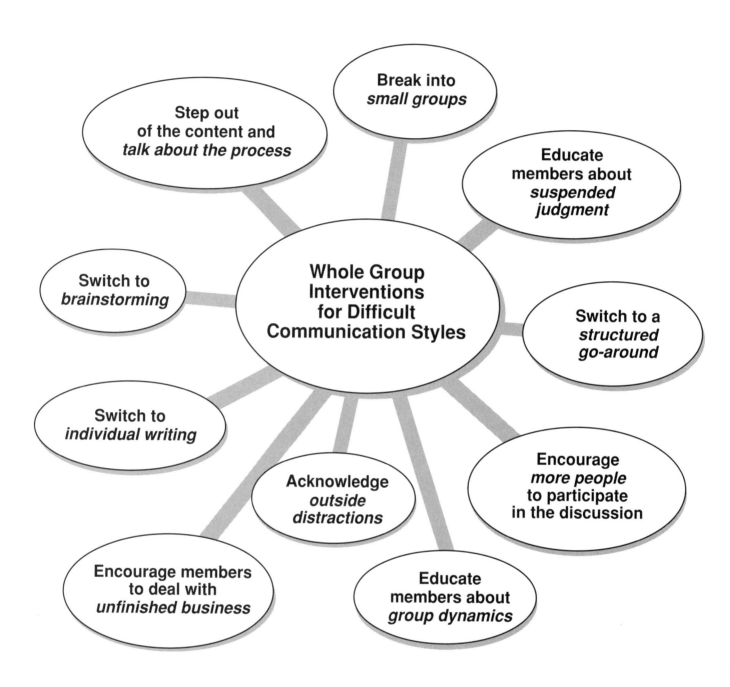

Facilitators who use the interventions shown here can handle many irritants and snags without abandoning their commitment to be respectful and supportive with *every* group member.

STEPPING OUT OF THE CONTENT AND TALKING ABOUT THE PROCESS

THE SITUATION

Meetings sometimes get bogged down for unclear reasons. For example, during a discussion some people keep bringing up a topic about which the group had already made a decision. At such times, a facilitator may be tempted to ask the group, "What's going on here? We appear to be stuck. Does anyone have any ideas why?"

One might expect such a comment to help a group reflect on their process. But it seldom works. The sudden "level shift" is too confusing. A few people will respond to the facilitator, but most will keep discussing the original topic. The problem is that some people don't realize they are being asked to step back from the discussion and talk about their process.

Here's a better strategy. First, point out that something isn't working. Next, obtain the group's agreement to step back from the discussion and talk about their process. *This is the crucial step.* Once members signal their readiness to proceed, everyone together can explore what's blocking them.

THE TECHNIQUE

1. Describe the predicament. Use facts to support your observations: "The group is having trouble staying on topic. Three people have asked us to stay focused on the budget, but someone keeps changing the subject."

2. Obtain agreement to proceed: "It might be useful to step back from the discussion for a moment and explore what's getting in the way. I have a simple way to do this and would like your agreement to proceed."

3. When agreement is obtained, ask a question that focuses on the process, not the content, of the preceding discussion. For example, "Does anyone have any thoughts about the way we are working together?"

4. After three or four responses, ask a more pointed question. For example, "What might be blocking us from working more effectively?"

5. When participants seem ready to return to the original task, prepare the group to make the shift. Ask, "Before we return to [the topic], are there any further reactions to what has just been said?"

6. Option: Call a short break at this point. The group's leadership will probably use the time to rethink the agenda.

HANDLING OUT-OF-CONTEXT DISTRACTIONS

THE SITUATION

Current events sometimes interfere with a group's ability to concentrate. After a terrible storm, for example, people need to talk about their flooded basements and leaking roofs. After an election, people need to discover how they feel about the potential impacts. During an organizational transition – a massive layoff, say – people need to let off steam and express their anxieties.

What should a group do when faced with distractions like these? Many people believe that the best response is to ignore their existence. This belief is grounded in value judgments, however, not empirical fact. Realistically, the presence of a serious distraction will lower a group's efficiency *regardless of what group members are officially allowed to talk about.*

This activity gives people the chance to spend a well-structured period of time talking about what's really on their minds. After expressing themselves, they are often better able to concentrate on the work at hand.

THE TECHNIQUE

1. If it's obvious that the group is having trouble focusing on the topic at hand, suggest that people talk about whatever might be the source of distraction. For example, "I notice we're having a hard time concentrating on this subject, and I'm aware that [the recent event] is on a lot of people's minds. Could we step back and spend a few minutes talking about [the event]?"

2. After securing agreement from the group to proceed, pose an open-ended question, such as, "What *are* people feeling about [the event]?" Ask everyone to respond.

3. When everyone has spoken, suggest a sequence for making the transition back to the main topic. For example, "What if we spend a few more minutes in this conversation, then take a short break and return to the main topic after the break?"

TEACHING A GROUP ABOUT GROUP DYNAMICS

1. *Set the frame.* Unveil a flipchart titled "GROUP DYNAMICS." The chart is blank except for the words "Discussion Begins" near the left margin and "Decision Is Made" near the right margin. Explain that you want to present a model which may help to explain why meetings can sometimes be so confusing and frustrating.

2. *Introduce the concepts of divergent thinking and convergent thinking.* On the left third of the flipchart, draw four or five arrows that signify divergent thinking. Describe what the arrows represent, and give some examples (e.g., listing causes, generating options, expressing different opinions). On the right third of the chart, (leaving the mid-section blank), draw arrows that signify convergent thinking. Give some examples (e.g., prioritizing, combining, evaluating).

3. *Discuss implications.* Label the two zones, and explain that this is a well-known model. Now ask for comments. A key point: A group of people can and should engage in very different behavior patterns at different points in a meeting – e.g., sometimes people can be creative, nonjudgmental, and free-thinking, while at other times the very same people can be focused, evaluative, and succinct.

4. *Introduce the Groan Zone.* Indicate that sometimes a group is neither diverging nor converging, but seems instead to be doing both at the same time. Embellish with examples and anecdotes. Explain the core problem: mutual misunderstanding. Assert that even though the *Groan Zone* can be an enormously confusing and frustrating phase, it is a normal, necessary phase in which people struggle to understand and be understood.

5. *Encourage reality-testing.* Ask people to share war stories and test the model against their actual experience. If feasible, use small groups for this step.

6. *Discuss implications.* Ask for questions and comments. In the ensuing discussion, make an effort to clarify the principle that if the group's eventual goal is to seek a sustainable agreement (i.e., a win/win decision based on an inclusive solution), then the resolution of the *Groan Zone* will occur when a framework of shared understanding has been built.

THE CHECK-IN
A PERSONAL WAY TO BEGIN MEETINGS

PURPOSE

A *Check-In* is a go-around that happens at the beginning of a meeting. People use it to share their mood and to briefly mention anything that might affect their participation. Each person takes a turn saying, in effect, "Here's how it feels to be me today."

Everyone faces non-work-related problems now and then. They range in degree from mild ("I'm having a bad hair day") to severe ("My mother is dying"). A Check-In allows people to tell each other what they're facing, in a way that informs without being obtrusive.

The Check-In is one of the most powerful methods for helping group members strengthen their relationships. Recognizing that they will devote most of their discussion-time to work-related issues, a Check-In provides members with a gentle format for getting to know one another in greater depth as multi-dimensional human beings.

PROCEDURE

1. Introduce the Check-In as a time for everyone to briefly report on the mood s/he is bringing to the meeting. Indicate that it is also appropriate for people to mention non-work-related issues that might be on their minds. If anyone questions the purpose of this activity, you can explain that this is a time to make the transition from "outside the meeting" to "inside the meeting." For many people, the act of sharing a little bit of personal information helps them make this transition.

2. Ask for a volunteer to go first. As with all go-arounds, ask this person to say, "I'm done" or "pass" when s/he is finished checking in.

3. If someone interrupts another group member's check-in, stop that person. Say, "This is not a time for comments from others. The person who is checking in is the only one who can talk."

4. When everyone has checked in, make a global statement that acknowledges what people have just said. For example, "Sounds like a lot of people are feeling overextended this week." Then move into the business section of the agenda.

A Check-In *builds group cohesion* by causing everyone to participate in a common activity right from the first moments of a meeting.

People use it to let each other know that they may have feelings lingering from the previous meeting.

It helps the group to be patient with someone who is having a "bad hair day."

REASONS FOR DOING A CHECK-IN

Everyone occasionally has to deal with a severe "outside problem," like the death or illness of a loved one. A Check-In lets people inform the group, without making a big issue of it.

It provides a transition from "outside the meeting," to "inside the meeting." It helps members shift the focus of their attention by expressing something in order to let go of it.

A regular Check-In is a solid investment in the long-term development of mutual trust.

A Check-In is a "go-around" that happens at the beginning of a meeting. People use it to share their mood and to briefly mention anything that might affect their participation. Each person takes a turn saying, in essence, "Here's how it feels to be me today."

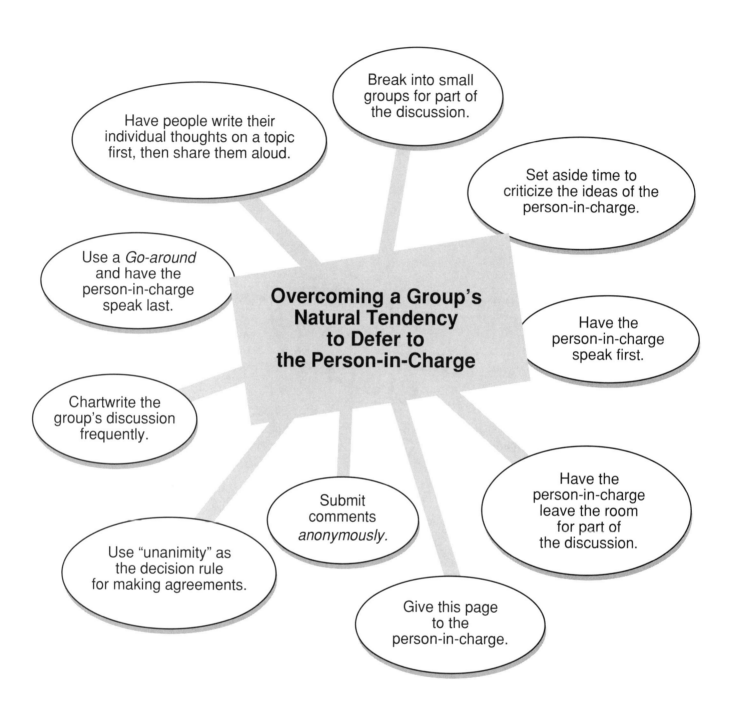

The most straightforward way to overcome a group's tendency to defer to the person-in-charge is to *identify the tendency and educate the group*. Acknowledge that it takes courage to speak truthfully in a hierarchy. Ask people to discuss what they might say differently if the person-in-charge were not in the room. Some people will respond defensively; others will be surprisingly honest. Remember that everyone – from the boldest risk taker to the most cautious diplomat – will need the facilitator's respect and support.

CLASSIC FACILITATOR CHALLENGES

(1)

PROBLEM	TYPICAL MISTAKE	EFFECTIVE RESPONSE
DOMINATION BY A HIGHLY VERBAL MEMBER	Inexperienced facilitators often try to control this person. "Excuse me, Mr. Q, do you mind if I let someone else take a turn?" Or, even worse, "Excuse me, Ms. Q, but you're taking up a lot of the group's time . . ."	When one or two people are over-participating, everyone else is under-participating. So, focus your efforts on the passive majority. Encourage *them* to participate more. Trying to change the dominant participants just sends even more attention their way.
GOOFING AROUND IN THE MIDST OF A DISCUSSION	Try to "organize" people by getting into a power struggle with them. Raise your voice if necessary. Single out the individuals who seem to be the ringleaders. "All right everyone, let's get back to work." (Or better yet, "Focus, people, focus!")	Often a break is the best response. People become undisciplined when they are overloaded or worn out. After a breather, they will be much better able to focus. Alternatively, ask for advice: "Is there something we ought to be doing differently?"
LOW PARTICIPATION BY THE ENTIRE GROUP	Assume that silence means consent. Don't ask whether everyone understands the key issues and agrees with what's being said. (That just wastes time unnecessarily.) Praise the group for all the work that's getting done, in the hope that flattery will motivate more people to participate.	Always be suspicious of low participation. Dependency, anger, or fear are often factors in play. The group, however, may not want to surface those feelings. If not, shift from *open discussion* to a format that lowers the anxiety level. Work in small groups, or build a list, or try a highly structured activity like a *fishbowl* or a *jigsaw*.

CLASSIC FACILITATOR CHALLENGES

2

PROBLEM	TYPICAL MISTAKE	EFFECTIVE RESPONSE
SEVERAL DIFFERENT TOPICS BEING DISCUSSED AT THE SAME TIME	"Come on, everyone, let's get back on track." "Focus, people, focus!!" Select the topic you think the group would most benefit from discussing, and do your best to sell your point of view: "I'm not at all attached to this, but . . ."	Use *tracking*: Name the various topics in play. "Let me see if I can summarize the key themes being discussed." Use *linking*: "Can you help us link your idea to the central issues before us?" Create a *parking lot* for ideas and issues to return to later.
MANY PEOPLE INTERRUPTING ONE ANOTHER, IN COMPETITION FOR AIRTIME	Take control. Don't be shy about interrupting the conversation yourself, in order to exhort people to be more respectful. Select one person to speak, but give no indication of whose turn will come next. That would undercut spontaneity.	If you must interrupt in order to restore decorum, say, "Pat, I'm going to cut in here. First, let's make sure your point is being heard. Then, I want to suggest a process that will cut down on further interruptions." After you complete your paraphrase, use *stacking*, *tracking*, and *sequencing* to organize the group.
PEOPLE TREAT ONE ANOTHER DISRESPECTFULLY	Ignore it altogether. No sense throwing fuel on the fire. Pretend that posting a ground rule imploring people to "be respectful" will somehow create respectful behavior.	Increase the frequency of your paraphrasing. People under pressure need support. If proposing a ground rule, be sure to create time for the group to reflect on what's happening and what they want to do differently.

CLASSIC FACILITATOR CHALLENGES

3

PROBLEM	TYPICAL MISTAKE	EFFECTIVE RESPONSE
MINIMAL PARTICIPATION BY MEMBERS WHO DON'T FEEL INVESTED IN THE TOPIC	Act as though silence signifies agreement with what's been said. Ignore them and be thankful they're not making trouble.	Encourage a discussion: "What's important to me about this topic?" Warm up in pairs, so everyone has time to explore his or her stake in the outcome. Before next meeting, ask the planners to assess why people don't seem more invested.
POOR FOLLOW-THROUGH ON ASSIGNMENTS	Give an ineffective pep talk. Ignore it. Excuse it: "Oh well, we didn't really need that information anyway."	Assign the work to teams. Build in a report-back process at a midpoint before the assignment is due. This gives anyone having trouble a chance to get help.
FAILURE TO START ON TIME AND END ON TIME	Announce, "We're going to start in five minutes." Then, five minutes later, repeat the same announcement, but this time say, "Just a few more minutes." Wait for the arrival of the "people who count," but don't bother waiting for anyone with lower ranking. When it's time to end, go overtime without asking. If anyone has to leave, they should know how to tiptoe out without disturbing anyone.	Option 1: Start the meeting when it is scheduled to begin. (Principle: Keep your word.) Option 2: Wait for everyone to arrive. (Principle: If someone's attendance isn't valuable, why is s/he coming in the first place?) Waiting for all will demonstrate that one person's tardiness can waste a lot of salaried staff time. Note: Make sure it is the person-in-charge, not you, who sets the policy and enforces it. If meetings chronically run late, improve your agenda planning.

CLASSIC FACILITATOR CHALLENGES

4

PROBLEM	TYPICAL MISTAKE	EFFECTIVE RESPONSE
TWO PEOPLE LOCKING HORNS	Put the focus exclusively on the interaction between the two disputing parties, as though no one else in the room has an opinion on the issue at hand. Or, treat the two like children. "Come on, you two, can't you get along?"	Reach out to others: "Who else has an opinion on this issue?" or "Are there any other issues that need to be discussed before we go too much further with this one?" Remember: When the majority is passive, focus your attention on *them*, not on the over-active few.
ONE OR TWO SILENT MEMBERS IN A GROUP WHOSE OTHER MEMBERS PARTICIPATE ACTIVELY	"Mr. Z, you haven't talked much today. Is there anything you'd like to add?" This may work when a shy member has nonverbally indicated a wish to speak. But all too often, the quiet person feels put on the spot and withdraws further.	"I'd like to get opinions from those who haven't talked for a while." Breaking into small groups works even better, allowing shy members to speak up without being pressed to compete for airtime.
SIDE CONVERSATIONS AND WHISPERED CHUCKLES	Ignore the behavior and hope it will go away. Chastise the whisperers, in the belief that humiliation is an excellent corrective.	With warmth and humor, make an appeal for decorum: "As you know, those who don't hear the joke often wonder if someone is laughing at *them*." If the problem persists, assume there's a reason. Has the topic become boring and stale? Do people need a break?

CLASSIC FACILITATOR CHALLENGES

5

PROBLEM	TYPICAL MISTAKE	EFFECTIVE RESPONSE
QUIBBLING ABOUT TRIVIAL PROCEDURES	Lecture the group about wasting time and "spinning our wheels." Space out, doodle, and think to yourself, "It's their fault we're not getting anything done."	Have the group step back from the content of the issue and talk about the process. Ask the group, "What is really going on here?"
SOMEONE BECOMES STRIDENT AND REPETITIVE	At lunch, talk behind the person's back. Tell the person-in-charge that s/he must take more control. Confront the person during a break. When the meeting resumes, raise your eyebrows or shake your head whenever s/he misbehaves.	People repeat themselves because they don't feel heard. Summarize the person's point of view until s/he feels understood. Encourage participants to state the views of group members whose views are different from their own.
SOMEONE DISCOVERS A COMPLETELY NEW PROBLEM THAT NO ONE HAD PREVIOUSLY NOTED	Try to come up with reasons to discourage people from opening up this new can of worms. Pretend not to hear the person's comments.	Wake up! This may be what you've been waiting for: the doorway into a new way of thinking about the whole situation.

CONTINUOUS IMPROVEMENT OF MEETINGS

STRENGTHS AND IMPROVABLES

1. Hang two sheets of paper. Title one page "Strengths." Title the other page "Improvables." *

2. Ask someone to call out a strength. Then ask someone else to call out an improvable. Build the two lists simultaneously.

3. Encourage participants to speak frankly in the spirit of constructive learning.

4. While the lists are being made, the ground rule of suspended judgment is in effect – no defending, explaining, or apologizing.

LEARNING FROM LAST WEEK'S EXPERIENCE

1. Ask participants to look back on the previous meeting and recall anything that made them feel uncomfortable.

2. Brainstorm a list: What can we do to handle this better in the future?

3. If everyone agrees to abide by one or more items on the list, fine. Often, however, agreement does not come easily because unresolved feelings may still be present. Rather than attempt to force an agreement prematurely, treat Steps 1 and 2 as a consciousness-raising activity. Often, simply naming a problem goes a long way toward changing it.

* Many facilitators substitute symbols for the words "Strengths" and "Improvables."
The plus-sign "+" and the Greek letter delta "Δ" (symbol for change) are both common.

11

EFFECTIVE AGENDAS: DESIRED OUTCOMES

CONCEPTS AND METHODS
FOR THINKING INTO THE FUTURE

SURE-FIRE METHODS FOR CREATING A PATHETIC AGENDA

☑

1. Time the agenda right down to the minute, and assume the meeting will start exactly on time.

2. Assume that everybody will know what you're trying to accomplish at the meeting – if they don't, they'll ask.

3. Plan to spend the first half of the meeting prioritizing what to do in the second half of the meeting.

4. Keep the meeting interesting by making sure the people who give reports use overheads and pie charts.

5. If you've got an agenda of difficult and important items, improve efficiency by skipping breaks and shortening lunch.

6. When the most important discussion is likely to be emotionally charged, save it for last. Maybe the group will be more ready to deal with it by then.

7. Since everyone prefers their meetings to stay on track, assume that no one will raise a topic that's not on the agenda.

8. When you know the agenda is too packed, assume the meeting will run overtime. But don't tell anyone in advance. People sometimes do their best thinking under pressure.

9. To maintain your flexibility, don't put the agenda in writing.

10. Don't waste time planning an agenda. Things never go the way you expect them to.

THREE COMPONENTS OF A MEETING

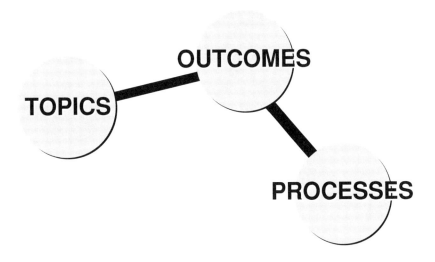

The work of a meeting consists of three components: the topics to be discussed, the desired outcomes for each topic, and the processes needed to achieve the desired outcomes. These three components can be thought of as the *building blocks* of meeting planning.

Each *topic* to be discussed can be viewed as a segment of the meeting. For example, if the group were going to discuss three topics – a marketing issue, a staffing issue, and a budget issue – each topic would be discussed separately and should thus be treated as a distinct segment.

The *desired outcome* of each topic can be viewed as the goal for that segment of the meeting. For example, the desired outcome of discussing the marketing issue might be a plan for developing a new website.

The *process* refers to the activity (or set of activities) the group will do to achieve the desired outcome. Such activities include brainstorming, categorizing, debating, and many more.

DESIGNING AN EFFECTIVE AGENDA

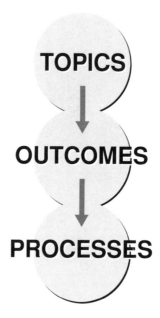

TOPICS

↓

OUTCOMES

↓

PROCESSES

The agenda is like a game plan. It describes how the work of the meeting will be done.

Creating an agenda involves identifying the topics to be discussed, defining the desired outcomes for each topic, and designing the processes to achieve the desired outcomes. Planning out the work of the meeting therefore means answering three questions, in the following sequence:

1. What topics do we want to address?

2. What outcome do we want for each topic?

3. What activity (or set of activities) will best support the group to achieve each desired outcome?

Assigning estimated times for each activity is done in tandem with Step 3.

The following pages provide concepts and tools for accomplishing some of the most challenging aspects of planning meetings effectively.

OVERALL GOALS AND MEETING GOALS

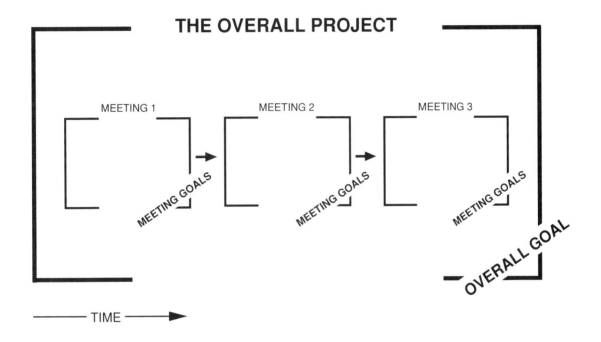

This graphic is known as a *Multiple Time Frames* map.* It was developed by the authors to depict the nesting of short-term goals within long-term goals.

As shown, the *overall goal* of a given project may take several meetings to achieve. By comparison, each meeting can be seen on its own terms, as a context within which the group can make progress toward the overall goal, by achieving two or three narrow *meeting goals*. As the following pages will clarify, *meeting goals* are specific, well-defined, realistic goals, designed to be achieved in the time frame of a single meeting.

* The graphic is also known as a *Milestone Map*. See S. Kaner and D. Berger, "Roadmaps for Strategic Change," unpublished manuscript, 2006.

TWO TYPES OF DESIRED OUTCOMES

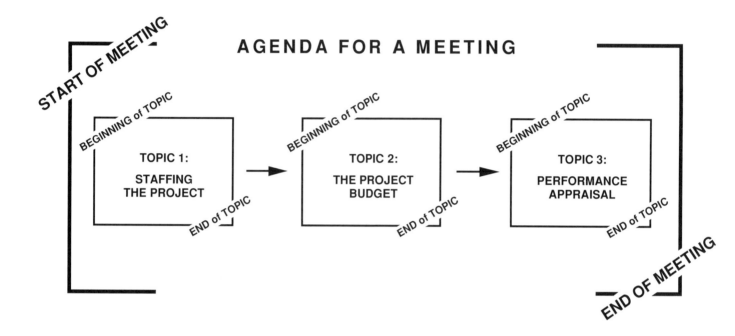

The diagram on the previous page depicted a project, with three meetings nested inside it. The picture above shows a single meeting, broken into three segments.

In the diagram, the goals for the segments are not yet defined. The following paragraphs demonstrate that an *overall goal* and a *meeting goal* can be defined for each topic.

Topic 1: Staffing the project. An example of a suitable *overall goal* is, "Hire suffcient staff to successfully complete our project." By contrast, the *meeting goal* would be much more limited. For instance it might be, "Agree on the criteria for potential staff, and draft a plan for recruiting them."

Topic 2: The project budget. A likely *overall goal* is, "Finalize the budget for this project." A *meeting goal* might be, "Identify budget items that need discussion, and assign someone to bring relevant data to the next meeting."

Topic 3: Performance Appraisal. A sample *overall goal* is, "Design a way to monitor and assess performance on this project." A much narrower *meeting goal* could be, "Set performance standards for key roles."

TWO TYPES OF DESIRED OUTCOMES

— COMMUNITY AT WORK —

THE OVERALL GOAL FOR THIS TOPIC

What *final result* do we want to achieve in order to be *completely done* with this topic?

THE MEETING GOAL FOR THIS TOPIC

What *narrowly-defined, specific objective* do we want to achieve for this topic at an *upcoming meeting*?

Defining the desired outcomes for each topic on the agenda is the most difficult task in planning a meeting. At the core of this difficulty is the necessity to distinguish between the *overall goal* for the topic and the *meeting goal* for that same topic.

The *meeting goal* for any given topic is the specific, narrowly-defined objective for working on that topic at an upcoming meeting. Descriptions of each of the seven types of meeting goals are presented in the following seven pages.

MEETING GOAL: SHARE INFORMATION

DESCRIPTION When someone makes an announcement, a report or a presentation, his or her meeting goal is to *share information.*

EXAMPLE Suppose a project team is working on their budget. Suppose also that the overall goal for that topic is, "Finalize the budget for this project." And further, suppose that the upcoming meeting is being designed by someone we'll call the meeting planner. If the meeting planner's objective is to give everyone access to last year's financial data, then the meeting goal is to *share information.* The planner might accomplish this goal by passing out a document and requesting that everyone read it by next meeting. Or he might have someone make a presentation and field questions along the way. Both of these processes are well within the boundaries of the basic meeting goal of sharing information.

KEY INSIGHT When the participants at a meeting understand that the goal is to share information, they tend to restrict their participation to questions of clarification – accompanied, perhaps, by brief statements of opinion or suggestions about what to do next. *However,* when people do not realize that the goal is to share information, they participate much more actively and substantively. This occurs when people believe they are expected to make progress on a topic – in other words, when they perceive that the meeting goal is to *advance the thinking* on the topic, not just to *share information.*

MEETING GOAL: OBTAIN INPUT

DESCRIPTION   When someone seeks feedback and/or suggestions, but does not want the group to make decisions, his or her meeting goal is to *obtain input.*

EXAMPLE   Let's continue with the example of a project team working on their budget. As before, suppose that the overall goal for that topic is, "Finalize the budget for this project." Now, imagine that the planner's objective is to find out how people will react to three different budget scenarios. He might create a questionnaire. Or he might ask people to call out their thoughts, brainstorm style. Or he might divide them into breakout groups. Thus he can use different participation formats to obtain input, but he has the same meeting goal, regardless of the process he uses.

KEY INSIGHT   When participants understand that the goal is to obtain their input, not to make decisions as a group, they are less prone to spend time attempting to influence one another. Instead, they focus their efforts on influencing the opinions of the person who is asking for input. More often than not, this person is their boss.

When participants don't realize that the goal is to obtain input, they might mistakenly believe that they're being asked to participate in making decisions. But that's a different goal altogether. The well-known complaint, "Why ask for my opinion if you don't want to use it?" reflects this confusion. Frustrations of this type can be avoided by planners who make it clear that the meeting goal is to *obtain input.*

MEETING GOAL: ADVANCE THE THINKING

DESCRIPTION   When a meeting planner wants the group to make progress on a topic, his or her goal is to *advance the thinking* on a specific step or task.

EXAMPLE   There are many types ways a group can *advance the thinking* at a single meeting. Here is a representative sample:

- Define a problem
- Analyze a problem
- Identify root causes
- Identify underlying patterns
- Sort a list of ideas into themes
- Rearrange a list of items by priority
- Draw a flowchart
- Identify core values

- Create a milestone map
- Create a work breakdown structure
- Conduct a resource analysis
- Conduct a risk assessment
- Define selection criteria
- Evaluate options
- Identify critical success factors
- Edit and/or wordsmith a statement

Note that clear deliverables can be defined for every task shown above. These are not just activities; they all produce tangible outputs.

KEY INSIGHT   Most projects involve several stages of work, and normally, many steps of thinking are embedded in each stage. Yet progress usually entails taking one step at a time. Thus, *advancing the thinking* is a legitimate meeting goal. This realization helps a planner become more precise in setting realistic and useful objectives.

MEETING GOAL: MAKE DECISIONS

DESCRIPTION   When a planner wants a group to address an issue and bring it to closure at the next meeting, the meeting goal is to *make a decision.*

EXAMPLE   Decisions that can be made at a meeting range from very simple to very difficult. The simple ones are those that are easy to think about – either because the stakes are low or because the issues are straightforward and familiar, with predictable consequences. For example, the majority of decisions in a budget-planning process turn out to be routine confirmations of ongoing programs and salaries. It's usually not problematic for groups to make simple decisions together at meetings.

By contrast, difficult decisions are quite challenging for groups to make. For example, a budget decision to cut a program or reduce payroll usually requires much more analysis and consideration. In other words, difficult decisions are best made *after* the issues have been well thought through.

KEY INSIGHT   Whether an issue is simple or complex, a commitment to make decisions at the next meeting means just that: the group is expected to bring the issue to closure. If a planner places a simple decision on the agenda, s/he can reasonably expect the group to achieve that goal. However, if a planner commits the group to make a difficult decision at the meeting, s/he is assuming that the challenging aspects have been adequately addressed. If they have not been, it probably makes more sense to commit the group to a meeting goal of *advancing the thinking*, not of *making decisions.*

MEETING GOAL: IMPROVE COMMUNICATION

DESCRIPTION When a meeting planner wants the members of a group to strengthen their working relationships by sharing feelings and/or dealing with interpersonal tension, the meeting goal is *improve communication.*

EXAMPLE A project team recently missed an important deadline. Some group members blamed the database coordinator for not finishing the data entry on schedule. Others blamed the project manager for creating a timetable that they felt was unrealistic to begin with. No one discussed their feelings openly at project meetings, but morale declined until the group set aside part of a meeting to raise these issues and clear the air.

KEY INSIGHT People normally do not consider their feelings to be appropriate subject matter for a meeting. Yet when a group schedules time to step away from task-related issues, so members can instead talk about their feelings and their relationships with one another, the benefits to a group can be significant. Unrecognized misperceptions and misunderstandings can be discovered and acted on. Paralyzing interpersonal grievances can be named, discussed, and reconciled. Dysfunctional group norms and patterns can be uncovered, explored, and replaced by more desirable procedures. But benefits notwithstanding, people normally do not engage in discussing this type of material *unless they are given explicit permission to do so.* And even then, it usually takes well-planned, well-structured activity to create the safe, supportive foundation this type of work requires.

MEETING GOAL: BUILD CAPACITY

DESCRIPTION   When a meeting planner schedules training time for members to focus on developing skills, the meeting goal is to *build capacity.*

EXAMPLE   A project team was working on their budget, with the overall goal of finalizing it. After two meetings on this topic, the project manager determined that key members did not understand basic accounting principles, causing them to become lost and confused during relevant discussions. The project manager decided to invite someone from the accounting department to spend a few hours with the group, teaching the relevant essentials of accounting.

KEY INSIGHT   Capacity-building is rarely viewed as something that can be done at a normal meeting. Instead, it is usually seen as training that should be done in classes offered by the training department, or by external programs and vendors. When instead it is treated as a meeting goal, many possibilities for increasing capacity arise. For example, team members can improve their problem-solving and decision-making capabilities; they can increase their knowledge of major trends in their industry; they can become more adept at a particular skill or best practice.

MEETING GOAL: BUILD COMMUNITY

DESCRIPTION   When a meeting planner wants to promote camaraderie, strengthen the bonds among people who work together, and generally boost morale, the meeting goal is to *build community*.

EXAMPLE   The project team decided that they would have a little celebration when they finalized their budget. They did not consider the achievement to be so major as to justify a grand celebration, yet neither did they want it to pass without some formal acknowledgment. The project manager decided to invite the project sponsor to come to the last hour of a late-afternoon meeting, at which time the group would present the budget to the sponsor for his final approval. By design, the sponsor would have seen the budget ahead of time. His main reason for coming to the meeting was to contribute to the goal of building community, which he did by offering some words of praise to the group – and by staying around for the food and drink, which the project manager then produced.

KEY INSIGHT   Community building is not normally considered to be a legitimate meeting goal.   Yet when it is seen as a meeting goal, it can achieve its purpose of strengthening bonds and boosting morale quite effectively. Celebrating birthdays can happen delightfully in 5-10 minutes. Likewise, the effect of sharing reactions as a group to a distressing current event is profound. Building community is not dependent on team-building offsites, as long as it is designed onto the agenda just like every other meeting goal.

– Community At Work –

Setting Outcomes for a Meeting

Facilitate the person-in-charge to:

1.   Identify all topics for the meeting.

2.   Select one to start with.

3.   List possible overall goals for that topic.

4.   Decide on an overall goal for that topic.

5.   Explore which type of meeting goal seems most suitable. Choose one.*

6.   Define the meeting goal precisely.*

Repeat Steps 1 to 6 with a new topic.

*Example: If the type of meeting goal is *Obtain input* (as chosen in Step 5), then the precise meeting goal might be something like, *Obtain input about Questions X and Y but not Z* (as defined in Step 6.)

Facilitators should keep in mind that this template is generic. When using it in real life, the person-in-charge will probably hop around from one step to another – or even from one topic to another – without completing the steps in the formal sequence. Follow his or her lead! Everyone has their own individual style of thinking.

DEFINING DESIRED OUTCOMES
FACILITATIVE QUESTIONS TO ASK A PERSON-IN-CHARGE

OVERALL GOALS

- What does success look like?

- How will you know when you're done?

- Fundamentally, what do you want to accomplish?

- Just to clarify, you're saying you'll be all done when . . .?

- What makes this important?

- What are you shooting for here?

- Tell me more about what you are trying to achieve.

- Suppose you had all the time and money you'd need. What do you *really* want to happen?

- Tell me more about your vision of the future.

MEETING GOALS

- Logically, what needs to be handled first?

- What part of this is urgent?

- What issues will need to be discussed in the future?

- What deliverables do you want this meeting to produce?

- Let's try breaking your overall goal into a few rough stages.

- At the end of this meeting, what do you want people to come away with?

- What could be done after the meeting?

- What could be done before the meeting?

- What could be done by people who are not at this meeting?

- What discussion needs everyone's involvement?

12

EFFECTIVE AGENDAS: PROCESS DESIGN

DESIGNING ACTIVITIES TO ACHIEVE
THE MEETING GOALS

- ▶ Designing a Process to Achieve
  a Meeting Goal

- ▶ Five Levels of Involvement

- ▶ Agenda Planning: Process Design

- ▶ Making Time Estimates for Activities

- ▶ Properties of an Effective Agenda

- ▶ Agenda Templates

- ▶ Agenda Planning Roles

DESIGNING A PROCESS TO ACHIEVE A MEETING GOAL

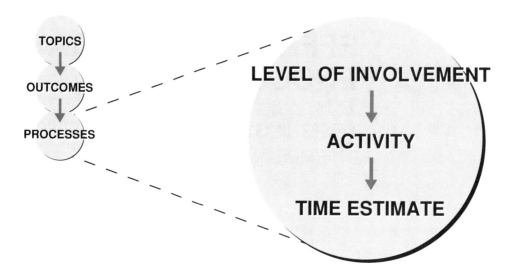

HOW INVOLVED DO YOU WANT PARTICIPANTS TO BE?   This is the first question a meeting planner has to answer, when s/he designs a process to achieve a meeting goal. For example, suppose *obtain input on a budget proposal* is the meeting goal. The planner might want the group simply to raise questions and make a few comments. Or s/he might prefer the group to engage in extensive discussion over key parts of the proposal. Obviously an extensive discussion will pull for more participation. Which level of participation does the planner consider to be most desirable, given the goal?

WHAT ACTIVITIES?   Once a planner sets the desired level of involvement, s/he can focus on designing an activity that encourages participation at the appropriate level. For example, if extensive discussion is desired, breakout groups might be a suitable activity. But if it is sufficient for the group to make a few comments, a single go-around might do the trick.

HOW MUCH TIME?   A planner can and should estimate the time it will take to achieve a given meeting goal *after* the two preceding steps have been explored. If it then appears that a given activity will require too much time, the planner can decide whether to change the activity or change the level of involvement desired.

FIVE LEVELS OF INVOLVEMENT

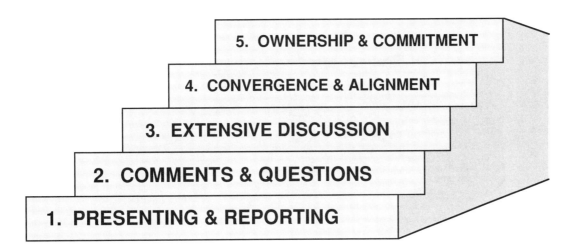

Here is a model that delineates five distinct levels of group participation and involvement. It can be used as a tool that assists meeting planners to design a process, once they have determined a meeting goal for a given topic.

If a planner does not want a group to spend very much time or energy on a particular goal, s/he should choose activities that correspond to the lower levels in this diagram. On the other hand, if s/he considers it important for group members to dig deeply into the issues at hand, then s/he would want to design a process that promotes the higher levels of involvement.

The processes that are associated with each of the lower three levels are self-evident. *Presenting and Reporting* is a one-way activity, which requires group members merely to sit and listen – and hopefully, to stay awake. *Comments and Questions* require active participation, but on a limited basis. *Extensive Discussion* requires sustained concentration and effort.

The two higher levels of involvement push a group into the *Groan Zone*. *Convergence and Alignment* requires participants to become able to think from each other's points of view, and to tolerate the tensions that arise during periods of misunderstanding, until they build a shared framework of understanding. *Ownership and Commitment* requires all of the above, with the added requirement that the participants persevere until they produce a solution that gains enthusiastic endorsement from all key participants.

This diagram is provided as a reminder of the many activities described in Chapter 7. When designing an agenda, a meeting planner can select participation formats from this page to encourage a suitable level of involvement from participants.

When a meeting goal calls for *presenting and reporting,* the process design is straightforward and self-evident. When a meeting goal calls for *questions and comments,* the planner has more latitude in selecting a suitable activity. All the simple formats – go arounds, small groups, open discussion, listing ideas, and individual writing – are candidates for facilitating involvement at the level of *questions and comments.*

When designing activities for meeting goals that pull for higher levels of involvement, planners can string together three or four different participation formats, one after the other, to produce the desired outcome. (See the next page.) Or they can create activities that are more sophisticated and intricate – such as the 40 activities provided in Chapters 14 -16 of this book.

AGENDA PLANNING: PROCESS DESIGN

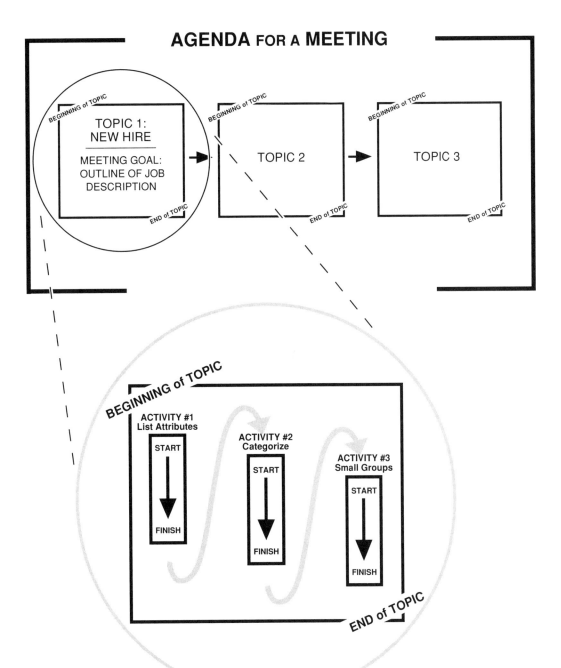

AGENDA FOR A MEETING

When a meeting goal pulls for high involvement, a planner can string together three or four different activities to produce the desired outcome. For example, if a meeting goal is to *advance the thinking* on a job description, a group could list attributes of the job; then categorize the list into themes; then break into small groups to write up each theme. This way of sequencing activities is called a *string*.

MAKING TIME ESTIMATES FOR ACTIVITIES

PROCESS	TYPICAL TIME	TIPS FOR ESTIMATING TIME
SMALL GROUPS	6-15 minutes	Decide how much time to give each person to speak. Multiply by the number of people in the group. Allow 3-4 minutes for instructions and the shuffling needed to form small groups.
GO-AROUNDS	5-20 minutes for an 8-person group, depending on topic	Assume 30 seconds per person for a simple question, and 2 minutes per person when the topic is deemed to be challenging or especially interesting.
LISTING IDEAS	7-10 minutes	The time limit for listing ideas is entirely arbitrary. However, more than 10 minutes without discussion is difficult for many to tolerate.
INDIVIDUAL WRITING	5-10 minutes	Allow 5 minutes for writing that is a "warm-up" to something else. Allow 10 minutes for writing that has a substantive purpose.
OPEN DISCUSSION	15-30 minutes	If high involvement is desired, assume the discussion will hit its stride after 5-10 minutes. When an open discussion runs longer than 20-30 minutes, attention will flag.
BREAKOUT GROUPS	30-90 minutes	Decide how much time to allow the groups to work. Then add 10 minutes for the shuffle to and from the breakout rooms.

PROPERTIES OF AN EFFECTIVE AGENDA

● Every topic to be covered at the meeting is clearly identified.

● Both the *overall goal* and the *meeting goal* for each topic have been defined. These may or may not be written onto the agenda, but they can and will be explicitly stated as needed.

● Each meeting goal is supported by a process that has been designed with the intention of encouraging an appropriate level of involvement. The process consists of one or more activities. In cases involving a highly substantive meeting goal, when no single activity will achieve the goal, a series of activities can be combined into a *string*.

● Realistic time estimates have been made for each activity. The estimated times may or may not be posted, but they will be reported when the process is described.

● The agenda begins with two items that bring people into the room: an overview (so everyone knows roughly what to expect for the rest of the meeting) and a brief welcoming activity, like a check-in. (See page 146.)

● The agenda ends with a way to provide participants with a sense of completion: a summary of accomplishments and a review of next steps, an evaluation of the meeting, or an opportunity for everyone to make a closing remark.

● A scheduled 10-minute break occurs whenever a meeting runs longer than 2 hours.

● The agenda is written and accessible – either as a printout distributed to everyone or as a flipchart posted on the wall.

AGENDA TEMPLATES

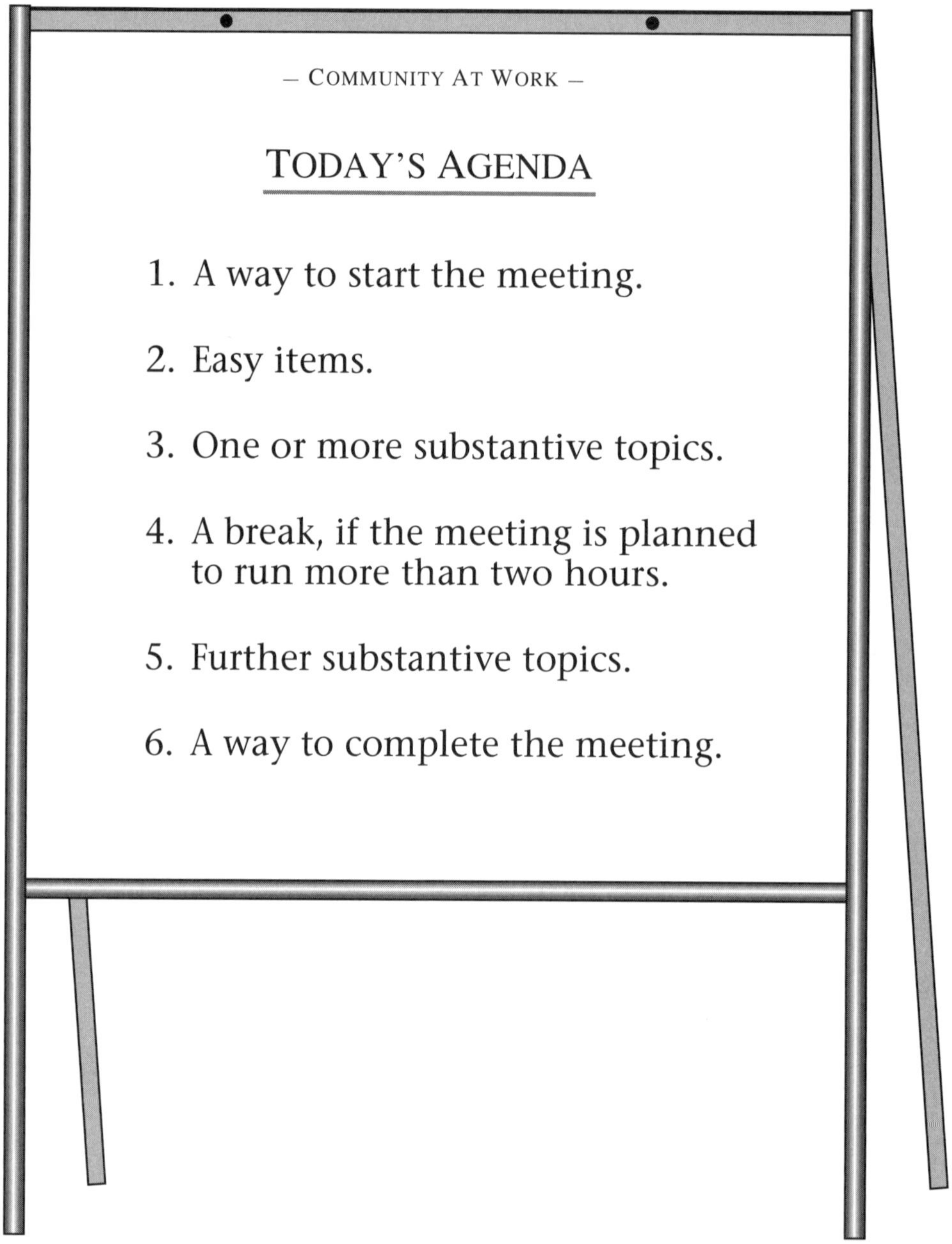

— Community At Work —

TODAY'S AGENDA

1. A way to start the meeting.

2. Easy items.

3. One or more substantive topics.

4. A break, if the meeting is planned to run more than two hours.

5. Further substantive topics.

6. A way to complete the meeting.

This diagram shows the underlying structure of an effective agenda. In the real world, each group customizes this structure to fit its own circumstances. The following pages present templates for six approaches in common use.

— COMMUNITY AT WORK —

QUICK BUSINESS & MAJOR TOPICS

1. Check-in and Agenda Review

2. Quick Business

3. First Major Topic
   - State today's meeting goal.
   - Describe the process to be followed.
   - Proceed until goal is met.
   - Identify action items.

— Break —

4. Second Major Topic
   - State today's meeting goal.
   - Describe the process to be followed.
   - Proceed until goal is met.
   - Identify action items.

5. Meeting Evaluation

BEST USE: This format is used for ongoing management-team meetings at which decisions are needed for several major items the same day.

TIMING: Quick Business in this format often takes 30-45 minutes. The items can be handled in a line-'em-up, knock-'em-down fashion. Each Major Topic will run at least 30 minutes – usually longer. Overall, a meeting with more than one major topic should be designed to last at least 2.5 hours. Major topics require more attention to process design than quick business items. Most quick business items can be handled by a simple open discussion.

— COMMUNITY AT WORK —

QUICK BUSINESS / MAIN EVENT

1. Check-in and Agenda Review

2. Quick Business

3. Main Event
   - State today's meeting goal.
   - Describe the process to be followed.
   - Proceed.
   - Take a short break every 90 minutes.
   - Continue until goal is met.

4. Action Plans
   - Identify action items.
   - For each item, determine *who?*
     what? and *by when?*
   - Is there a need to disseminate
     information from today's discussion?
     If so, *what?* and *how?*

5. Meeting Evaluation

BEST USE: This format works best when a group has been convened for a special purpose: to problem-solve a complex issue that has a beginning, middle, and end. Examples include developing a strategic plan, setting an annual budget, planning a sizable layoff, or designing a reorganization. This type of meeting requires planners to design a well-thought-out process.

TIMING: These meetings typically last 3-6 hours per session. The project often runs for several weeks or more. Quick business is best done by giving each person 5-7 minutes to use as s/he wishes. Unfinished items are recorded on a back burner, to be dealt with off line or at the next meeting.

– COMMUNITY AT WORK –

OLD BUSINESS / NEW BUSINESS

1. Adoption of Last Meeting's Minutes

2. Announcements and Reports

3. Old Business
   - Begin with oldest outstanding item recorded in *the minutes*, which lists items tabled from prior meetings.
   - Deal with the item or table it again.
   - Continue until every *old business* item is either handled or tabled.

4. New Business
   - *New business* items must be listed on the agenda ahead of time.
   - All *new business* items must be handled or tabled until next meeting.

5. Meeting Evaluation

BEST USE: This format – a simplified Robert's Rules – is used in volunteer organizations, especially in board meetings. Since members are not regular co-workers, they tend not to spend much time thinking about the agenda items between meetings. Therefore, minutes from prior meetings are used as the key tool to structure the agenda.

TIMING: The meeting lasts as long as it takes to complete old business and new business. Under time pressure, groups tend to defer many items.

— COMMUNITY AT WORK —

LINE 'EM UP & KNOCK 'EM DOWN

1. Check-in

2. Announcements

3. Today's Business Items
   - List all items
   - Rank items by priority
   - Begin with highest-priority item
   - Clarify desired outcome
   - When discussion is complete, identify and record any next steps.
   - Continue process until all items are dealt with, or time runs out.

4. Review Next Steps

5. Meeting Evaluation

BEST USE: This format is used at an ongoing staff meeting, at which most business items are straightforward. This format requires no advance planning, and therefore the desired outcome must be clarified in real time during the meeting. When complex topics are raised, they may be discussed as input, but they are rarely decided at the meeting.

TIMING: Today's Business Items lasts for a fixed time, usually 45 minutes. Overall, this type of meeting is usually scheduled to last 1 hour.

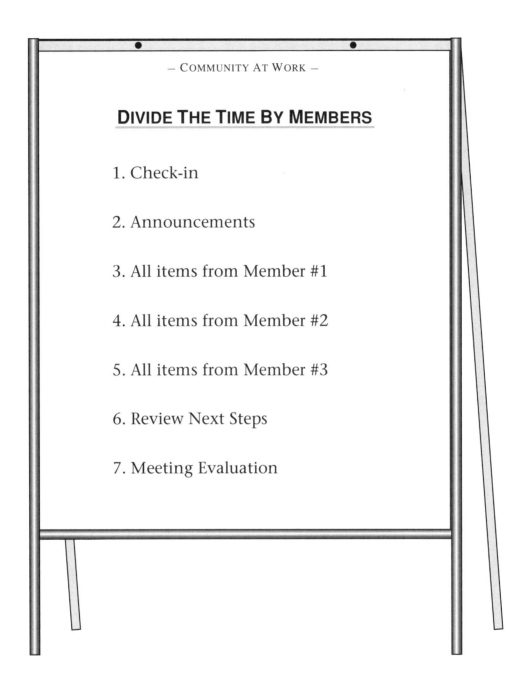

BEST USE: This format is especially suitable for groups whose members have different areas of responsibility. It can be used both to obtain input and to make decisions. Note, however, that this format will work only if each member prepares in advance by defining the overall goal and meeting goal for each topic s/he raises.

TIMING: Each group determines for itself how much time to allot each member. Everyone receives equal time unless someone negotiates for more.

— COMMUNITY AT WORK —

STATUS REPORTS

1. Check-in

2. Announcements

3. Status Reports

For each project being reported on:
- Summarize the project's overall goal and current targets.
- Report on significant events that have occurred since last review.
- List all action items identified when project was last reviewed.
- For each action item, report on what was done or not done.
- Field questions.
- As a group, list new action items with brief discussion as needed.

4. Meeting Evaluation

BEST USE: This format is useful for meetings of project teams. It's also useful for program staff meetings at which most staff members are working independently, and want to keep one another updated.

TIMING: To keep people engaged, status reports should take no more than 10-15 minutes per report. Half that time should be spent discussing action items. This type of meeting takes less than 1 hour. To shorten the meeting further, not everyone has to report at every meeting.

AGENDA PLANNING ROLES

THE FACILITATOR	THE PERSON-IN-CHARGE
Explains the importance of reserving time to plan the agenda.	Decides how much time to invest in agenda planning.
Asks the person-in-charge to list all possible topics.	Identifies possible topics and decides which to include.
Asks the person-in-charge to set the *overall goal* for each topic.	Clarifies the *overall goal* for each topic.
Encourages the person-in-charge to define *meeting goals* for each topic.	Sets the *meeting goal* for each topic on the agenda.
Suggests thinking activities for the group to engage in during each segment of the meeting.	Considers the options and makes decisions regarding the process design for each segment.
Puts together a draft agenda, complete with time estimates.	Makes any revisions to the draft and validates the final agenda.
Does not present the agenda at the meeting. (The person-in-charge is the owner of the outcomes.)	Presents the agenda at the meeting and explains the objectives for each item.

Part Three

BUILDING
SUSTAINABLE
AGREEMENTS

13

PRINCIPLES FOR BUILDING SUSTAINABLE AGREEMENTS

MAKING DECISIONS THAT INCORPORATE
EVERYONE'S POINT OF VIEW

▶ **What Makes an Agreement Sustainable**

▶ **Case Example: A Typical Tale of Woe**

▶ **Case Example: Success Story**

▶ **Business-as-Usual Compared with Participatory Decision-Making**

▶ **Two Mind-Sets: Either/Or and Both/And**

▶ **Facilitating Sustainable Agreements**

WHAT MAKES AN AGREEMENT SUSTAINABLE ?

IDEALIZED SEQUENCE

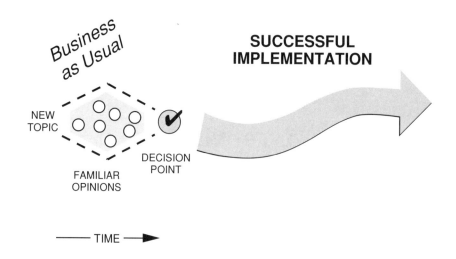

The diagram shown above represents an idealized sequence of the relationship between the discussion that precedes a decision, and the implementation that follows a decision. The discussion is quick and direct, and the implementation is straightforward.

Many people – perhaps most people – really do believe in this model. No struggle. No *Groan Zone*. No problems. Just a clean, linear, predictable forward movement from the inception of an idea to the end of its implementation.

And the reason the model is so widely credible is simple: *most of the time, it works!* In other words, most of the decisions a group makes *are* routine. The issues are familiar, the solutions are obvious, and the implementation can be accomplished with a bare minimum of planning and organizing.

Not all problems are routine, though. And what most people don't realize is that *this model does not work when the problem is a difficult one.*

WHAT MAKES AN AGREEMENT SUSTAINABLE ?

TOUGH PROBLEMS DON'T SOLVE EASILY

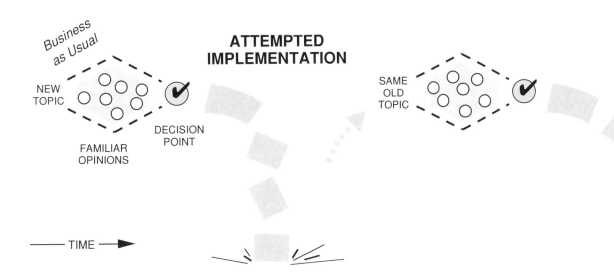

When a group attempts to solve a *difficult* problem as though it were a routine problem, they will very likely make a decision that simply does not work. The implementation will break down, and the group will find itself, sooner or later, back where it began.

Groups that pressure themselves to solve a tough problem with a conventional business-as-usual discussion frequently produce "pseudo-solutions" – ideas that sound good at the time, but are ridiculous in retrospect. Here are some common pseudo-solutions:

- Agree on the top 20 priorities
- Delegate a job to someone who is already too overworked to do it
- Establish a policy that has no accountability built into it
- Create a committee to do the same work all over again
- Create a program and don't fund it
- Make an agreement that will be vetoed by someone who is not present
- Agree to "try harder" from now on

Pseudo-solutions don't solve anything; they merely provide participants with an illusory feeling of closure, so people can believe they accomplished something without having to go through the *Groan Zone*.

UNSUSTAINABLE AGREEMENTS

A TYPICAL TALE OF WOE

It's a mistake to expect a business-as-usual discussion to solve a difficult problem. Here's a case in point.

CASE STUDY

The owner of a large urban department store had a problem: his salespeople were consistently late for work. The owner had tried everything he could think of – fines, threats, pleading – but nothing worked. So he called a storewide staff meeting to tackle the problem.

The meeting began in good spirits. Many participants had an opinion about what the "real problem" was, and they were eager to state their views.

There appeared to be two camps. One group, including most floor managers and supervisors, believed that the owner hired too many students to work part-time. Students, they said, are transient – not committed to the long-term health of the business. If supervisors were free to hire more full-time employees, they could instill the staff with more loyalty, better morale, and higher standards of discipline.

The other group, including most salespeople, said that the problem was caused by the way they were paid. They were on commission, and very few shoppers appeared before mid-morning. Therefore, said the salespeople, they rarely earned any money for the first hour of the day. They recommended that those who opened the store should be paid a few extra dollars per day for their work.

The store owner listened as the two sides debated each other. After a while, people's patience began to wear thin. No one seemed to be changing their mind, and the group hadn't found any new ideas. The group saw no point in continuing. Someone said, "Everyone can't always get what they want. Sometimes there are winners and losers, and we just have to bite the bullet." So the owner said, "Here's my proposal. For the next four months, everyone who works on the first floor will be paid extra for coming on time. If it works, I will do it storewide. If it doesn't work, I will switch policies and hire more full-time employees. How does this sound?" A few people said, "Fine" or "Let's try it." The owner asked for objections, got none, and said, "All right, we're agreed."

After the meeting most people felt that the salespeople "won" and the managers "lost." The salespeople were glad for the extra pay and pleased that their concerns had been heard. But the supervisors were irritated. They felt the owner had not respected their judgment and that their authority had been undermined.

Over the next few months, the part-time students were treated very poorly. If someone asked to work Thursday and Friday, that person was scheduled to work Monday and Tuesday. If they asked to work evenings, they got mornings. The students reacted predictably: by taking long breaks; by spending too much time on personal phone calls; by calling in sick at the last minute; by quitting on two days' notice. The full-time sales staff saw what was happening and reacted by complaining more than ever. Morale on the first floor dropped to an all-time low.

Four months later, the owner ended the experiment and told the managers to hire more full-time staff. They were relieved. Now, with a better workforce, they could move forward on their goals of improving morale and loyalty and instilling higher standards of discipline. But the sales staff were resentful. They felt they'd been robbed of extra income by a management that had sabotaged the agreement. They told newly hired employees, "Don't trust your boss; he is a jerk." Tensions lingered for years. And the original problem – coming to work late – grew even worse, and was never resolved.

SUSTAINABLE AGREEMENTS

SUCCESS STORY

When a group makes a commitment to engage in participatory decision-making, the process can produce meaningful, integrated, broadly supported solutions to exceedingly difficult problems. The keys are to resource it properly, and stay committed to the process. Here's a real-life example.*

CASE STUDY

In Mendocino County, California, local authorities brought together a group of loggers, environmentalists, and government officials to try to resolve a longstanding quarrel over the fate of privately owned redwood groves.

Until 1975 the property tax on privately owned forest land was based on the number of standing trees. The more trees on your property, the more tax you paid. To give the lumber companies an incentive to replant, all redwood trees under forty years old were exempt from the tax. But this policy had an unintended consequence: it created an incentive to cut down all older redwood trees, including ancient redwoods, whether or not the wood was in demand.

Environmentalists proposed taxing *all* redwoods, regardless of age. Lumber companies opposed this proposal. They argued that it would discourage them from replanting. Further, it would induce them to cut down even more trees – fewer standing trees would mean fewer taxes. Many residents of Mendocino County were advocates for preserving old-growth forests, and the county politicians felt pressured to find a workable solution.

Accordingly they created a task force with representatives from all factions. The task force was charged with developing a proposal for revising the tax code. The proposal would then be submitted to the California State legislature for approval.

The first meetings of the task force were polarized. The loggers insisted that the environmentalists' proposal would wreak havoc on the local economy, which depended heavily on the viability of the lumber business. Environmentalists retorted that the lumber companies were mercenary and short-sighted, and that they failed to protect the needs of the local ecosystem.

Many observers doubted that the group could produce a proposal that would make it through the legislative gauntlet. (Ten committees had to approve the bill – providing special-interest lobbyists ample opportunity to stall a proposal they didn't agree with.) But the conveners of the task force were determined to overcome the odds. They provided encouragement and staff support, so the group could keep working to find a solution that would be agreeable to all parties. They knew that letting

the dispute persist would lead to costly legal battles, a divided community, and various potential disruptions in the local economy.

Over the next few months, the task force met regularly. They gradually relaxed their posturing and became more willing to search for common ground. As they became more familiar with each other's points of view, their discussion became more interesting and more insightful.

It took them several months, but they found a creative framework: What if they stopped calculating property tax based on standing trees and switched to a tax based on *cut lumber?* This would discourage lumber companies from logging more than they could immediately market. By removing the tax on standing trees, land owners were no longer penalized for preserving ancient redwoods.

They developed a formal proposal and sent it to the legislature. Since it was supported by all sides, the proposal sailed through all ten legislative committees without opposition. The bill passed quickly, became law, and the entire community benefited.

* This case study was told to Sam Kaner by a former lumber industry lobbyist who was a member of the task force described here.

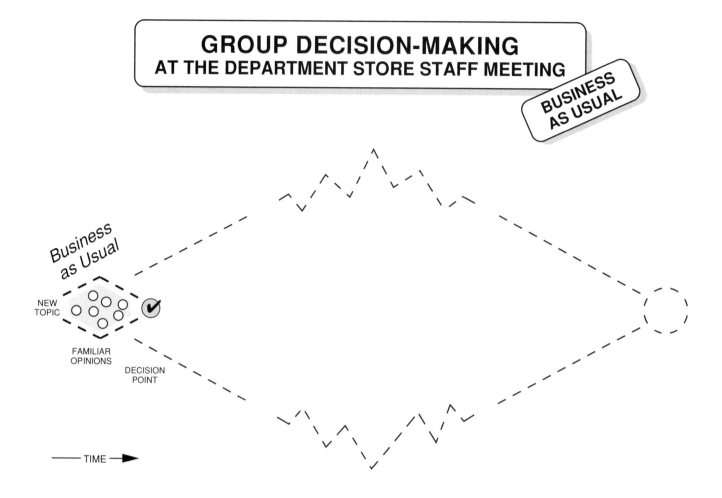

What went wrong at the department store staff meeting? Not only did the participants fail to solve the tardiness problem, but their course of action bred long-lasting animosity and cynicism. The above diagram offers insight into the reasons their meeting produced such poor outcomes.

Not realizing how much effort it would take to find a sustainable agreement, the group engaged in a *business-as-usual* decision-making process. They arrived at a decision without ever breaking out of the narrow band of familiar opinions to hunt for creative options. No one, for example, even raised the possibility of opening the store an hour later. Nor did anyone suggest simple but offbeat ideas, such as offering free cappuccino to early-morning shoppers. Rather than search for alternatives, the group focused on two conventional approaches: people stated their own points of view without thinking too deeply about the larger implications of their opinions, or they repeated their arguments until nothing new was being said. No one attempted to take the other side's needs into account. The owner, who expected to reach closure at that meeting, suggested a proposal and then made a superficial effort to check for group agreement. Thus, the group reached a quick decision – quick, but entirely ineffective.

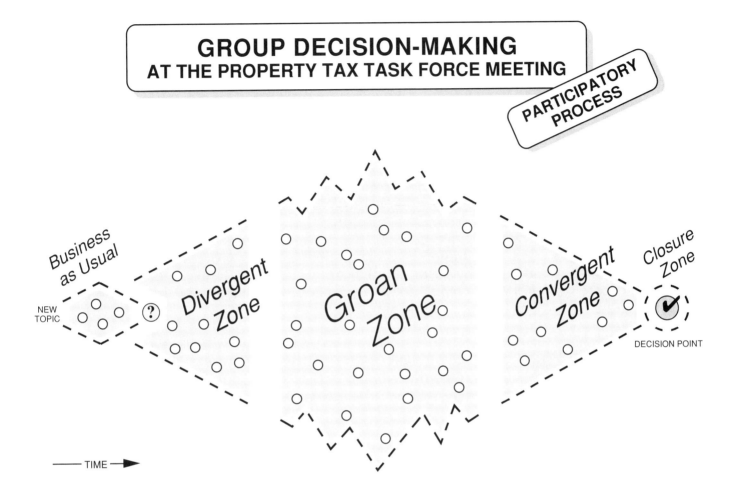

GROUP DECISION-MAKING
AT THE PROPERTY TAX TASK FORCE MEETING

PARTICIPATORY PROCESS

Business as Usual

NEW TOPIC

Divergent Zone

Groan Zone

Convergent Zone

Closure Zone

DECISION POINT

TIME →

What made the second case turn out so differently? After all, the problem itself was much more difficult: the stakes were higher, the competing interest groups were more powerful, and the overall structure for reaching closure was incomparably more complicated. Yet the parties were able to find a creative solution that was genuinely acceptable to all sets of stakeholders. The diagram above is a rough schematic representation of the type of decision-making process *this* group engaged in.

Recognizing that they had a difficult problem on their hands, this group did not try to solve the problem in a meeting or two; instead they created a structure that allowed them to keep working for as long as it took to solve the problem. As for the decision-making authority, they saw that all parties would have to agree to the final decision or it wouldn't work. This, in turn, allowed them to survive the rocky start. Once they broke out of the narrow band – which in their case was marked by arguments between factions – it was inevitable that they would enter the *Groan Zone*. They had to struggle, sometimes for entire meetings, to understand one another's perspectives. Over time, they built a shared framework of understanding, which allowed them to create a solution that incorporated everyone's point of view.

TWO MIND-SETS FOR SOLVING PROBLEMS

Why did the results of the department store staff meeting turn out so poorly, compared to the results of the property tax task force? Part of the answer to this question is obvious: *they organized themselves differently*. The people at the department store held a single meeting: business as usual. They gave themselves a chance to air familiar opinions; then they brought the issue to closure. In contrast, the members of the property tax task force designed a participatory process that allowed their problem-solving process to unfold in stages. They too began by airing familiar opinions – but they created a structure that supported people to move beyond their starting positions and build a shared framework of understanding.

But this tells us *what* they did, not *why* they did it. Why, in other words, did the two groups organize themselves so differently? The answer is that each group was operating from a different *mind-set* for solving problems: one group had an *Either/Or mind-set*; the other group had a *Both/And mind-set*.

From an *Either/Or mind-set*, solving a problem is a matter of making a choice among competing alternatives. Either you choose option "A" or you choose option "B" – someone wins and someone loses, and that's how it goes. From a *Both/And mind-set*, solving a problem is a matter of finding an inclusive solution – one that encompasses everyone's point of view. Rather than choosing between options "A" and "B," you search for a brand-new alternative that is satisfactory to everyone.

Groups that operate from an *Either/Or mind-set* are in a hurry. They want to get the decision over with. After all, what's the point of going over and over the same territory? Once the range of options has been clarified, further discussion becomes irrelevant. But groups that operate from a *Both/And mind-set* place a higher value on effectiveness than on expedience.

If the original range of options can provide the group with a workable solution, then great! Decisions that can be made quickly *should* be made quickly. But if the original range of options does not provide a workable solution, then more work lies ahead. The goal in such groups is not merely to reach a decision, but to reach a *sustainable agreement* – that is, to find a solution that works.

Several characteristics of these two mind-sets are contrasted on the next page.

TWO MIND-SETS FOR SOLVING PROBLEMS

	EITHER / OR	BOTH / AND
VALUE SYSTEM	Competitive	Collaborative
TYPE OF OUTCOME EXPECTED	Win / Lose	Win / Win
ATTITUDE TOWARD "WINNING"	To the victor goes the spoils.	Your success is my success.
ATTITUDE TOWARD "LOSING"	Someone has to lose.	If someone loses, everyone loses.
ATTITUDE TOWARD MINORITY OPINIONS	Get with the program.	Everyone has a piece of the truth.
WHY EXPLORE DIFFERENCES BETWEEN COMPETING POSITIONS?	To search for bargaining chips, in preparation for horse trading and compromise.	To build a shared framework of understanding, in preparation for mutual creative thinking.
ESSENTIAL MENTAL ACTIVITY	Analyze: break wholes into parts.	Synthesize: integrate parts into wholes.
HOW LONG IT TAKES	It's usually faster in the short run.	It's usually faster in the long run.
WHEN TO USE IT	When expedience is more important than durability, *Either/Or thinking* will usually produce satisfactory results.	When all parties have the power to block any decision, and the issue is for high stakes, *Both/And thinking* is usually the only hope for resolution.
UNDERLYING PHILOSOPHY	Survival of the fittest.	Interdependence of all things.

WHAT MAKES AN AGREEMENT SUSTAINABLE ?

SHARED UNDERSTANDING

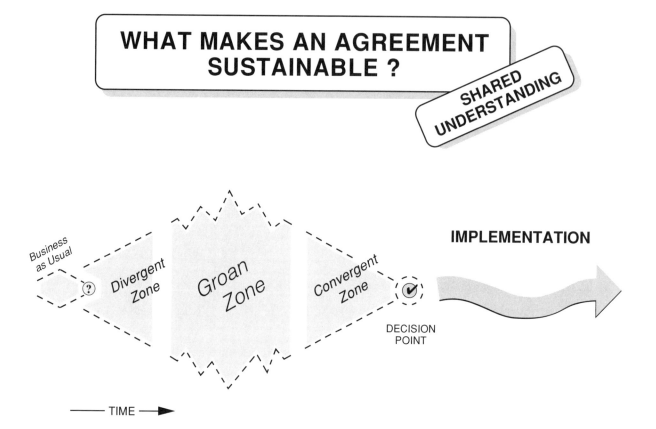

This diagram represents the process of building sustainable agreements. Up to the point of decision, progress is slow – much slower than anyone expects – as the members of the group struggle to develop a shared framework of understanding. The implementation, on the other hand, is often interesting, exciting, and challenging – rather than painful. Bringing a sustainable agreement to fruition is like swimming with the tide instead of against it. People feel confident that their efforts are headed toward results.

What is it that makes a sustainable agreement sustainable? The answer is that the agreement is based on a solution that incorporates everyone's point of view. Participants would say, "Yes, this works! From my perspective, this proposal actually does solve the problem."

How does a group achieve this? By patient, persistent effort. People keep working to understand one another's goals and needs and fears and frames of reference. They face conflicts and overcome them; they explore possibilities by putting themselves in each other's shoes; they challenge their underlying assumptions; they search for imaginative solutions. And they share responsibility for reaching a result that works for everyone.

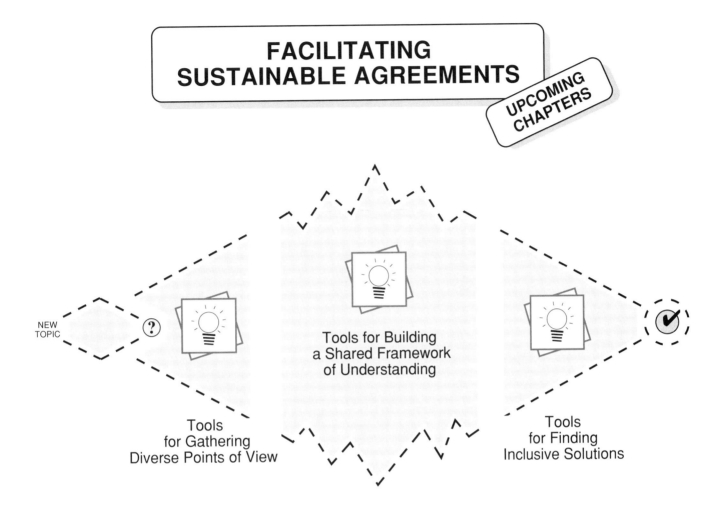

FACILITATING
SUSTAINABLE AGREEMENTS

UPCOMING
CHAPTERS

NEW
TOPIC

Tools
for Gathering
Diverse Points of View

Tools for Building
a Shared Framework
of Understanding

Tools
for Finding
Inclusive Solutions

*G*roups need different types of support at different points in the process. Facilitators who understand this will vary their technique accordingly. Different zones call for different tools and skills.

For example, it is unwise to promote convergent thinking in a group whose members have not yet built a shared framework of understanding. They will probably not trust solutions proposed by their opponents, because they do not yet feel personally understood by one another. On the other hand, if members are *able* to take each other's needs into account, they might benefit greatly from a structured thinking activity that helps them hunt for inclusive solutions.

The preceding chapters of this book have introduced the fundamental skills of group facilitation. Skills like listening, chartwriting, and process management are useful in *every* zone. But there are also many facilitation tools that are designed to work in a *specific* zone. Dozens of these tools are presented in the next three chapters.

14

GATHERING DIVERSE POINTS OF VIEW

PRINCIPLES AND TOOLS THAT PROMOTE FREE EXPRESSION

▶ **Introduction to the Divergent Zone**

▶ **Six Tools for Surveying the Territory**

▶ **Six Tools for Generating Alternatives**

▶ **Three Tools for Raising Difficult Issues**

▶ **Summary**

GATHERING DIVERSE POINTS OF VIEW

INTRODUCTION

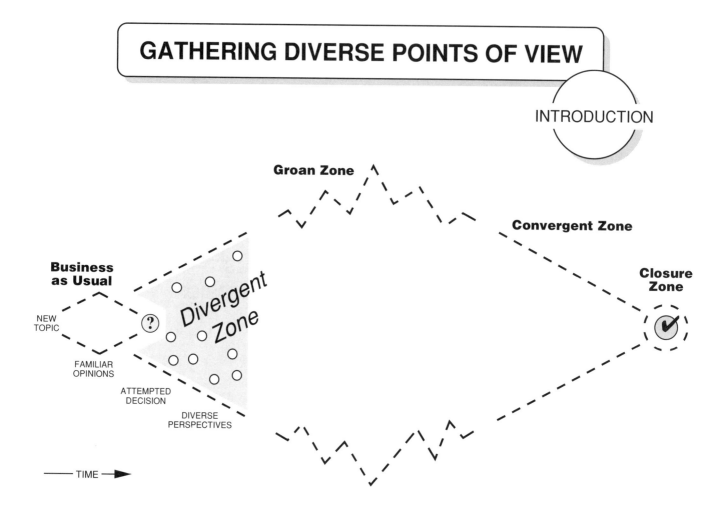

The facilitator's main task in the *Divergent Zone* is to create opportunities for everyone to express their views on the topic at hand. At this phase of the discussion, the facilitator does not even try to resolve disagreements. S/he honors everything everyone says and refrains from asking participants to revise or reconsider their opinions.

Structured thinking activities like the ones presented in this chapter can be very helpful in the *Divergent Zone*. Structure serves as a container. It can allow members to express a wide range of opinions without fearing that their diversity will overwhelm the group's resources. People sense this, and they feel relief at the thought that the process is "under control." For this reason, many groups are pleased to be given an opportunity to do structured thinking in the *Divergent Zone*. Facilitators can offer their suggestions with confidence that they will usually be well received.

GATHERING DIVERSE POINTS OF VIEW

THREE TYPES OF THINKING IN THE DIVERGENT ZONE

Whenever a group is engaged in divergent thinking, the members are *increasing the diversity* of the material they can work with. Divergent thinking expands the range of the ideas that can be discussed further. This principle holds true whether group members are engaged in a boisterous round of brainstorming or whether they are nervously sharing their individual reactions to a painful controversy. In either case, their activity will result in the emergence of a greater diversity of perspectives. This is the defining property of the *Divergent Zone.*

Nonetheless, not all divergent thinking is the same. There are different *types* of divergent thinking, and each has its own characteristics. The three most common types are: *Surveying the Territory, Searching for Alternatives,* and *Raising Difficult Issues.*

Type 1: Surveying the Territory

Surveying the Territory involves identifying the components of the problem under discussion. For example, suppose a group is facing a contentious dispute. If every group member takes a turn stating his or her position, everyone will get an initial impression of the complexity of the conflict. The essence of this type of divergent thinking is *collecting perspectives.*

Type 2: Searching for Alternatives

Searching for Alternatives refers to the creative activity of listing unusual, innovative ideas. Some ideas on the list will prove to be realistic; many will not. The essence of this type of divergent thinking is *generating ideas.*

Type 3: Raising Difficult Issues

Raising Difficult Issues involves the discussion of a troubling – often threatening – subject. Some groups treat the members who raise difficult issues as troublemakers; deviations from the party line are squelched. But other groups make an effort to respond to someone who raises a difficult issue by sharing the risk and encouraging everyone to disclose his or her individual perspective. The ensuing discussion usually turns out to be quite meaningful. The essence of this type of divergent thinking is *speaking freely.*

SURVEYING THE TERRITORY
DIVERGENT ZONE THINKING ACTIVITY: TYPE 1

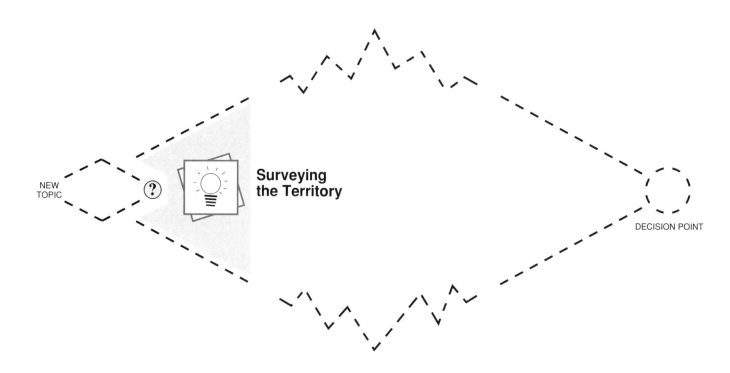

Surveying the Territory is the most common – and the most essential – type of divergent thinking. It involves identifying components of the problem under discussion. The basic question on people's minds is something like, "How complex *is* this problem?" or "What are we dealing with here?"

The simplest way to help a group survey the territory is by suggesting a go-around. This gives people the opportunity to hear the range of different objectives, problems, questions, and feelings that might be connected to the subject at hand. By the time the go-around ends, the overall scope of the group's task will have become much more visible.

Sometimes a simple go-around will not provide the group with enough direction. For example, one group might need to find out whether there are different goals in the room; another group might need to find out whether the right people are in the room. This is a perfect opportunity for the facilitator to suggest a structured thinking activity that can help the group *Survey the Territory*. Six such activities are described in the following pages.

SURVEYING THE TERRITORY

SPEAK FROM
YOUR OWN PERSPECTIVE

WHY

This is a basic, straightforward activity that encourages participants to offer their own points of view on the topic at hand.

The purpose of this activity is to enable members to quickly gain a picture of the breadth of the group's thinking. By seeing all the parts, the group gains a sense of the whole.

Another purpose of the activity is to legitimize and validate every perspective. By allowing the group to hear each person's contribution, this activity sends the message that "Everyone has something to offer."

HOW

1. Pose an open-ended question such as:

   • How would you describe what's going on?
   • How does this problem affect you?
   • What is your position on this matter?
   • Why, in your opinion, is this happening?

2. Ask each person to answer the question without commenting on each other's ideas.

3. Close the activity by asking participants for their reactions, general comments and learnings.

4. Optional Step:
   When everyone has had a chance to express their views, ask,
   "Is there anyone absent today who might have a significantly different perspective? What might that person tell us?"

SURVEYING THE TERRITORY

SPECIFYING REQUIREMENTS

WHY

When tackling a difficult problem, different stakeholders bring different requirements to the table. To be sustainable, the eventual solution must take into account every stakeholder's requirements. For example, an appliance manufacturing company held a product design meeting to discuss the development of a new, low-energy light bulb. The purchasing department wanted the bulb to be built from parts and materials that were readily available. The marketing department insisted that the shape of the bulb had to fit in standardized packaging. The engineering department wanted precise timetables from research and development so they would know how to schedule their staff. And the company president wanted assurance that the new product would be a salable commodity.

For groups like these, the challenge is to take stock of *all* requirements before getting bogged down in specifics. This activity helps a group to gain a preliminary understanding of everyone's conditions for success.

HOW

1. Hang two sheets of chart paper, one titled "Requirements and Necessary Conditions" and the other "Topics for Further Discussion."

2. Break the group into pairs. Ask each person to take a turn describing his or her own requirements and necessary conditions for success.

3. Reconvene the large group. Give each person three minutes to state his or her requirements and five minutes to answer questions. Record each requirement on the chart paper. Questions that would require further discussion are also recorded.

4. After repeating Step 3 for each person, have the group examine the lists and decide how to organize the subsequent discussion.

SURVEYING THE TERRITORY
WHO, WHAT, WHEN, WHERE, AND HOW?

WHY

When solving problems in groups, people come to the table with *very different questions* based on their individual perspectives. Since everyone wants their own questions answered, they often have trouble recognizing that many, many questions – not just their own – need to be answered. This element of divergent thinking is one of the most difficult aspects of group decision-making.

At a recent meeting, for example, one person who was mystified by the budgeting process requested clarifications and explanations repeatedly. Another asked several questions about the reasons why certain people had been invited to the meeting while others had not. A third person appeared to understand everything but one little detail, about which he kept asking questions. Each was focused on his or her own questions and could not see that others were struggling with entirely different questions.

This activity supports a group to identify *the whole range of questions* before they get too focused on wrestling with any single question.

HOW

1. Hang five sheets of paper titled respectively, "Who?" "What?" "When?" "Where?" and "How?"

2. Start by naming the general topic. For example, "We're now going to start planning the annual staff retreat."

3. On the "Who?" page, brainstorm a list of questions that begin with "Who?" For example, "Who will set the agenda?" "Who knows someone who can rent us a conference room?" "Who should be invited?" "Who said we can't spend more than $500?"

4. Repeat Step 3 for each of the other sheets.

5. When all five lists are complete, identify the easy questions and answer them. Then make a plan to answer the rest.

This tool was inspired by an exercise called "Five W's and H" in A. B. VanGundy, Jr., *Techniques of Structured Problem Solving,* 2nd ed. (New York: Van Nostrand Reinhold, 1988), p. 46.

SURVEYING THE TERRITORY

FACTS AND OPINIONS

WHY

This activity enables a group to trade a lot of information without getting bogged down in a discussion of who is right or what is true.

For example, suppose a group needed to begin thinking about next year's budget. *Facts and Opinions* would help them to generate numerical statistics ("last year we spent $4,000 on legal fees") and speculation ("we might want to initiate two new lawsuits next year") both within a short period of time.

Note that in this example, *Facts and Opinions* postpones the debate over the budget. Instead, the thrust of the exercise is to gather a lot of material on many different subjects. Once group members see the big picture, they can decide which topics to discuss and in what order.

HOW

1. To prepare for this activity, hang two large pieces of paper on a wall. Title one "Facts" and the other "Opinions." Also, make available sticky notes in two colors, with enough for every member to receive at least ten of each color.

2. Ask the group members, "What do you know about this topic?" Have each group member write his or her answers on the sticky notes, using one color for "Facts" and the other color for "Opinions." (If asked how to know whether something is a fact or an opinion, answer, "Please decide for yourself. If you're not sure, write it both ways.")

3. Have each person post his or her sticky notes on the wall. The notes should be posted as soon as they are written, so everyone can read the posted notes whenever they like. Reading often prompts new thinking. Participants can continue posting ideas until time is up.

4. After all data have been collected, ask the group for their observations and reflections.

STARTING POSITIONS

WHY

This activity is perfect for helping people deal with a contentious issue – especially when their conflict is fueled by a wide range of opposing perspectives.

When people are brought together to resolve a dispute, many participants arrive with strong opinions and well-rehearsed arguments. They need to be given a chance to express their opinions fully, so they can let everyone else see where they stand.

When people aren't able to speak without being interrupted or discounted, it is predictable that they will insert their positions into the discussion at every opportunity. Conversely, when people *are* supported to state their positions fully, they frequently become more able to listen to one another. This often leads to better mutual understanding, which is a precondition for finding creative solutions to difficult problems.

HOW

1. Introduce the activity by indicating that there may be several diverse perspectives in the room. Encourage everyone to give each other the time and the attention each person needs to express his or her views.

2. Using a go-around format, ask each speaker to take a turn answering the following questions from his or her individual perspective:

   • What is the problem and what solution is s/he advocating?
   • What are his or her reasons for taking this particular position?

   Note: This step is often done by having each speaker come up to the front of the room and present his or her ideas standing up.

3. When each person has had a turn, ask the group for observations and reflections.

SURVEYING THE TERRITORY

UNREPRESENTED PERSPECTIVES

WHY

People in a group often share so many assumptions in common that they may not recognize their own blind spots. Yet omitting a key perspective can ruin the outcome of an otherwise participatory process.

For example, in the 1980s, urban-based environmental organizations, in collaboration with state and federal agencies, drew up many unpopular and ultimately unacceptable proposals for rural conservation. These plans were rarely supported by the loggers or miners whose livelihoods were being threatened. In many cases, the plans were unworkable because they had been designed without adequate understanding of the needs and goals of the working people in the affected communities.

This activity assists a group to determine whether there are stakeholders whose perspective should be better represented at future meetings.

HOW

1. List every group of stakeholders that might be affected by this problem. Don't forget to include less-than-obvious stakeholders. For example, does your issue affect trainees? Suppliers? Neighbors? Does it affect the families of employees? For this activity, every affected stakeholder group matters.

2. One by one, go down the list considering each group in the following way: "How does the situation at hand affect this stakeholder group?" Example: "How does our project expansion for next year affect our trainees?"

3. When the list is complete ask, "Has anyone spotted a problem that wasn't previously identified?" and "Is there someone missing from these meetings who should be included from now on?"

SEARCHING FOR ALTERNATIVES
DIVERGENT ZONE THINKING ACTIVITY: TYPE 2

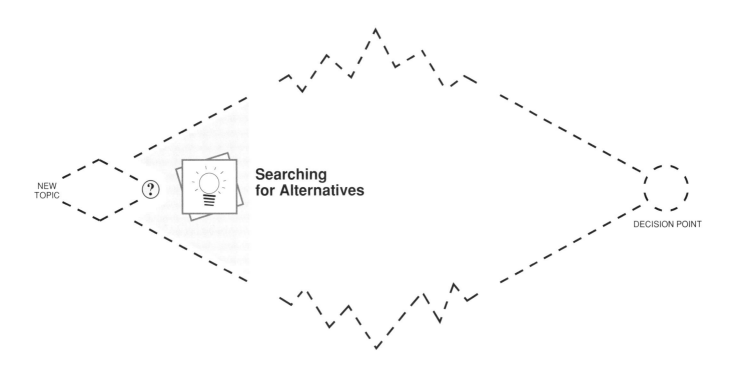

Searching for Alternatives involves generating lists of creative ideas for the purpose of discovering new ways of approaching the problem at hand.

The most straightforward way to help a group search for alternatives is by leading them through a brainstorming session. To do this, ask the group to state the question they want the brainstorm to answer. Record that question on a flipchart, then review the ground rules of brainstorming, and begin. Have someone else do the chartwriting if possible, so you can focus on using your facilitative listening skills: *mirroring, paraphrasing,* and *gathering ideas.*

Often a brainstorming session will produce exactly what is needed: some new rough ideas that are worth further discussion. But there are times when people are so stuck in their fixed positions that not even brainstorming can help them break free of their rigid mental models. Many structured creative thinking activities are available to help deal effectively with this exact situation. A sampling of these activities can be found on the next pages. Many others, along with a wonderfully lucid and useful explanation of the underlying cognitive process of creative thinking, can be found in the work of Edward de Bono, including his masterpiece, *Lateral Thinking* (1970).

SEARCHING FOR ALTERNATIVES
BRAINSTORMING VARIATIONS

THE TRIGGER METHOD

1. Have the group formulate a statement of the problem.

2. Have everyone silently write their questions and/or solutions on sheets of paper for 5 minutes.

3. Ask someone to read his or her ideas to the group.

4. Have the group discuss these ideas for 10 minutes, with the goal of generating variations or totally new ideas. Suspend judgment for this 10-minute period.

5. Repeat Steps 3 and 4 for each member.

6. When everyone has had a turn, have the group select the most promising ideas for further analysis.

Source: A. B. VanGundy, Jr., *Techniques of Structured Problem Solving, 2nd ed.* (New York: John Wiley and Sons, 1998).

BRAINWRITING

1. Seat members around a table.

2. Have someone state the problem to be solved.

3. Ask each person to silently write down four ideas for solving the problem on one sheet of paper.

4. Explain to group members that as soon as anyone has listed four ideas, s/he should exchange that page with someone else.

5. When someone has obtained a new sheet of paper, s/he should add one or two more ideas to it. Then trade this page for another.

6. Repeat for 15 minutes, or until most people run out of ideas.

7. Compare notes and discuss.

Source: H. Geschka, G.R. Schaude, and H. Schlicksupp, "Brainwriting Pool," <u>Chemical Engineering</u> (August 1973).

SEARCHING FOR ALTERNATIVES
CREATIVE THINKING ACTIVITIES

ROLESTORMING

1. Have everyone select a character. It can be a great leader, a fictional character, a typical customer – anyone who is not in the room.

2. Pose the question, and review the ground rules for brainstorming.

3. Instruct half the members to participate in the brainstorming from the perspective of their imaginary character, while the other half give contributions from their own real-life perspectives.

4. After a few minutes, switch roles. Thus, the former roleplayers now leave their roles, and the others assume the roles chosen earlier.

5. Debrief. Discuss any insights obtained.

Source: R. E. Griggs, "A Storm of Ideas," *Training*, 22 (1985):56.

ANALOGS

1. Have participants generate a list of situations or conditions that are analogous to the problem at hand. For example, suppose a group's goal is to increase its funding. Members could list *other types of growth* – plant growth, growth of a city, and so on.

2. Have the group pick one of the analogs and describe it in detail, listing uses, functions, parts, and so on. Continuing the preceding example: plants have roots; they reproduce via seeds; and their growth is seasonal and cyclical.

3. Now encourage the group to consider each analogy in the light of the original problem. Example: Are any new ideas for fundraising suggested by thinking about a plant's seasonal cycles? Its root structure? Its reproduction by seeds?

Source: E. de Bono, *Lateral Thinking* (New York: Harper and Row, 1970).

RAISING DIFFICULT ISSUES
DIVERGENT ZONE THINKING ACTIVITY: TYPE 3

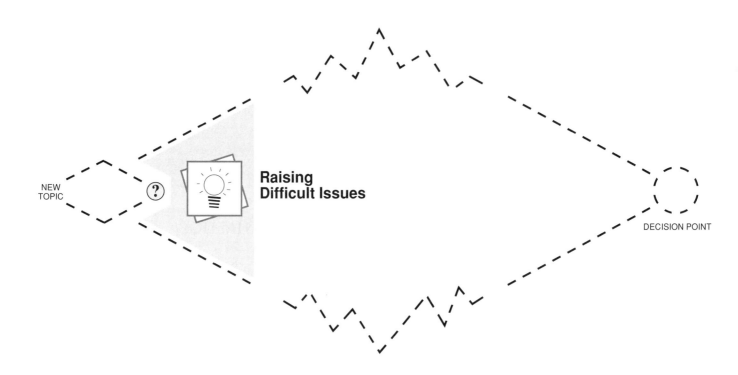

Raising Difficult Issues refers to the initial surfacing of risky subjects – the act of bringing them up for the first time. Issues such as an ongoing feud between key parties or a poor decision that everyone dislikes but no one wants to revisit are seldom placed on an agenda forthrightly. Rather, they typically surface in the cracks of a related discussion. Someone might say, "Can we talk about what is *really* causing this problem?" Then s/he names the unspeakable issue, hoping that others will participate in exploring the subject. But often, they do no such thing! People frequently become anxious and change the subject or withdraw. This places the person who *did* speak up in a tough position – as though s/he were the only one who felt that his or her points were relevant.

The following activities provide an alternative. Rather than treat this situation as a dilemma that occurs *after* one person takes a risk, each activity offers participants the opportunity to share the load of *surfacing* difficult issues. Each activity offers a structured, low-pressure forum in which members can give voice to the difficult topics that might be on their minds.

RAISING DIFFICULT ISSUES

IS THERE ANYTHING I'M NOT SAYING?

WHY

People refrain from saying what they're really thinking for a wide variety of reasons. Sometimes they hold back because the risk is too great. But people also keep quiet because they aren't sure whether their ideas are worth saying or because they can't turn the kernels of their ideas into fully formed presentations. In other words, there are many occasions when group members – if they were given a little support, a little permission, a little nudge – might go ahead and say what's on their mind. Yet without that support, they often stay quiet.

This activity helps group members take a look at the thoughts they've been having (but not speaking) during a discussion. It also gives members an opportunity to reflect on whether the group would be served if a person did open up and share his or her perspective.

HOW

1. Describe this activity. Explain why people can benefit from structured activities that give them permission to speak up. Obtain agreement from the group to proceed.

2. Have the group break into pairs. Ask each partner to answer this question: "During this discussion, have I had any thoughts I haven't said aloud?" Assure people that no one is required to say anything they don't want to say.

3. Next, ask everyone (still in pairs) to answer this question: "Would the group benefit from hearing your partner's thinking?"

4. Return to the large group. Ask for volunteers to share any of their own thoughts that might be useful for others to hear.

RAISING DIFFICULT ISSUES

HOW HAS THIS AFFECTED ME?

WHY

This activity supports people to react to a problem on a personal level by giving people permission to express their fears, confusions, hurts, or resentments openly. The activity helps people become more aware of what they're feeling so they can discuss the situation in more depth.

Also, this activity enables people to step back from their own individual perspective and see a bigger picture. It is frequently surprising and highly informative for them to hear what other people are feeling.

HOW

1. Ask people to reflect on the following questions:

    - "How do I feel about this situation?"
    - "How has it affected me so far?"

2. Ask each person to take a turn sharing his or her reflections and feelings with the whole group. A go-around format works best for this activity because it discourages back-and-forth discussion.

3. When everyone has spoken, ask the whole group, "Now that you have heard from everyone else, what reactions are you having?"

4. If responses indicate that this activity has surfaced a lot of emotion, encourage the group to do a second go-around. Say something like, "Use this time to let the rest of us know whatever is on your mind."

5. End by summarizing the main themes. Validating everyone's self-disclosure helps provide people with a temporary sense of completion, even when the source problems remain obviously unresolved.

RAISING DIFFICULT ISSUES
THREE COMPLAINTS

WHY

Giving people the opportunity to complain about their situation has two powerful results. People have a chance to say things that are normally not acceptable. Often useful information is revealed about a situation that would otherwise remain hidden.

Second, when people have a chance to vent their negative feelings instead of stewing in them, they are more able to move forward on a task.

After an activity like this one, it is common for people to make significant progress on the topic under discussion.

HOW

1. Give the group an overview of the upcoming steps. Then have each individual write on a separate slip of paper three complaints about the situation under discussion.

2. Have everyone throw the slips of paper into a hat.

3. Pull out one note, read it aloud, and ask for comments. The author may or may not wish to identify himself or herself.

4. After three or four comments, pull out another complaint and repeat the process.

5. After 10 or 15 minutes, ask the group how much longer they would like this activity to continue.

6. When time runs out, ask people to close by saying what the experience was like for them.

GATHERING DIVERSE POINTS OF VIEW

SUMMARY

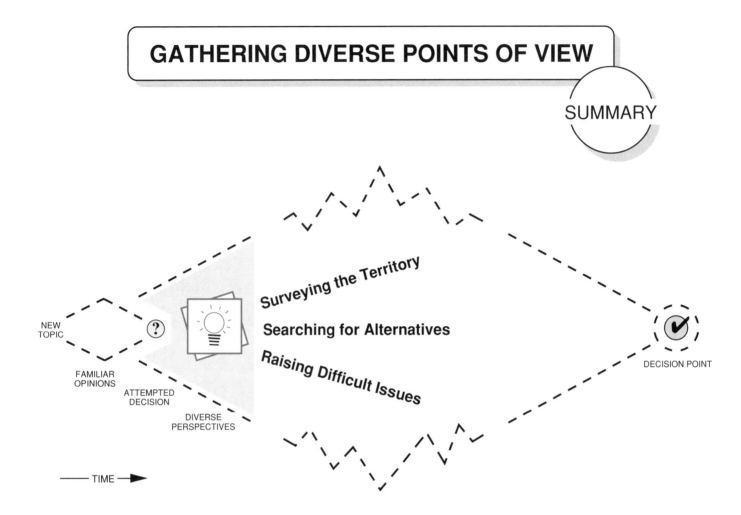

Surveying the Territory

Searching for Alternatives

Raising Difficult Issues

NEW
TOPIC

FAMILIAR
OPINIONS

ATTEMPTED
DECISION

DIVERSE
PERSPECTIVES

DECISION POINT

TIME

The most common types of divergent thinking are shown above. Each type can be supported by activities like those presented in this chapter. Some activities help a group gain a better picture of the scope of the task at hand. Others enable a group to create a list of unusual ideas. Still others support participants to uncover and then discuss topics that are uncomfortable.

Structured activities are often useful in the *Divergent Zone* – but because they are so highly directive, they are not always the preferred approach. Sometimes people simply want to engage in conversation. On those occasions, the facilitator can rely on nondirective techniques, using listening skills like *paraphrasing, drawing people out, stacking, encouraging,* and *making space,* all of which support divergent thinking.

No matter what approach s/he takes, the facilitator's main task in the *Divergent Zone* is to support everyone to speak up and state his or her point of view. This is a prerequisite for building sustainable agreements.

15

BUILDING A SHARED FRAMEWORK OF UNDERSTANDING

PRINCIPLES AND TOOLS THAT
SUPPORT GROUPS TO STRUGGLE
IN THE SERVICE OF INTEGRATION

- ▶ Introduction to the Groan Zone

- ▶ Seven Tools for Creating Shared Context

- ▶ Six Tools for Strengthening Relationships

- ▶ Summary

BUILDING A SHARED FRAMEWORK OF UNDERSTANDING

INTRODUCTION

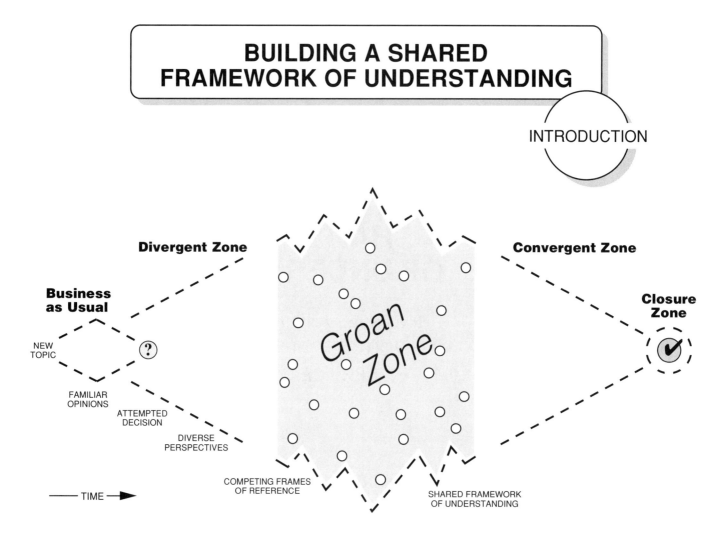

The facilitator's main objective in the *Groan Zone* is to help the group develop a shared framework of understanding. This is anything but easy. The greater the divergence of opinions in the room, the greater is the chance for confusion and misinterpretation. The facilitator should concentrate on *promoting mutual understanding.* This takes a lot of careful, responsive listening; at times, the facilitator may be the only person in the room who is listening at all.

Whether the facilitator is helping one person stand up to pressure from others, or helping two people clear up a misunderstanding between them, or helping a whole group focus on the same thing at the same time, the overall goal remains constant: *support the group to keep working.* Don't let the group give in to the temptation to make a pseudo-decision. Instead, help them keep struggling to integrate each other's points of view.

BUILDING A SHARED FRAMEWORK OF UNDERSTANDING

TWO TYPES OF THINKING IN THE GROAN ZONE

After a period of divergent thinking, most groups enter the *Groan Zone.* Suppose, for example, the members have just finished a brainstorming process. In theory, the group's next task seems simple: sift through all the ideas, and discuss a few more in depth. But in practice that task is often grueling. Everyone has his or her own unique frame of reference, and communication can easily break down. Moreover, when people misunderstand one another, their behavior often becomes more confused, more impatient, more self-centered – more unpleasant all around.

This phase of work is truly difficult to tolerate. It is a normal, natural period – but it's still a struggle. The effort to understand one another's perspectives and build a shared framework of understanding – this *struggle in the service of integration* – is the defining work of the *Groan Zone.*

Most groups flee from the *Groan Zone* long before they have developed the capacity to think together. This is reflected in the quality of their decisions. Those who *do* persevere discover that what enabled them to survive the struggle were the periods they spent learning to understand each other.

The development of a shared framework of understanding centers around two types of thinking: *Creating Shared Context* and *Strengthening Relationships.* Both types are discussed in this chapter.

Type 1: Creating Shared Context

Creating Shared Context refers to activities that directly advance mutual understanding. This can be done in a variety of ways: by acquiring shared experiences, by developing shared language, by surfacing background information, and by making efforts to put oneself in the other person's shoes. In all cases the purpose is to enable people to think from each other's point of view. The essence of this type of activity is *understanding.*

Type 2: Strengthening Relationships

Strengthening Relationships refers to activities that support people to get to know each other. It is easier to listen to a person's thinking when one has experienced that person's humanity. The essence of this type of activity is *interpersonal communication.*

CREATING SHARED CONTEXT
GROAN ZONE THINKING ACTIVITY: TYPE 1

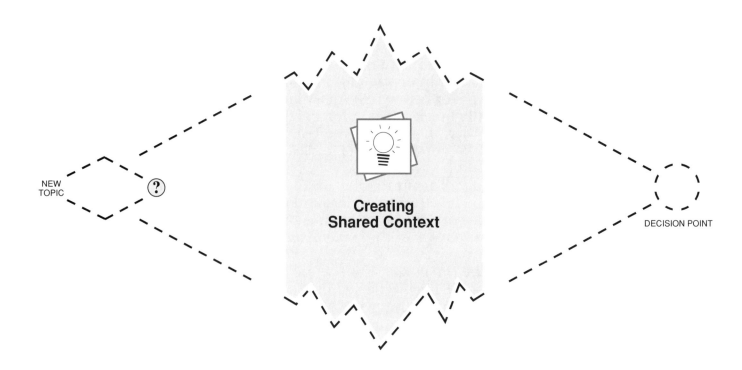

NEW
TOPIC

(?)

Creating
Shared Context

DECISION POINT

In order for a group to develop sustainable agreements that take everyone's interests into account, the participants must be able to think from one another's points of view. They do not have to *agree* with someone else's perspective, but they do have to *understand* it.

The simplest way to help group members gain a deeper understanding of each other's perspectives is to encourage them to ask direct questions of one another and listen carefully to the answers.

But some participants fear that asking questions might appear confrontational or rude, especially when the speaker's statements were controversial or difficult to understand. Furthermore, many people simply can't tolerate the ambiguity of unstructured inquiry and dialogue for very long. Thus many groups require structured thinking activities to help them learn more about each other's frames of reference. The following pages present seven tools that support group members to create shared context.

CREATING SHARED CONTEXT

LEARNING MORE ABOUT EACH OTHER'S PERSPECTIVES

WHY

The most basic method for promoting mutual understanding is to ask questions. Sometimes, however, people hesitate to ask questions about each other's perspectives because questioning is so often perceived as criticism. By providing structure, this activity helps people understand that the questions are not intended as attacks.

Facilitators often hesitate to use a tool like this one because it eats up precious meeting time. But the alternative – trying to proceed in the absence of understanding – ends up consuming much more time, with much worse results. Using this simple tool builds trust and patience, and it significantly improves mutual understanding.

HOW

1. Ask for a volunteer to be the "focal person." S/he begins by saying, "Here's the point I want to make." S/he has three minutes to talk.

2. When s/he is done, encourage someone to ask a question, like, "What do you mean by . . . ?" or, "Can you explain why . . . ?" or something similar.

3. The focal person then answers the first question.

4. Turn to the questioner, and ask, "Is this clear to you now?" If so, continue to Step 5. If not, ask the questioner to state, first, what s/he believes the focal person has said, and then what s/he still finds unclear. For example, someone might say, "I hear the focal person saying that we should all share the cleanup chores equally. But I still don't understand why he feels so strongly about it."

5. When both the questioner and the focal person feel understood, ask for another questioner to take a turn.

6. After three or four people have had a chance to ask questions, ask for another person to volunteer to be the new focal person.

   The goal of this activity is to promote understanding, not to resolve differences. This should be emphasized beforehand and, if necessary, throughout the activity.

CREATING SHARED CONTEXT

IF I WERE YOU

WHY

Another straightforward way to promote mutual understanding is to have people look at the world through each other's eyes.

Exploring someone else's perspective helps people to suspend their own points of view. This activity thus provides some participants with insights that they may not have acquired through conventional discussion.

Furthermore, the process supports participants to feel understood and "seen." If necessary, it allows them the opportunity to correct any misperceptions.

HOW

1. Have the group choose a statement to work with. The statement should begin with the words, "If I were you . . ." For example, two common choices are, "If I were you, a main concern of mine would be . . ." or "If I were you, one of my goals would be . . ."

2. Write each member's name on two separate slips of paper, and put them into a hat.

3. Have each person draw out two slips, so that each person has the names of two different people. (If a person pulls his or her own name, s/he puts it back or trades with someone.)

4. Give everyone a turn being the focal person. When someone is the focal person, the two people who have that person's name say to him or her, "If I were you . . ."

5. After listening to both people, the focal person may respond.

6. When everyone has had a turn, ask the group members to reflect on the activity and share any new insights they have gained.

CREATING SHARED CONTEXT

BACKING UP
FROM SOLUTIONS TO NEEDS

WHY

When an argument seems to be going around in circles, it can be *extremely helpful* for everyone to stop arguing over proposed "solutions" and start talking about their individual needs instead.

For example, consider a dispute between three administrators over whether to schedule an important meeting in New York or Boston. The problem (where to meet) had two solutions (New York or Boston). But beneath the superficial solutions were everyone's individual needs. One person needed to stay near his office as much as possible because his assistant was on vacation. A second needed to keep her commitment to attend three other meetings that had long been planned. A third was expecting a drop-in visit from the regional director; she needed to be available "just in case." Once everyone understood each other's needs more clearly, they stopped imagining that the disagreement was due to "power struggles" and "turf battles." They realized that meeting on a Saturday would work for everyone no matter *where* they met.

As the example shows, it becomes easier to develop proposals that meet a *broader range of needs* when those needs have been made explicit – and, therefore, understandable to everyone.

HOW

1. Make sure everyone understands the difference between "their proposed solution" and "their actual need." For example, "holding the meeting in Boston" is a proposed solution; "honoring prior commitments to attend three other meetings" is a need. Take time, if necessary, to teach this distinction to group members.

2. Ask everyone to answer these questions: "What are my needs in this situation?" and "What do I think *your* needs are?"

3. Continue until everyone feels satisfied that their own needs have been stated clearly. Then ask the group to generate new proposals that seek to incorporate a broader range of people's needs.

CREATING SHARED CONTEXT

MEANINGFUL THEMES

WHY

Each participant comes to a meeting with his or her own unique set of interests and concerns. And in many cases, the participant wants to find out where others stand on the area of his or her special concern. For example, one person may need to know whether other members are committed to remaining in the group. Someone else may need to hear how people feel about the group's track record on diversity issues. Another member may want to know people's attitudes toward retaining a consultant.

Often, however, it is not clear how or when to raise those issues for discussion. Any of these themes might be very meaningful to a few people yet not very meaningful at all, to others. This creates a dilemma. How can a group devote sufficient time to such concerns – enough to prevent individual participants from becoming impatient or distracted and withdrawn – yet not so much that the agenda becomes derailed by focusing on topics that seem tangential or low-priority to other members? This activity offers a method for balancing the two sets of concerns by providing members with a chance to make a *preliminary assessment* of the attitudes and biases pertaining to their area of interest.

HOW

1. Begin by having each group member identify one or two questions that, if everyone's answer were known, would enable that group member to participate more effectively. For example, "Do others think we should be prepared to spend a lot of money on this project?"

2. Ask each person to write his or her question on a sheet of paper. Collect everyone's questions and put them in a hat.

3. Draw out one sheet of paper, read that question, and ask the person who wrote that question to spend up to two minutes explaining why he or she wants to understand everyone's position on that question.

4. Ask for brief responses from everyone: "I feel this way because . . ." When everyone has spoken, draw another question. If time is short, the remaining questions can be carried over to the next meeting.

CREATING SHARED CONTEXT

HOW WILL THIS PROPOSAL AFFECT OUR JOBS?

WHY

Sometimes a participant is clearly unhappy with a proposal but s/he cannot seem to communicate his or her concerns effectively. The difficulty may be rooted in the fact that most proposals affect different roles in different ways. When participants do not understand the nuances of one another's roles – a common state of affairs – they may have trouble understanding one another's concerns about a given proposal.

This activity helps the group focus their whole attention on how a proposal will affect each participant. As a result, many confusions and misunderstandings clear up as people gain insight into the subtle realities of each other's situations.

HOW

1. Identify which members are likely to be affected by the proposal on the floor. Ask for a volunteer to become the focal person.

2. For 3 to 5 minutes, have the group brainstorm answers to the question: "If we implement our proposal, how will it affect this person's role?" While the brainstorm is in effect, no disagreements are allowed.

3. When time is up, ask the focal person to come to the front of the room. S/he educates the group by elaborating on the items s/he thinks are important for everyone to understand. Encourage participants to ask questions.

4. Have the group choose a second focal person. Repeat Steps 2 and 3.

CREATING SHARED CONTEXT

DEFINING GOALS AND MILESTONES

WHY

Thinking into the future is one of the hardest challenges for any group. We don't have good points of reference to distinguish between a large-scale goal and a small-scale goal. Yet every complex project contains many levels of goals-within-goals.

For example, consider the project of rebuilding an impoverished neighborhood. Suppose the overall large-scale goal were to restore the vitality and economic viability of that neighborhood. That goal would no doubt contain many stages and milestones (such as attracting new business to the area). Furthermore, each stage would contain various steps that must be taken before the milestone could be achieved.

Since we lack good points of reference to make the distinctions described above, most groups find it difficult to engage in a planning process that requires them to set overall goals and define stages and milestones.

HOW

1. Hang a long sheet of paper across the front of the room. At the far right-hand end of the paper, write the group's goal – for example, "Goal: Open a new office in Denver."

2. Ask the group to generate three to five milestones that must be completed in order to reach the goal – for example, "Complete our financial projections."

3. Write the milestones from left to right across the long sheet of paper. Leave as much space as possible between milestones.

4. Break into small groups, and assign one milestone to each group. Each group now identifies and lists each step it would take to complete that milestone, and writes each step on a sticky note.

5. Have everyone come up to the front and put his or her sticky notes up on the wall, each step in sequence, leading up to their milestone. At the same time, people can review each other's work and add any steps that may be missing.

CREATING SHARED CONTEXT

TAKING TANGENTS SERIOUSLY

WHY

Tangents are a major cause of the frustration and confusion of the *Groan Zone*. When someone raises an issue that seems peripheral to the discussion, other participants often become nervous. They don't want the speaker to derail the conversation and take the group off track. But the speaker may believe that s/he has identified a crucial "side problem" that the group must face before the "main problem" can be resolved.

This dilemma comes up regularly. Because everyone has a unique perspective, it's not unusual for one person to spot a hidden problem that no one else has noticed. Group members may think that the speaker is wasting their time on a tangent, when in fact the speaker might be *ahead* of the group in articulating hidden complexities. And when that happens, the group is plunged into the *Groan Zone*.

Taking Tangents Seriously helps overcome mutual misunderstanding because it supports the group to gain a deeper appreciation of each person's perspective.

HOW

1. At the beginning of a discussion, or when the first tangential issue arises, post a blank sheet and title it "Side Issues." Add to it as tangents are identified.

2. At every meeting, ask the group to choose one topic from the list and discuss it for 15 minutes.

3. After 15 minutes ask, "Are we done, or would you prefer to extend the time?"

4. When time is up, finish with a quick summary. Ask, "What have you learned? Are there any next steps you should take?"

5. Repeat Steps 2 to 4 at subsequent meetings.

STRENGTHENING RELATIONSHIPS
GROAN ZONE THINKING ACTIVITY: TYPE 2

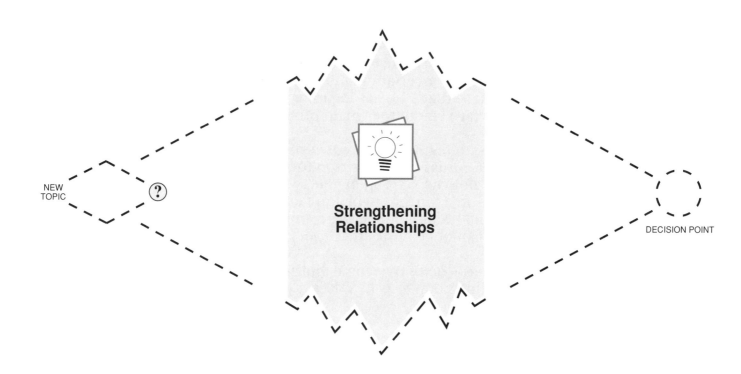

NEW TOPIC

Strengthening Relationships

DECISION POINT

People who know one another are more likely to overcome their differences and find common ground than people who remain personally isolated from one another. This principle is noticeable in business and in politics, where leaders often make a practice of building friendly relationships with their colleagues and the families of their colleagues. It holds true for grassroots movements, where activists – progressives and conservatives alike – intentionally design events to provide participants with a mixture of community building and social action. Yet this principle is undervalued in the realm of group decision-making. Bringing photographs of one's family members to a meeting, for example, or taking time to tell each other a little about the neighborhood where one grew up – these activities are hard for some people to imagine in the context of group decision-making.

The facilitator's task is to seek opportunities to strengthen relationships, in order to counterbalance the struggles that make the *Groan Zone* so painful. Participants need relief, even if temporary, from long, frustrating meetings. More important, broadening the context of working relationships allows people to see one another as real people, not just as "opponents" or "allies." Relationship building strengthens the foundation of mutual understanding.

STRENGTHENING RELATIONSHIPS

GETTING TO KNOW EACH OTHER

ANECDOTES & MEMENTOS

1. Ask everyone to come to the next meeting prepared to share something personal – a memento, a photograph, or an anecdote.

2. At the next meeting, ask for volunteers to share their memorabilia with the group.

3. Before starting, establish an order for the presentations. Also, clarify what will happen if the group runs out of time. For example, "We only have thirty minutes for this today. If we don't finish, we'll do the remaining people next time."

4. Give each presenter five minutes to speak. Allow time for two or three questions.

TWO TRUTHS AND A LIE

1. Describe the activity.* Explain that all members will tell the group three things about themselves: two truths and a lie. The lie must be a bald-faced lie, not a half-truth. For example, someone who has one brother may not say, "I have two brothers." S/he *could* say, "I have twelve brothers."

2. After all have told their tales, have everyone quickly raise hands to indicate which "fact" they think was the lie. Ask, "How many people think the lie was such-and-such?"

3. Have the person reveal the lie. Then call on the next person to take a turn.

4. After everyone has gone, applaud those who did the best job of fooling the group.

THE SUPPORT SEAT

1. Arrange the chairs in a semi-circle, and put one chair in front, facing the rest.

2. Describe the activity. Explain that each person will sit in the support seat for 20 minutes, while everyone else asks that person about his or her life away from work. Members may ask whatever they wish. The person in the center can always say, "I prefer not to answer that question."

3. Ask for someone to sit in the support seat.

4. Anyone can ask the first question. S/he may ask one follow-up question, but must then pass until everyone has had a turn.

Note: This activity is often spread over several meetings.

* This activity is a variation of "Two Truths and a Lie" presented by Bill Schmidt, instructor in Organizational Psychology at the Wright Institute, Berkeley, California, 1993.

STRENGTHENING RELATIONSHIPS

GIVING AND RECEIVING FEEDBACK

OBSERVATIONS AND INTERPRETATIONS

1. Ask everyone to find a partner.

2. Allow each person five minutes to give his or her partner feedback as follows: First: "Something I *observe* about you is..." Then: "What I make up in my head about this observation is..."

3. When five minutes have passed, remind each pair to switch roles. The speaker becomes the listener, and vice versa.

4. Optional: When time is up, ask everyone to find a different partner. Repeat Steps 2 and 3 with the new partner.

5. Debrief in large group.

APPRECIATIONS

1. Count the number of group members and subtract one. Then distribute that many sheets of blank pages to each participant. For example, each person in an eight-person group would receive seven sheets.

2. Ask everyone to write one thing they appreciate about each group member. This can be something simple, or something more personal and thoughtful.

3. When everyone has written one message to each member, ask everyone to fold their messages, stand up, and put each note on its proper chair.

4. When all messages have been delivered, have people return to their seats and read.

5. Debrief, allowing at least fifteen minutes.*

HOW DO I COME ACROSS?

1. Describe the activity. Explain that one person will ask the group, "How do I come across in our meetings? What are my strengths and weaknesses?" People can respond with statements like, "I see you protecting Jim when he misses a deadline." Or, "You're the only person who really listens to everyone's opinions."

2. Ask for a volunteer. Set a firm time limit for this person to hear how s/he comes across. Allow at least 15 minutes.

3. While people state their perceptions, make sure the recipient listens without speaking. When time is up, give him or her at least 5 minutes to respond.

4. Move to another volunteer. If members prefer to continue interacting with the first person, set another limit.

* Source: Nancy Feinstein, Ph.D. organization development specialist, as told to Sam Kaner, May 1995.

BUILDING A SHARED FRAMEWORK OF UNDERSTANDING

SUMMARY

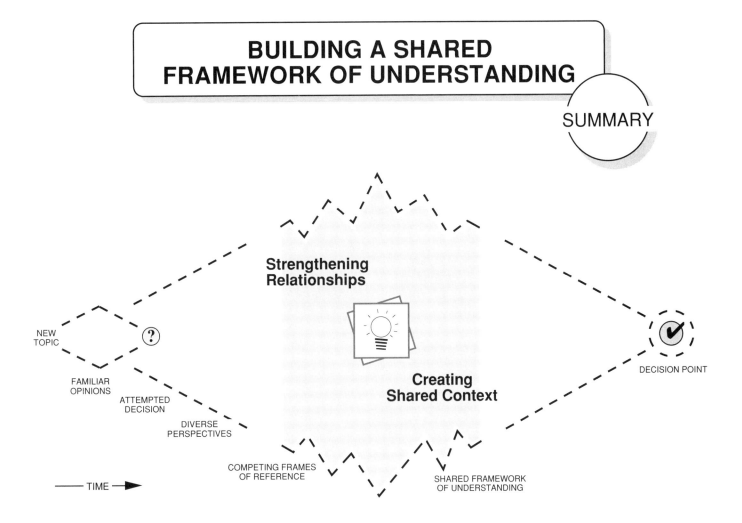

Strengthening Relationships

Creating Shared Context

NEW TOPIC

FAMILIAR OPINIONS

ATTEMPTED DECISION

DIVERSE PERSPECTIVES

COMPETING FRAMES OF REFERENCE

SHARED FRAMEWORK OF UNDERSTANDING

DECISION POINT

TIME ➤

Structured activities like those presented in this chapter are very helpful during periods of misunderstanding. They help people focus on the same thing at the same time. But it's not easy for a facilitator to obtain a group's agreement to *do* a structured activity. People oppose facilitators regularly – and this is particularly true in the *Groan Zone*, when the trust levels are low and the tension levels are high. Thus, someone may oppose a suggestion because s/he imagines it was proposed as a direct, personal response to something s/he said. Someone else may interpret a facilitator's suggestion as a power play. Others may feel that the proposed activity would slow the pace of discussion or move the group in the wrong direction. For all these reasons and more, facilitators must expect the group to challenge, and probably reject, a high percentage of such suggestions.

When this happens, remember to *honor objections and ask for suggestions.* In the *Groan Zone,* everyone's ideas are frequently misunderstood – and yours will be too. Keep in mind that your role is to help, not to be "right." Be patient, be tolerant, be flexible; don't be attached to what you suggest. Here's the general rule: in the *Groan Zone* people are under pressure – *they need the facilitator's support.*

16

DEVELOPING INCLUSIVE SOLUTIONS

PRINCIPLES AND TOOLS FOR FINDING SOLUTIONS THAT TAKE EVERYONE'S INTERESTS INTO ACCOUNT

DEVELOPING INCLUSIVE SOLUTIONS

INTRODUCTION

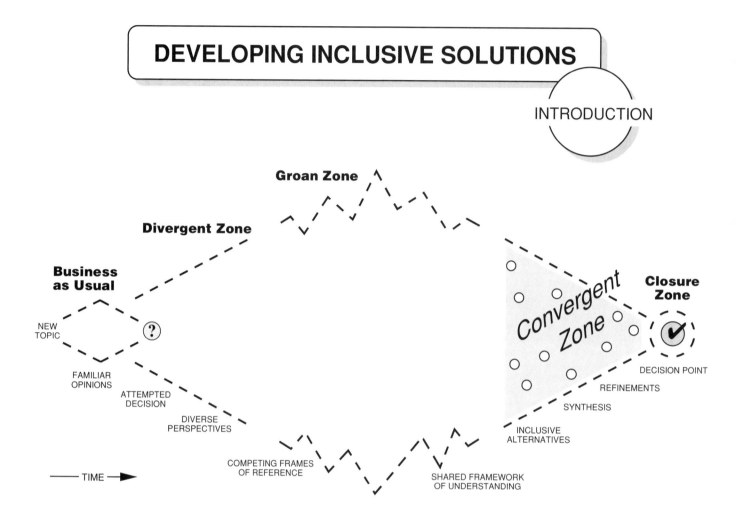

In the *Convergent Zone,* the facilitator's main task is to help the group develop inclusive alternatives and synthesize them into a solution that will work for everyone. This is often easier than it sounds. Once a group has managed to build a shared framework of understanding, the discussion can move pretty quickly, and quite comfortably, with little intervention.

There are many exceptions, however. Some groups have trouble thinking creatively. They need help breaking out of their habitual mental categories. To spur their imagination, a facilitator may wish to provide them with case studies of inclusive solutions like the ones presented in this chapter. The power of discussing a real-life example is that it can stimulate insights that may apply to the group's current situation.

There are other groups that become almost intoxicated with the excitement of fast-paced thinking. They are prone to make hasty decisions that are destined to become underfunded and overcommitted. Those groups need a facilitator's help to be rigorous, not impulsive, as they fine-tune their thinking and strengthen the logic and the quality of their ideas.

DEVELOPING INCLUSIVE SOLUTIONS

THREE TYPES OF THINKING IN THE CONVERGENT ZONE

A group enters the *Convergent Zone* when it has developed a shared framework of understanding. Its discussion then becomes much easier. Here's a sample of what happens. First someone offers an interesting idea, and others try it on for size. Someone else adds to it or blends it with a completely different idea. People are able to say to themselves, "I know why so-and-so would not like that idea; I wonder if I can think of a way to meet that need." The whole group is operating within a shared context of meaning. When this happens – when the members of a group can realistically include one another's perspectives in their own thinking – they are on their way to finding a solution that will incorporate everyone's needs and goals. This is the work of the *Convergent Zone.*

Three types of convergent thinking are discussed in this chapter: *Applying Inclusive Principles, Creative Reframing,* and *Strengthening Good Ideas.*

Type 1: Applying Inclusive Principles

Applying Inclusive Principles entails identifying and discussing principles that promote creative problem solving. A group can use these principles to develop a solution that works for everyone. A fine way to develop a *both/and* mind-set is to study case examples and discuss their relevance to the situation at hand. The essence of this type of thinking is *application.*

Type 2: Creative Reframing

Creative Reframing involves altering one's beliefs about the nature of the problem at hand. Members identify core assumptions and deliberately replace or reverse them in order to gain an alternative perspective. The goal is to acquire a "breakthrough experience," a significant change in outlook. The essence of this type of thinking is *paradigm shifting.*

Type 3: Strengthening Good Ideas

Strengthening Good Ideas refers to the group's efforts to evaluate and refine the logic and quality of their thinking. The process is iterative. Every new insight causes the basic idea to strengthen and grow. The essence of this type of thinking is *critical reasoning.*

APPLYING INCLUSIVE PRINCIPLES
CONVERGENT ZONE THINKING ACTIVITY: TYPE 1

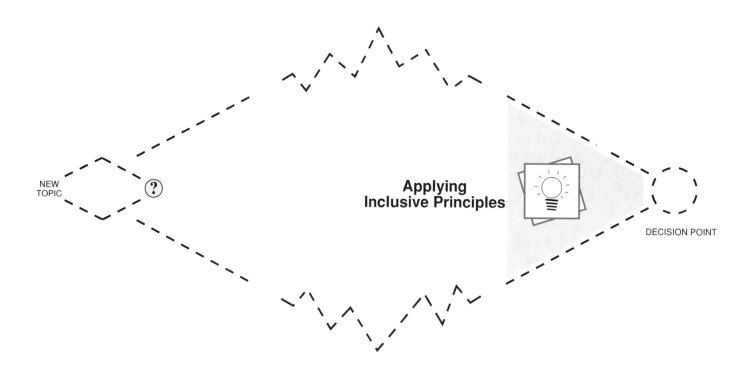

NEW
TOPIC

**Applying
Inclusive Principles**

DECISION POINT

Inclusive, nonadversarial, problem-solving principles, like those listed on the next page, are often at the heart of sustainable agreements. For example, consider the previously discussed case of the Mendocino County timber tax committee. After years of disagreement over the rate of logging, they found an inclusive solution when they realized that a change in the tax code would benefit everyone. Thus, they switched from taxing *standing trees*, a method used for forty years, to taxing *cut trees*. Underlying this change was a creative problem-solving principle: *challenge fixed assumptions – just because something has always been done one way doesn't mean it has to be done that way in the future.*

A facilitator can encourage group members to identify and discuss inclusive principles that might apply to their current situation. This will foster creative thinking. For example, you might show a group the Mendocino case, discuss it, and then ask, "What are *our* group's fixed assumptions? Are there any *we* can challenge?" As this example shows, real-life cases are an excellent vehicle for helping groups explore inclusive principles. Several more case studies are presented in the following pages.

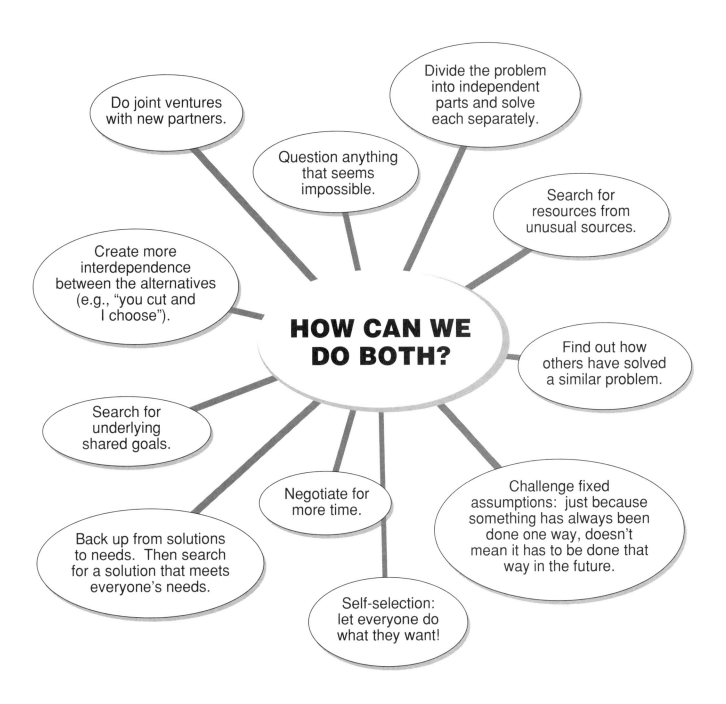

These problem-solving principles help people synthesize seemingly opposing alternatives into an integrated solution. Note that none of these requires group members to use adversarial methods to resolve their differences. *They all lead to solutions that work for everyone.*

APPLYING INCLUSIVE PRINCIPLES

USING CASE STUDIES

WHY

The next six pages present capsule summaries of inclusive solutions to difficult real-life problems. Each case demonstrates the use of an *inclusive principle* – that is, a problem-solving principle that enables participants to develop a creative solution that takes everyone's interests into account.

Left to their own inclinations, few groups make the effort to keep looking for fresh ideas. Thus, the facilitator has a key role in motivating people to search for inclusive solutions. But this creates a challenge. Some facilitators offer their groups potential solutions, but many groups don't respond well to facilitators who attempt to "join the group." There is a surprisingly high likelihood that a group will reject a facilitator's solution without even considering its merits.

Fortunately, there are alternatives. One particularly useful method is to present real-life examples of inclusive solutions to difficult problems, and encourage discussion. For many people, discussing a case study is more effective than listening to a lecture. This approach preserves the facilitator's neutrality even as it inspires group members to keep working toward sustainable agreements. Accordingly, the following examples have been designed to be used as tools that can stimulate discussion.

HOW

1. Photocopy and distribute some or all of the following case studies.

2. Ask everyone to read one or two cases.

3. Have everyone find a partner and discuss their case studies. Ask, "What reactions are you having to what you just read?"

4. After five minutes, reconvene the large group and ask, "Has anyone found a principle that might shed new light on *our* situation?" Allow ample time for discussion.

APPLYING INCLUSIVE PRINCIPLES

CASE STUDY: BREAKING WITH TRADITION

PROBLEM

At San Jose National Bank, many of the employees were women. One year, 10 percent of the staff became pregnant. A high rate of maternity leave would clearly cause a serious drop in productivity. Management pondered the options. Should maternity leave be limited? Should some of the employees be laid off? The expectant mothers recognized that the bank could suffer, but they also felt it was important to be with their babies during their first months of life. Each group understood the other's point of view, but no one felt able to change positions.

SOLUTION

Mothers were allowed to bring their infants to the office and keep them by their desks. They stayed at work the whole day and tended to their infants' needs as necessary. Their pay was slightly reduced to reflect the actual hours they worked. When the infants became toddlers, they were placed at a nearby day care center sponsored by the bank.

PRINCIPLE

The solution to this problem was to break with the tradition that parents must choose between working and being with their children. Here, the bank's needs (getting the work done) and the mothers' needs (staying with their infants) were combined. In your situation, is there a tradition that locks you into an *either / or* position? Why is that tradition seen as "sacred"? If it were challenged, what new options might open up?

Source: *San Jose Mercury News*, March 6, 1994.

APPLYING INCLUSIVE PRINCIPLES

CASE STUDY: YOU CUT AND I CHOOSE

PROBLEM

Representatives from many nations met to develop international policies regarding the mining of oceanic resources. One problem they addressed was how to best allocate underwater mining sites. The Enterprise, a U.N. organization representing poorer countries, charged that rich countries had an unfair advantage. They feared that private companies from wealthy countries could identify the superior mining sites because they had better radar and mining equipment and superior expertise. With this knowledge, the rich countries could propose an unequal allocation of mining resources, and the poorer countries would have no way to evaluate the fairness of the allocation.

SOLUTION

The representatives decided to ask a private company to identify two mining sites of equal value, using its sophisticated equipment and expertise. The Enterprise would then choose one of the sites for the poorer countries to mine. The private company would get the other one. In this way, the private companies would have an incentive to identify two sites of equal value, thus giving poorer nations the benefit of their expertise.

PRINCIPLE

This situation involved competition for a fixed resource: high-quality mining sites. The inclusive principle they employed was to tie the interests of the more powerful party to those of the less powerful party. In your own situation, what incentives might induce the more powerful party to participate?

Source: R. Fisher and W. Ury, *Getting to Yes* (New York: Penguin Books, 1983), p. 58.

CASE STUDY: DISCOVERING COMMON GROUND

PROBLEM

A suburb of a large city was becoming more and more racially diverse. Residents formed a community council to preserve the neighborhood's character while simultaneously promoting racial integration. The council suspected that financial institutions were cutting back on their investment in the neighborhood because of the demographic changes. After investigating several local lending institutions, the council found evidence that lenders were indeed using discriminatory tactics. The council demanded more investment in its neighborhood, and it threatened to boycott the lenders. The lenders denied the charges and refused to cooperate with further monitoring.

SOLUTION

At first the two sides locked horns and argued over who was to blame for the disinvestment. Their breakthrough came when they realized they all shared a common concern: preserving the neighborhood. Together they founded a local development corporation that promoted commercial revitalization, and they created a foreclosure rehabilitation program for which the lenders raised funds.

PRINCIPLE

Affixing blame, polarizing into opposing camps, and calling for help from the powers-that-be is a typical strategy for dealing with the problems created by changing circumstances. In this case, participants followed a different principle. They focused on discovering shared concerns, and they aimed at developing a shared vision. This helped them collaborate effectively and take constructive, self-empowered action.

Source: B. Gray, *Collaborating* (San Francisco: Jossey-Bass, 1989), p. 95.

CASE STUDY: INCLUDING THE "TROUBLEMAKERS" IN THE SOLUTION

PROBLEM

A community had a problem with its high school youth, whose public behavior was becoming increasingly unruly, especially at night. The city administration decided to increase police patrols and impose a curfew for the youth in the neighborhood. Community members rejected this decision. They felt that the curfew would restrict everyone's freedom, and the increased police presence would probably *increase* violence in the neighborhood.

SOLUTION

Neighborhood residents met and discussed ideas for solving this problem. They decided that a midnight basketball program would provide the youths with an alternative to hanging out and getting in trouble. The community members saw this as a way to improve neighborhood safety without requiring outside intervention. The city administrators were pleased because the program would help keep youth off the streets at night.

PRINCIPLE

Normally we try to "fix" the people who make trouble – whether by incarcerating them, hospitalizing them, expelling them, going to war with them, or controlling their behavior. By contrast, it sometimes can be advantageous to treat the troublemakers as stakeholders, and involve them in the problem-solving process. If their needs can be understood, they might become allies in transforming the problem.

Source: Marshall Rosenberg's workshop on Compassionate Communication, February 1995, as related by Liz Dittrich to Sam Kaner's Group Facilitation Skills class, June 1995.

APPLYING INCLUSIVE PRINCIPLES

CASE STUDY: UNUSUAL PARTNERSHIP

PROBLEM

A small western city had a one-time-only budget surplus. Two groups immediately began vying for the funds. On one side, a coalition of women's groups wished to use the money to expand the city's inadequate day care facilities. On the other side, homeowners and the city's firefighters wanted to upgrade their antiquated firefighting equipment to protect homes and lower insurance costs.

SOLUTION

A small portion of the money was used to convert the city's old fire stations into day care centers. The new centers were used to attract state and federal matching funds to operate them. The majority of the money was then used to build three new fire stations. The new stations raised the city's fire rating from AA to AAA, thus lowering insurance rates and raising property values – which in turn enabled new equipment purchases.

PRINCIPLE

Competing for funding is the normal way to proceed when finances are limited. Yet the groups in this case partnered in order to identify additional resources from sources that were foreign to their own contexts.

Can your group partner with its competitors? Are there other unusual alliances to explore?

Source: M. Doyle and D. Straus, *How to Make Meetings Work* (New York: Jove Press, 1982), p. 56.

CASE STUDY: LOCATING RESOURCES TO SUPPORT LONG-TERM STABILITY

PROBLEM

In a rainforest in New Guinea, the indigenous people were approached by a large lumber corporation. The company offered to pay a lump sum for the right to clear-cut the forest and extract the hardwood trees. The deal sounded fantastic to many members of the impoverished forest tribe; they wanted to sell their only marketable commodity in exchange for money, which they could use to buy things they could not produce themselves. Local environmentalists, however, were alarmed; the forests would be completely and irreplaceably destroyed.

SOLUTION

Environmentalists helped the indigenous people start their own lumber company with a small, portable sawmill that could process trees one at a time. The cut lumber was worth significantly more than the company had offered for the trees, so the people did not feel pressured to log more than was appropriate for the health of the forest. The logging company purchased the lumber, which it then resold at a profit overseas.

PRINCIPLE

Group problem-solving often seeks simple, direct solutions that focus on the near term, and the immediate need. But it sometimes makes more sense to search for solutions that take a longer view. As this case example illustrates, a consideration of long-term sustainability can lead to the emergence of creative strategies that would not have been entertained in a search for a quick fix.

Source: Told to Sarah Fisk by John Seed, environmentalist and author.

CREATIVE REFRAMING
CONVERGENT ZONE THINKING ACTIVITY: TYPE 2

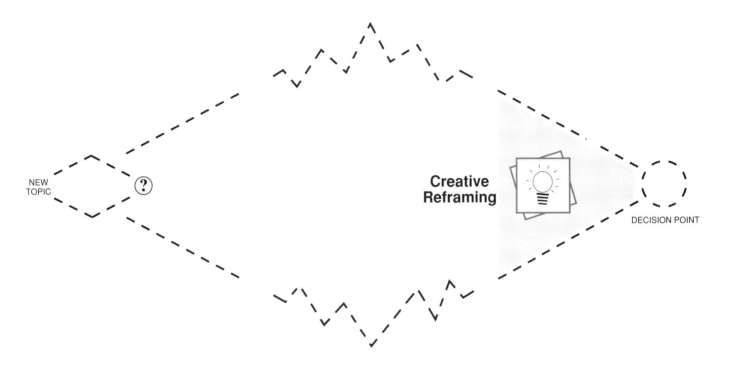

NEW TOPIC

Creative Reframing

DECISION POINT

Creative Reframing involves breaking out of our normal categories of analysis and reexamining our beliefs and assumptions. This type of thinking requires us to make a deliberate mental shift in order to look at a problem from a completely different angle. Making such a shift can lead a group to see choices to which they were blind just moments before.

Because it is counterintuitive and "unnatural," *creative reframing* is a type of thinking that rarely happens spontaneously. A facilitator can guide a group toward this type of thinking in two ways – either with structured thinking activities or through informal technique that helps participants shift their thinking. As an example of the latter, one could ask questions like, "Is that the only way to do this?" or "Suppose this had never happened. Would that change your choice of action?" Simple questions like these can be posed with relatively little forethought. Alternatively, one can use the activities provided on the following pages.

TWO WAYS OF LOOKING AT THE SAME PROBLEM

PERCEIVED PROBLEM	REFRAMED PROBLEM
It's them.	It's all of us.
It's a problem.	It's an opportunity.
Our goal is unachievable.	We don't have our goal broken into realistic steps.
Our product won't sell.	We're trying to sell our product to the wrong people.
We don't have enough resources.	We are wasting the resources we do have.
We need to gather more input.	We need to pay more attention to the input we're already getting.
Our employees are incompetent.	Our employees don't have enough time to do a quality job.
We don't have enough money.	We haven't figured out how to find new sources of money.
We can't get along with each other.	We haven't made the commitment to work through our feelings toward one another.
We don't have any power in this system.	We haven't found our leverage points in this system.
We don't have enough time to do all of these things.	We have to decide what to do now and what to do later.

CREATIVE REFRAMING

INTRODUCING REFRAMING TO A GROUP

WHY

Once someone perceives a problem in a particular way, s/he may find it difficult to see that problem in any other way. Our minds tend to lock into a pattern of thought. For example, many job recruiters routinely decline to hire a talented applicant because of the applicant's appearance; yet in some companies, this habit persists even when recruiting for technical positions, when appearance has no impact on performance.

When tackling difficult problems, most people reach conclusions quickly. They believe they have explored every option for a solution and that it would be pointless to waste more time. The idea that it might be possible to reframe a problem – that is, to dramatically alter their understanding of the nature of the problem – is, for most people, a paradigm shift.

Thus, facilitators who decide to encourage their groups to undertake creative reframing often find it quite challenging to motivate people to invest the time. This tool is designed to help facilitators overcome that initial wall of resistance.

HOW

1. Hand out copies of page 250, *Two Ways of Looking at the Same Problem.*

2. Ask people to discuss the differences between a perceived problem and a reframed problem. Remember that many people will be thinking about this concept for the first time ever; as part of digesting a new idea, they may say things that sound rigid or naive. Expect remarks like, "As far as I'm concerned, this whole idea is ridiculous." Remember to honor all points of view and remain supportive throughout the discussion.

3. After several minutes say, "Now let's apply this theory to our own situation. Could someone please state *our* perceived problem?" Write the perceived problem on a flipchart. Then ask the group to brainstorm a list of *reframes* of the problem. Record all answers on flipcharts.

4. After the brainstorm, encourage members to discuss the implications of their new ideas. Say, "As you review this list, what are your reactions?"

CREATIVE REFRAMING

WHAT'S UNCHANGEABLE ABOUT THIS PROBLEM?

WHY

Habits of thought are as hard to break as habits of any other kind. Suppose, for example, that someone thinks his or her boss is afraid of confrontation. That person may find it very difficult to change this opinion, even if the boss has actually changed.

Entire groups fall into these habits of thought, too. For example, a management team had to refill a specific staff position five times in less than a year. Yet every time they lost another person, the managers simply recruited someone else for the job and crossed their fingers. Not until the end of the year did they consider reorganizing the department and doing away with that job altogether.

What's Unchangeable About This Problem allows a group to explore hidden assumptions and biases in the way they have defined a problem. Once a group has identified a self-limiting assumption, they often discover a new line of thought that leads to a creative, innovative solution.

HOW

1. At the top of a flipchart, write "What's unchangeable about our problem?"

2. List everyone's answers.

3. Ask the group to look over the list and identify any hidden assumptions and biases. Encourage open discussion.

4. Based on these insights, list any aspects of the problem that may be changeable after all.

CREATIVE REFRAMING

KEY WORDS

WHY

Everyone makes assumptions. People often take it for granted that everyone else is making the same assumptions about such things as the meanings of words, the likelihood that an event will occur, and the motives behind a person's actions – to name just a few. When members are unaware of differences in their assumptions, they may find it very difficult to understand each other's thinking and behavior.

For example, the director of a city agency asked her staff for input on a proposed reorganization. A few people took her request seriously, but many others treated it lightly. This caused turmoil at staff meetings until the explanation was found. Several people had heard a rumor that the director was leaving; they doubted the reorganization would ever occur. The few who worked hard to give input were those who had not heard the rumor. These differences in assumptions were never mentioned, but they influenced everyone's commitment to the task.

Key Words helps people explore the meaning of the statements they make to one another. By discussing the meanings of key words, people can identify unspoken assumptions that are causing miscommunication.

HOW

1. Have the group compose a problem statement. For example, "New computers are too expensive to purchase." Write it on a flipchart.

2. Ask group members to identify the key words in the statement. Underline all key words. For example, "<u>New computers</u> are too <u>expensive</u> to <u>purchase</u>."

3. Have the group identify which word to focus on first. Then ask, "What questions does this word raise?" Record all responses. Then ask, "Does this word suggest any assumptions that can be challenged? For example, is 'purchase' the only way to obtain new computers?"

4. Repeat Step 3 for each key word. Note: Encourage discussion throughout this activity.

This tool was inspired by an exercise called "Lasso" in M. Doyle and D. Straus, *How to Make Meetings Work* (New York: Jove Books, 1982).

TWO REFRAMING ACTIVITIES

REVERSING ASSUMPTIONS

1. Hang a sheet of chart paper titled, "Assumptions About This Problem."

2. Have the group list assumptions about
   • The causes of the problem
   • The connections between different aspects of the problem.

3. Ask someone to select an item from the list, and reverse it. For example, consider an item like "We are losing our best employees." Reverse this to, "We're *keeping* our best employees."

4. Ask, "How could we bring about this new, opposite state of affairs?" Encourage a brainstorm of answers.

5. Choose another assumption and repeat Steps 3 and 4. When done, discuss ideas that seem promising.

A version of this activity appears in M. Michalko, *ThinkerToys* (Berkeley, CA: Ten Speed Press, 1992), p. 45.

REMOVING CONSTRAINTS

1. Have the group generate constraints by asking, "What is keeping us from developing the best solution to this problem?"

2. Upon completing the list, consider each item one at a time, asking, "What if *this* were not a problem?" For example, "What if we had plenty of funds available? How would we solve our problem in *that* case?"

3. Keep each discussion brief for now. The goal is to scan the list in search of promising options.

4. When finished with the first pass, have the group identify potential high-payoff ideas in preparation for extended discussion.

CREATIVE REFRAMING

TWO MORE REFRAMING ACTIVITIES

RECENTERING THE CAUSE

1. Ask the group to break the problem into its major components. For example, consider the problem of keeping public libraries open. This might divide into such components as "funding," "usage," "staffing," "civic priorities," and so on.

2. Ask a volunteer to select any component. For example, suppose someone picks "staffing."

3. Treat that selection as the central cause of the problem. Ask, "How might this affect our view of the problem?" For example, suppose "staffing" is viewed as the central cause of the problem. Someone might now suggest a new approach to the problem: perhaps volunteers could help staff the library during busy hours, enabling the library to remain open with less funding.

CATASTROPHIZING
(WE'RE DOOMED NO MATTER WHAT WE DO)

1. Ask everyone to think about the problem from their own perspective, imagining anything and everything that could go wrong.

2. Have each person in turn state his or her worst-case scenario.

3. Encourage each new speaker to build on the previous ideas until the situation seems doomed. Whining and complaining are an integral part of the activity at this point.

4. When the humor has subsided, have the group identify obstacles that merit further discussion.

5. Go down the list of obstacles one at a time, asking "Is *this* one capable of producing a catastrophe?" If so, ask, "What could be done to reduce its potential impact?"

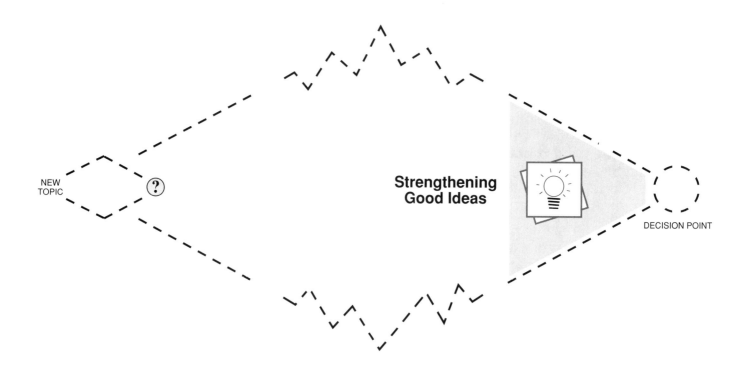

STRENGTHENING GOOD IDEAS
CONVERGENT ZONE THINKING ACTIVITY: TYPE 3

NEW TOPIC

Strengthening Good Ideas

DECISION POINT

Strengthening Good Ideas is a type of thinking that encompasses such questions as, "What resources will we need to make this work? Do we have them?" and "Who else should take a look at this idea? What would *they* say?" and "If we actually decide to move forward, who will do what by when?" During this period of critical thinking, the facilitator's job is to help group members analyze potential problems with their game plan. Are there flaws in the reasoning? Are there other options that have not been adequately explored? Does the idea really meet the group's stated criteria for success? The more questions like these a group can discuss, the better will be the quality of the group's eventual decisions. And that translates into sustainability.

As a rule, groups who have built a shared framework of understanding can evaluate and refine their ideas without formal structure – and without much facilitation, either. But occasionally – especially when the stakes are high – a facilitator will want to ensure the caliber of the work by offering a structured thinking activity, such as those provided in the following pages.

STRENGTHENING GOOD IDEAS

CLARIFYING EVALUATION CRITERIA

WHY

How should a group choose one proposal over another? One way is to agree on the criteria to use in evaluating each proposal. For example, suppose a group agreed that its most important criteria were "easy to do" and "inexpensive." These criteria could help them reject a proposal that would be expensive or difficult, even if the project seemed interesting.

This activity helps group members to discuss and reach agreement on a list of five or fewer criteria, by defining criteria *before* specific proposals are brought up for consideration.

HOW

1. Have the group brainstorm a list of answers to this question: "By doing this project (or solving this problem, or developing this plan, for example), what are we trying to accomplish?"

2. Start a new chart titled "Selection Criteria." Facilitate the group to reword the items on the first list so that each item is now a statement of a possible selection criterion. For example, if an item from the brainstorm list is, "We're trying to get two opposing factions to work together," the rewording might be, "It allows both factions to work together." Another rewording might be, "It appeals to both factions."

3. Explain that the list will soon be reduced to no more than five items. To prepare members for that judgment, have people break into small groups and discuss which criteria seem most important, and why.

4. Reconvene the large group. Have people select items from the list of criteria, and ask them to advocate for retaining those items on a final list of five or fewer criteria.

5. Give everyone five votes. Tally the results, and eliminate all but the top five vote-getters. This may not be a final decision on criteria. It will provide the membership with a sense of what people value most.

STRENGTHENING GOOD IDEAS

PAYOFFS AND RISKS

WHY

This activity improves the viability of a proposal by reducing the costs and risks that are associated with it.

For example, the mayor of a large city recently received several million dollars to improve public transportation. The public favored a proposal to spend the money on new bus routes. But the mayor was committed to upholding a previously announced hiring freeze: no new city employees were to be hired until the budget was balanced. On one hand, without new bus drivers, no more routes could be added. On the other hand, if new bus drivers were hired, the other government agencies would lobby for exemptions for *their* programs.

Payoffs And Risks helped the mayor's planning staff explore in detail the risks they would face if they went ahead with a route expansion. Through the analysis, they discovered a way to reduce their risk. They enlisted the local newspapers in an editorial campaign to build political support for this exception to the hiring freeze. It was successful, and they were able to add three new bus routes without opposition.

HOW

1. Hang three sheets of flipchart paper. Title the first page "Payoffs" and the second page "Risks." Leave the third page untitled.

2. On page one, list the payoffs associated with the proposal.

3. On page two, list the risks associated with the same proposal.

4. Now title page three "Ways to Reduce Risk." For each risk listed on the "Risks" page, discuss options for reducing the costs and the extent of the risk. Record the discussion on page three.

5. After the costs are more fully understood, ask for new proposals that preserve the payoffs while incorporating some of the risk-reducing options.

RESOURCE ANALYSIS:
CAN WE REALLY MAKE THIS WORK?

WHY

Sometimes groups agree to proposals that sound wonderful but have not been thought through very well. This is usually not a problem, because most such agreements pertain to matters of small importance. But occasionally, a group will agree to a huge undertaking with absolutely no sense of what they're in for.

For example, a group of eight nurses once agreed to organize a large conference that would bring together representatives from more than one hundred agencies in Los Angeles. The purpose of the conference was to build a coalition that could influence state and county funding policies. The organizers did not have the slightest grasp of the effort it would take them, yet they publicized the conference and kept taking on new responsibilities as they came up. Eventually one person lost her job, and another got very sick. The conference itself was disorganized, poorly attended and, ultimately, insignificant. In retrospect the nurses said, "We should have been more realistic to begin with."

HOW

1. Ask the group to list the major tasks that must be achieved if the proposal under consideration is to be implemented.

2. Assign two or three people to think about each task. Have them choose a record keeper and a spokesperson.

3. Give the small groups the following instruction: "For the next 10 minutes, think about the steps necessary to complete your assigned task. Break the task into small, doable action steps."

4. When time is up, reconvene the large group and ask the spokesperson from each group to report on his or her group's work.

5. After all committees have reported, ask everyone to discuss whether the overall proposal is adequate or requires modification.

STRENGTHENING GOOD IDEAS

WHO ELSE NEEDS TO EVALUATE THIS PROPOSAL?

WHY

Most decisions do not just affect the people who make them. Obviously, not everyone who will be affected can participate in making a decision and planning its implementation. Nonetheless, it can be very, very costly to overlook the perspectives of those who did not participate in developing the reasoning that led to the decison.

This activity helps a group to think proactively about the question, "Who else needs to be consulted?" *It usually takes a group two or three hours – sometimes longer – to go through all the steps.* Obviously this is a significant investment of group time. To decide whether to do this activity, ask, "How much time will we lose if we don't do this thinking?"

HOW

1. Have group members generate lists of people who:

   - Will be directly affected by this decision.
   - Have final sign-off authority.
   - Have to implement the decision.
   - Could sabotage the process.

2. Take a few moments to examine the list. Discuss the following questions: "What's the likelihood that any of these stakeholders would disagree with our ultimate decision? If any of them did not support the decision, how might that affect our ability to implement?"

3. Next consider each person or group on the list. Who needs to be consulted before the final decision is made?

4. For each person or group who will be consulted, decide on the best method for doing so. Some methods for including other stakeholders are interviews, focus groups, questionnaires, and an invitation to a core group meeting.

STRENGTHENING GOOD IDEAS

WHO DOES WHAT BY WHEN?

WHY

Group decision-making is often viewed as an exercise in futility. In the experience of many, agreements reached during meetings are likely to be implemented poorly, if at all.

The odds of successful implementation increase when a group takes the time to spell out specifically what needs to be done, who will do it, by when, and with what resources. But often this step does not occur. Instead, people act as if they assumed that once an agreement has been reached, the follow-through will happen magically. "Someone else" will tend to the details later.

When a group stays fuzzy about the specifics of implementing an agreement, two or three people will probably wind up with all of the tasks – often without adequate resources. Alternatively, no one takes responsibility, and nothing happens.

This activity supports group members to consider, in advance, the resources needed to undertake these efforts and commit to well-defined tasks by specific times. Moreover, the responsibilities often are distributed more evenly, because the issues are discussed openly when everyone is listening.

HOW

1. Draw a matrix with four vertical columns. Title the columns: "Tasks," "Who," "By When," and "Resources Needed."

2. Under the first heading, "Tasks," list all tasks that need to be done. If additional tasks are identified later, add them to the list.

3. Number each task listed. Then discuss: *"Who will do this? By when? What resources are needed?"* Often this thinking is done in an open discussion format, in which group members flip back and forth from one question to another.

4. As specific agreements are made, write them on the chart.

DEVELOPING INCLUSIVE SOLUTIONS

SUMMARY

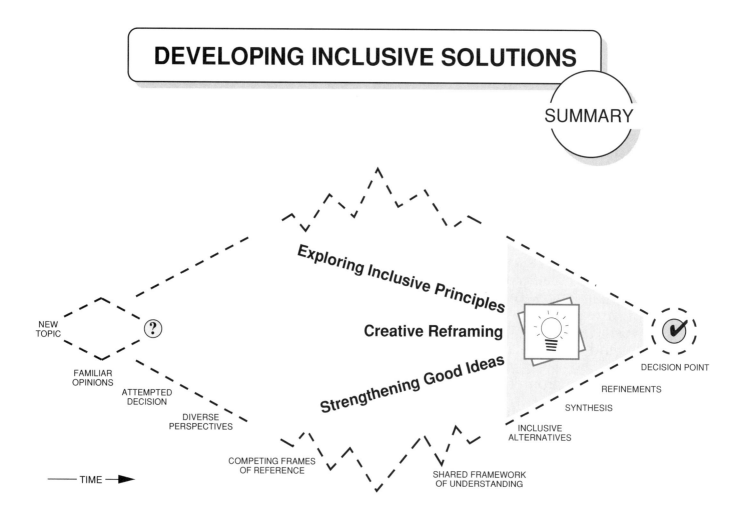

Exploring Inclusive Principles

Creative Reframing

Strengthening Good Ideas

NEW TOPIC

FAMILIAR OPINIONS

ATTEMPTED DECISION

DIVERSE PERSPECTIVES

COMPETING FRAMES OF REFERENCE

SHARED FRAMEWORK OF UNDERSTANDING

INCLUSIVE ALTERNATIVES

SYNTHESIS

REFINEMENTS

DECISION POINT

TIME ➡

Three common types of convergent thinking are shown above. Each type can be supported by activities like those presented in this chapter. Some activities help a group gain insight into the principles underlying inclusive solutions. Others enable a group to manipulate their assumptions in order to break out of fixed positions. Still others support participants to evaluate and refine the quality and the logic of their thinking.

Structured thinking activities are useful when a group appears to be trapped in an *either/or* mentality. Groups in this condition need inspiration and stimulation. Structured activities also support groups to do the nitty-gritty work of making sure their ideas can be implemented. But it would be misleading to suggest that groups in the *Convergent Zone* spend much time engaged in structured thinking. The truth is the opposite. *Convergent Zone* discussions are largely self-managing. For many facilitators, the hardest part is learning to sit down and get out of the group's way!

Sustainable agreements require well-thought-out ideas that incorporate everyone's needs and goals. If the struggle of the *Groan Zone* is the heart of a sustainable agreement, the ingenuity of the *Convergent Zone* is the brain.

Part Four

REACHING CLOSURE

17

IMPORTANCE OF CLEAR DECISION RULES

CLARIFYING THE SINGLE MOST
IMPORTANT STRUCTURAL ELEMENT
OF GROUP DECISION-MAKING

- ▶ **The Significance of Having a Clear Decision Rule**

- ▶ **Common Decision Rules**

- ▶ **Decision-Making Without Decision Rules**

- ▶ **Uses and Implications of Major Decision Rules**

- ▶ **How Different Decision Rules Affect Participation**

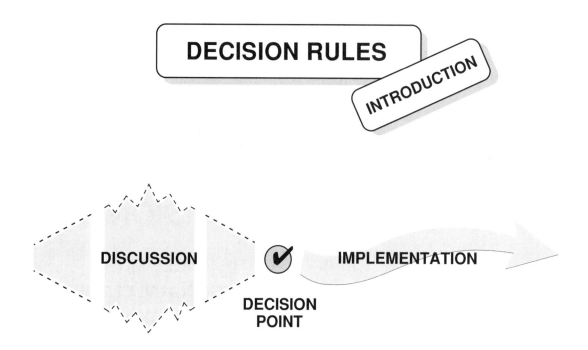

This diagram depicts two entirely different domains of group behavior: the period of discussion and the period of implementation. During a discussion, people think. They discuss. They consider their options. During the implementation, people act on what they've decided. Thus, for example, during a discussion, participants might *figure out the budget* for a project; in the implementation of that project, *people spend the money*.

During the discussion, in other words, a group operates in *the world of ideas;* after the decision has been made, that group shifts into *the world of action.*

In the world of ideas, people explore possibilities; they develop models and try them on in their imagination. They hypothesize. They extrapolate. They evaluate alternatives and develop plans. In the world of action, the group has made a commitment to take an idea and make it come true. Contracts are signed. People are hired. Departments are restructured, and offices are relocated.

The *Decision Point* is the point at which a decision is made. *It is the point that separates thinking from action.* It is the point of authorization for the actions that follow. Discussion occurs *before* the point of decision; implementation happens *after* the point of decision.

The *Decision Point* is the formal marker that says, "From this moment on, our agreement will be treated as the officially authorized reality. Disagreements will no longer be treated as alternative points of view. From now on, objections are officially out of line."

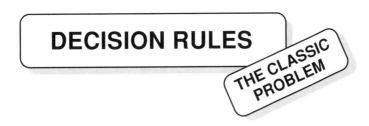

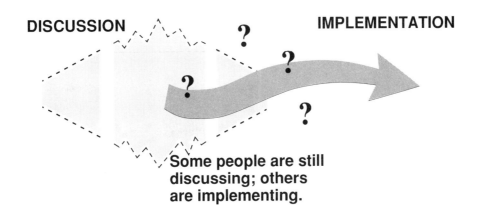

DISCUSSION   **IMPLEMENTATION**

Some people are still discussing; others are implementing.

In practice, however, group members are often not sure whether a decision has actually been made.

This can produce much confusion. Someone who thinks a decision has been made will feel empowered to take action in line with that decision. But if others think the decision has not yet been made, they will view the person who took the action as "impulsive" or "having their own agenda" or "not a team player." In such cases, however, the person accused of acting prematurely will frequently justify his or her action by saying, "I was sure we decided to go ahead with that plan."

The same is true in reverse. Inaction after the point of decision is often perceived as "insubordinate" or "passive-aggressive" or "disloyal." In such cases, it is common to hear people defend themselves by saying, "I don't recall us making an actual decision about that" or "I never agreed to this!"

These examples remind us that people need a clear, explicit indicator that a decision has been made. Some groups *can* clearly tell when a decision has or has not been made. For instance, groups that make decisions by majority rule know they are still in the discussion phase until they vote and tally the results. But most groups are fuzzy about how they make decisions. *They lack clear rules for bringing their discussion to closure.*

This chapter describes the six most common *decision rules* and explores the implications of each one.

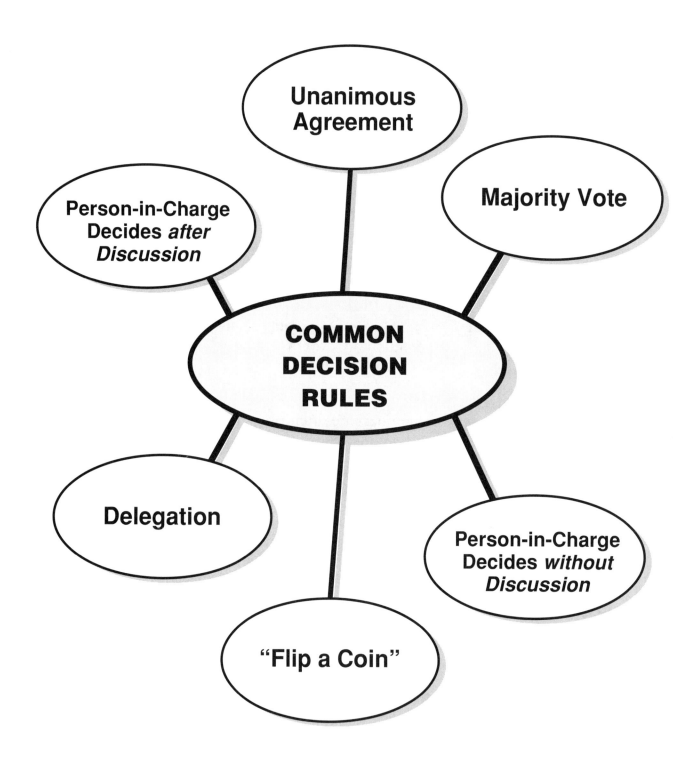

A decision rule is a mechanism that answers the question, "How do we know when we've made a decision?" Each of the six rules shown above performs this basic function.

Individual members act on their own idiosyncratic perspectives. Soon, the left hand doesn't know what the right hand is doing.

Those who whine or raise their voice get what they want.

Someone says, "Let's put this on next month's agenda and pick up where we left off." But at the next meeting, the item is superseded by urgent new business.

Just as time runs out, someone makes a new suggestion. This becomes "the decision."

DECISION-MAKING WITHOUT A DECISION RULE

People assume that since the issue was discussed, a decision was made.

After the meeting ends without agreement, a few people meet behind closed doors and make the real decisions.

Someone's name gets vaguely attached to a poorly defined task (as in, "Duane, why don't you check into that?") Later, that person gets blamed for poor follow-through.

The person who has the most at stake makes an independent decision; later, people resent him or her for taking actions that did not meet other people's needs.

Certain people *always* get their way.

When a quick decision has to be made or an opportunity will be lost, conservative members exercise a pocket veto by stalling the discussion. Thus, "no decision" becomes a decision not to act.

The person-in-charge says, "Is everyone okay with this idea?" After a few seconds of silence, the person-in-charge moves to the next topic, believing that every member's silence meant "yes," rather than "no" or "I'm still thinking."

The meeting goes overtime; the discussion drags on and on. . .

MAJOR DECISION RULES: USES AND IMPLICATIONS

» UNANIMOUS AGREEMENT

High-Stakes Decisions

In groups that decide by *unanimous agreement,* members must keep working to understand one another's perspectives until they integrate those perspectives into a shared framework of understanding. Once people are sufficiently familiar with each other's views, they become capable of advancing innovative proposals that are acceptable to everyone. It takes a lot of effort, but this is precisely why the unanimous agreement decision rule has the best chance of producing sustainable agreements when the stakes are high.

The difficulty with using unanimous agreement as the decision rule is that most people don't know how to search for Both/And solutions. Instead, people pressure each other to live with decisions that they don't truly support. And the group often ends up with a watered-down compromise.

This problem is a function of the general tendency of groups to push for a fast decision: "We need unanimous agreement because we want everyone's buy-in, but we also want to reach a decision as quickly as possible." This mentality undermines the whole point of using unanimous agreement. Its purpose is to channel the tension of diversity, in service of creative thinking – to invent brand-new ideas that really do work for everyone. This takes time. In order to realize the potentials of unanimous agreement, members should be encouraged to keep working toward mutual understanding until they develop a proposal that will receive enthusiastic support from a broad base of participants.

Low-Stakes Decisions

With low-stakes issues, unanimous agreements are usually comparable in quality to decisions reached by other decision rules. Participants learn to go along with proposals they can tolerate, rather than hold out for an innovative solution that would take a lot of time and effort to develop.

One benefit of using the unanimous agreement rule to make low-stakes decisions is that it prevents a group from making a decision that is abhorrent to a small minority. Other decision rules can lead to outcomes that are intolerable to one or two members, but are adopted because they are popular with a majority. By definition, such a decision will not be made by unanimous agreement.

MAJOR DECISION RULES: USES AND IMPLICATIONS

» MAJORITY VOTE

High-Stakes Decisions

Majority vote produces a win/lose solution through an adversarial process. The traditional justification for using this rule when stakes are high is that the competition of ideas creates pressure. Thus, the quality of everyone's reasoning theoretically gets better and better as the debate ensues.

The problem with this reasoning is that people don't always vote based on the logic of the arguments. People often "horse-trade" their votes or vote against opponents for political reasons. To increase the odds that people will vote on the merits of a high-stakes proposal, the use of secret ballots is worth considering.

Low-Stakes Decisions

When expedience is more important than quality, majority vote strikes a useful balance between the lengthy discussion that is a characteristic of unanimous agreement, and the lack of deliberation that is a danger of the other extreme. Group members can be encouraged to call for a quick round of pros and cons and get on with the vote.

» "FLIP A COIN"

High-Stakes Decisions

"Flip a coin" refers to any arbitrary, random method of making a decision, including common practices like drawing straws, picking numbers from a hat or "eeny-meeny-miney-moe." Who in their right mind would consider using this decision rule to make a high-stakes decision?

Low-Stakes Decisions

Knowing the decision will be made arbitrarily, most members stop participating. Their comments won't have any impact on the actual result. However, this is not necessarily bad. For example, how much discussion is needed to decide whether a lunch break should be 45 minutes or an hour?

MAJOR DECISION RULES: USES AND IMPLICATIONS

» PERSON-IN-CHARGE DECIDES *AFTER DISCUSSION*

High-Stakes Decisions

There is strong justification for using this decision rule when the stakes are high. The person-in-charge, after all, is the one with the access, resources, authority, and credibility to act on the decision. Seeking counsel from group members, rather than deciding without discussion, allows the person-in-charge to expand his or her understanding of the issues and form a wiser opinion about the best course of action.

Unfortunately, some group members give false advice and say what they think their boss wants to hear rather than express their true opinions.*

To overcome this problem, group members can design a formal procedure to ensure or include "devil's advocate" thinking, thus allowing people to debate the merits of an idea without the pressure of worrying whether they're blocking the group's momentum. Or group members can schedule a formal discussion without the person-in-charge. They can then bring their best thinking back to a meeting with him or her to discuss it further.

Low-Stakes Decisions

There are three decision rules that encourage group discussion: unanimous agreement, majority rule, and person-in-charge decides after discussion. With low-stakes issues, all three decision rules produce results that are roughly equivalent in quality.

Low-stakes issues provide a group with the opportunity to practice giving honest, direct advice to the person-in-charge. When the stakes are low, the person-in-charge is less likely to feel pressured to "get it right," and is therefore less defensive and more open-minded. Similarly, group members are less afraid of being punished for taking risks.

---

* Irving Janis, in his ground-breaking classic on the group dynamics of conformity, *Victims of Groupthink* (Boston: Houghton Mifflin, 1972), describes many case studies demonstrating this problem. For more suggestions on ways to overcome this problem, see pages 207-224.

MAJOR DECISION RULES: USES AND IMPLICATIONS

» PERSON-IN-CHARGE DECIDES WITHOUT DISCUSSION

High-Stakes Decisions

When a person-in-charge makes a decision without discussion, s/he assumes full responsibility for analyzing the situation and coming up with a course of action. Proponents argue that this decision rule firmly clarifies the link between authority, responsibility, and accountability. Detractors argue that this decision rule creates a high potential for blind spots and irrationality.

The most appropriate time for a person-in-charge to make high-stakes decisions without discussion is in the midst of a crisis, when the absence of a clear decision would be catastrophic. In general, though, the higher the stakes, the riskier it is for anyone to make decisions without group discussion.

How will group members behave in the face of this decision rule? The answer depends on one's values. Some people believe that good team players are loyal, disciplined subordinates who have the duty to play their roles and carry out orders. Other people argue that group members who must contend with this decision rule should develop a formal mechanism, like a union, for making sure their points of view are taken into account.

The fundamental point is that whenever one person is solely responsible for analyzing a problem and solving it, the decision-maker may lack essential information. Or those responsible for implementation might sabotage the decision because they disagree with it or because they don't understand it. The more the person-in-charge understands the dangers of deciding without group discussion, the more capable s/he is of evaluating in each situation whether the stakes are too high to take the risks.

Low-Stakes Decisions

Not all decisions made this way turn out badly. In fact, many turn out just fine. And when the stakes are low, even bad decisions can usually be undone or compensated for.

THE EFFECTS OF DIFFERENT DECISION RULES ON PARTICIPATION

Person-in-Charge Decides *Without* Group Discussion

This decision rule gets group members in the habit of "doing what they are told."

At meetings, they listen passively to the person-in-charge, who talks and talks without being challenged.

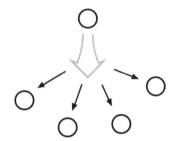

Person-in-Charge Decides *After* Group Discussion

When the person-in-charge is the final decision-maker, s/he is the main person who needs to be convinced. Everyone tends to direct their comments to the person-in-charge.

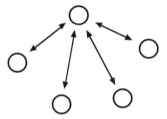

Majority Vote

Since the goal is to obtain 51% agreement, the influence process is a battle for the undecided center. Once a majority is established, the opinions of the minority can be disregarded.

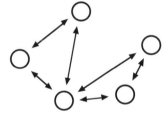

Unanimous Agreement

When everyone has the power to block a decision, each participant has the right to expect his or her perspective to be taken into account. This puts pressure on members to work toward mutual understanding.

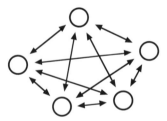

Each decision rule has a different effect on group behavior. Individual group members adjust the quantity and quality of their participation depending on how they think their behavior will influence the decision.

18

STRIVING FOR UNANIMITY

WORKING WITH
GRADIENTS OF AGREEMENT

- ▶ **Unanimity and Consensus**

- ▶ **Intro to the Gradients of Agreement Scale**

- ▶ **Using the Gradients of Agreement Scale**

- ▶ **Gradients of Agreement in Action:**
  Enthusiastic Support
  Lukewarm Support

- ▶ **When to Seek Enthusiastic Support**

- ▶ **What Level of Support is Optimal?**

- ▶ **Gradients of Agreement in Action:**
  Ambiguous Support
  Majority Support with Outliers

- ▶ **Adapting the Gradients of Agreement Scale**

- ▶ **Methods of Polling the Group**

STRIVING FOR UNANIMITY

INTRODUCTION

THE POWER OF UNANIMOUS AGREEMENT

The word *unanimous* comes from two Latin words: *unus*, meaning "one," and *animus*, meaning "spirit." A group that reaches unanimous agreement is a group that acts from one spirit. By this understanding, a unanimous agreement can be expected to contain wisdom and soundness of judgment, because it expresses an idea that is felt by each person to be true. As the Quakers say, the decision speaks for everyone.

To reach unanimity, everyone must agree. This means that everyone has an individual veto. Thus, anyone who perceives that his or her interests are *not* being taken into account can keep the discussion alive for as many hours or weeks or months as it takes, to find a solution that works for everyone. This veto capacity is the crux of the power of unanimous agreement. When a group is committed to reaching unanimous agreement, the members are in effect making a commitment to remain in discussion until they develop a solution that takes everyone's needs into account.

UNANIMITY AND CONSENSUS

Consensus also has Latin origins. Its root word is *consentire*, which is a combination of two Latin words: *con*, meaning "with" or "together with," and *sentire*, meaning "to think and feel." *Consentire* thus translates as "to think and feel together."

Consensus is *the process* – a participatory process by which a group thinks and feels together, *en route to* their decision. Unanimity, by contrast, is the point at which the group *reaches closure*. Many groups that practice consensus decision-making use unanimity as their decision rule for reaching closure – but many groups *do not*. For example, the Seva Foundation uses "unanimity minus one." So does the renowned collective, the Hog Farm. Some chapters of the Green Party use 80% as their acceptable level of agreement. Yet all such groups consider themselves to be sincere adherents of a consensus decision-making process.

In these cases, no single member has personal veto power. Nonetheless, individual voices wield significant influence – enough to ensure that the group will engage in a genuine process of thinking and feeling together.

STRIVING FOR UNANIMITY
IDEALISM vs REALITY

A SILENCE IS NOT AN AGREEMENT

Many managers want their teams to be strongly aligned in relation to the high-stake, high-impact issues that most affect their work. When tackling such issues, these managers come to meetings with statements like, "I need to get everyone's buy-in today." Clearly, these managers *want* their groups to achieve unanimous agreement.

Yet if we look at how such meetings play out, what actually happens? The discussion may go well for a time, but once the group becomes mired in the *Groan Zone,* the person-in-charge often feels pressure to bring the discussion to closure and make a decision.

To close discussion, it's common for a person-in-charge to summarize a key line of thought and say something like, "It sounds like people want to do such-and-such." Then s/he will follow with, "Does everyone agree with this proposal?" Typically, after a few seconds of silence, this person will say, "All right, we're agreed. That's what we'll do. Now let's move on."

Is this actually a unanimous agreement? Not really. The manager has no idea, really, what the people who didn't respond were thinking.

THE PROBLEM WITH YES AND NO

Unanimity means that every person has said "yes." But "yes" does not necessarily mean, "Yes, this is a great idea." It could also mean, "Yes... well... I have reservations, but I guess I can work them out when we implement it," or even, "Yes, though actually I don't much care for this idea, but I'll go along with the majority. I want to be seen as a team player."

Moreover, someone who says "no" is saying, in effect, "I require the group to spend more time on this discussion." This causes most group members to be very hesitant to say "no." They do not want to feel responsible for dragging out a discussion.

Thus, the "yes-no" language is a fundamental problem. To strive for unanimity, group members need a way to accurately and authentically convey the extent of their support (or nonsupport) for a proposal.

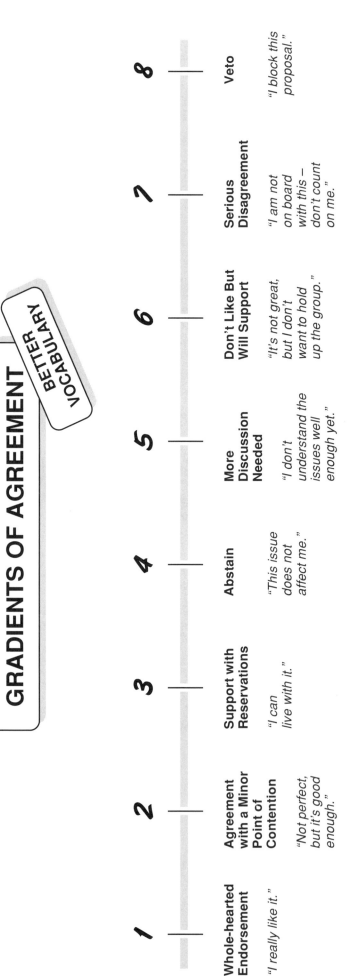

GRADIENTS OF AGREEMENT

BETTER VOCABULARY

1	2	3	4	5	6	7	8
Whole-hearted Endorsement	Agreement with a Minor Point of Contention	Support with Reservations	Abstain	More Discussion Needed	Don't Like But Will Support	Serious Disagreement	Veto
"I really like it."	"Not perfect, but it's good enough."	"I can live with it."	"This issue does not affect me."	"I don't understand the issues well enough yet."	"It's not great, but I don't want to hold up the group."	"I am not on board with this – don't count on me."	"I block this proposal."

This is the *Gradients of Agreement Scale.* It enables members of a group to express their support for a proposal in degrees, along a continuum. Using this tool, group members are no longer trapped into expressing support in terms of "yes" and "no."

The *Gradients of Agreement Scale was* developed in 1987 by Sam Kaner, Duane Berger, and the staff of Community At Work. It has been translated into Spanish, French, Russian, Mandarin, Arabic and Swahili, and it has been used in organizations large and small throughout the world.

Community At Work © 2007

HOW TO USE
THE GRADIENTS OF AGREEMENT SCALE

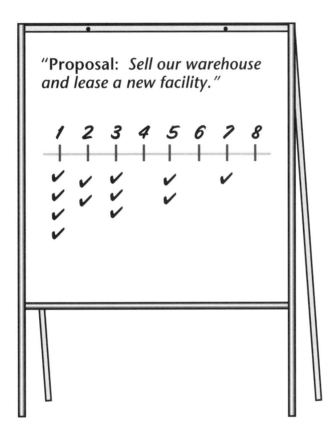

Before the meeting, post the *Gradients of Agreement Scale* on a flipchart. Some facilitators show the chart to the group at the beginning of the meeting and obtain the group's agreement to use it. Other facilitators don't introduce it until the group is ready to make a decision.

When the time comes to take a poll, follow these steps:
- Step 1: Record the proposal under discussion on a flipchart.
- Step 2: Check to see that everyone understands the proposal.
- Step 3: Ask for final revisions in the wording of the proposal.
- Step 4: Draw a scorecard below the proposal, as shown on this page.
- Step 5: Ask, "How do you like this proposal?"
- Step 6: Take the poll. Capture everyone's positions on the scorecard.

Note that the result is not a vote or a decision; it's just the record of a poll. It indicates the extent to which a group supports a proposal.

GRADIENTS OF AGREEMENT IN ACTION: ENTHUSIASTIC SUPPORT

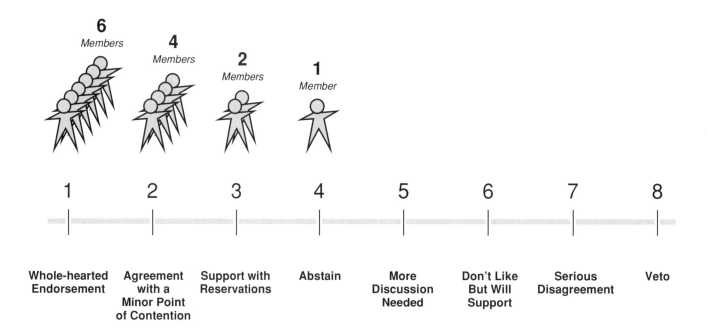

This diagram portrays the result of a hypothetical poll, taken in a group of 13 members. The pattern of responses – also known as "the spread" – indicates a high level of enthusiastic support for the proposal.

An agreement based on this much support will usually produce a successful implementation. After all, six members of the group are whole-hearted in their endorsement, and the others are not too far behind. One could reasonably expect that these participants would care about the results they produce.

Words like *buy-in* and *ownership* carry the same connotation as *enthusiastic support* – they express the depth of enthusiasm and commitment groups experience when they engage in a high-quality thinking process that results in high levels of endorsement.

GRADIENTS OF AGREEMENT IN ACTION: LUKEWARM SUPPORT

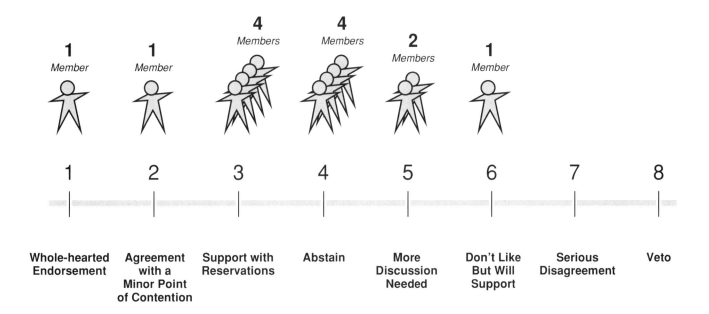

1	2	3	4	5	6	7	8
Whole-hearted Endorsement	Agreement with a Minor Point of Contention	Support with Reservations	Abstain	More Discussion Needed	Don't Like But Will Support	Serious Disagreement	Veto

This diagram portrays the result of a different poll, taken of the same 13-person group. Here, the spread indicates significantly less enthusiasm for the proposal. Nonetheless, this spread also indicates unanimous agreement. Not one person would veto this proposal and block it from going forward. In fact, there is no serious disagreement with it whatsoever.

For many purposes, lukewarm support is perfectly adequate. For example, when the stakes are low, it is usually not worth pushing for a higher level of support.   But in other cases, when achieving a goal will require high motivation and sustained effort, lukewarm support just won't do the trick.

WHEN TO SEEK ENTHUSIATIC SUPPORT

When does a group need to seek enthusiastic support? And when is lukewarm sufficient? Here are some variables that help to answer this question:

Enthusiastic support is desirable whenever the stakes are so high that the consequences of failure would be severe. By contrast, when the stakes are lower, a group may not wish to invest the time and energy it takes to develop enthusiastic support.

Some decisions are not easily reversible – for example, the decision to relocate headquarters to a new city. Decisions like these are worth spending whatever time it takes to get them right. But others decisions – such as the question of how to staff a project during an employee's two-week vacation – have a short life-span. To get such a decision perfectly right might take longer than the entire lifetime of the decision.

The chief factors that make problems hard to solve are complexity, ambiguity, and the severity of conflict.* The tougher the problem is, the more time and effort a group should expect to expend. Routine problems, by contrast, don't require long-drawn-out discussions.

When many people have a stake in the outcome of the decision, it is more likely to be worth the effort to include everyone's thinking in the development of that decision. When the decision affects only a few people, the process need not be as inclusive.

The more likely it is that members will be expected to use their own judgment and creativity to implement a decision, the more they will need to understand the reasoning behind that decision. The process of seeking enthusiastic support pushes people to think through the logic of the issues at hand.

*Source: Paul C. Nutt, *Solving Tough Problems* (San Francisco: Jossey-Bass, 1989).

WHAT LEVEL OF SUPPORT IS OPTIMAL?

Enthusiastic Support
is necessary
when the issue
involves:

Lukewarm Support
is good enough
when the issue
involves:

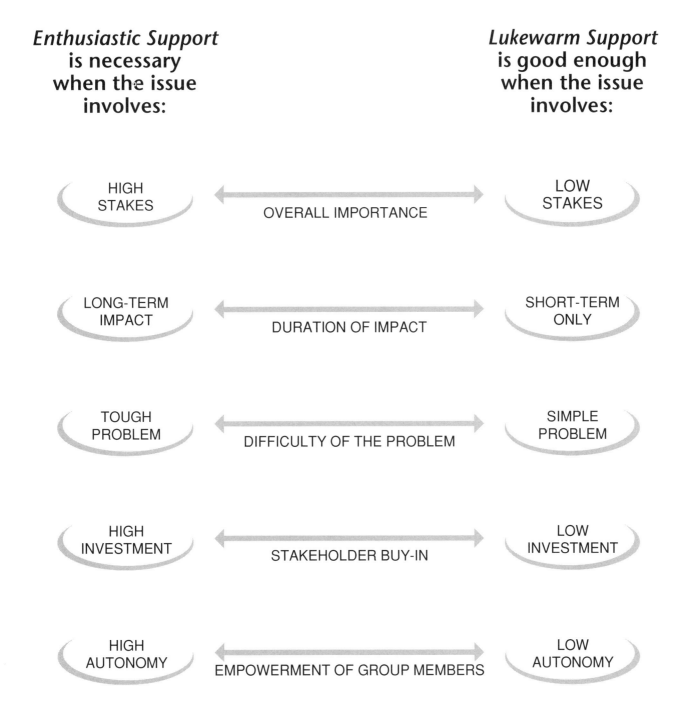

| HIGH STAKES | OVERALL IMPORTANCE | LOW STAKES |

| LONG-TERM IMPACT | DURATION OF IMPACT | SHORT-TERM ONLY |

| TOUGH PROBLEM | DIFFICULTY OF THE PROBLEM | SIMPLE PROBLEM |

| HIGH INVESTMENT | STAKEHOLDER BUY-IN | LOW INVESTMENT |

| HIGH AUTONOMY | EMPOWERMENT OF GROUP MEMBERS | LOW AUTONOMY |

GRADIENTS OF AGREEMENT IN ACTION: AMBIGUOUS SUPPORT

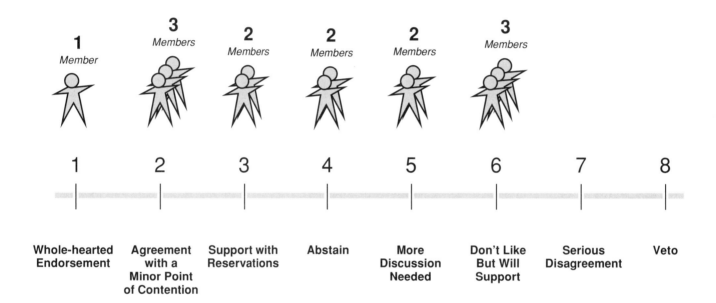

This diagram portrays a group of people who are all over the map in their response to the proposal. Ambiguous results frequently indicate that the original problem was poorly defined. Michael Doyle and David Straus say, "You can't agree on the solution if you don't agree on the problem."* This group would definitely benefit from more discussion. Yet many groups would treat this result as indicating unanimity, since no vetoes were exercised.

* Source: M. Doyle and D. Straus, *Making Meetings Work* (New York: Berkeley Books, 1993).

GRADIENTS OF AGREEMENT IN ACTION: MAJORITY SUPPORT WITH OUTLIERS

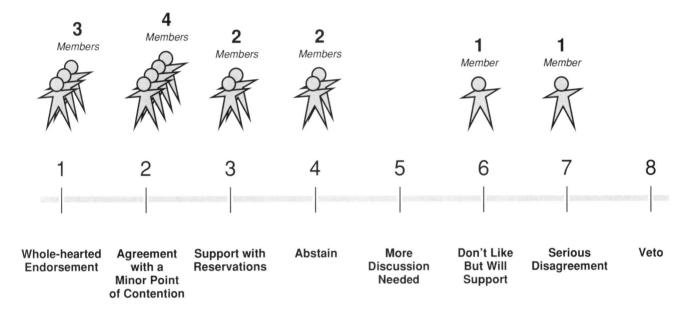

3 Members	**4** Members	**2** Members	**2** Members		**1** Member	**1** Member	
1	2	3	4	5	6	7	8
Whole-hearted Endorsement	Agreement with a Minor Point of Contention	Support with Reservations	Abstain	More Discussion Needed	Don't Like But Will Support	Serious Disagreement	Veto

This spread is surprisingly common. When it occurs, the question arises as to whether the group should disregard the objections of the outliers or whether the group should keep making efforts to resolve those objections.

Often the person-in-charge of the group will try for a compromise, asking those with objections if they can suggest remedies that would increase their level of support. Sometimes this works.

But not always. It depends on whether the situation requires enthusiastic support. When everyone's strong support is needed, lukewarm compromises will not do. In those cases, the group must continue searching for a genuinely inclusive solution.

ADAPTING THE GRADIENTS OF AGREEMENT SCALE

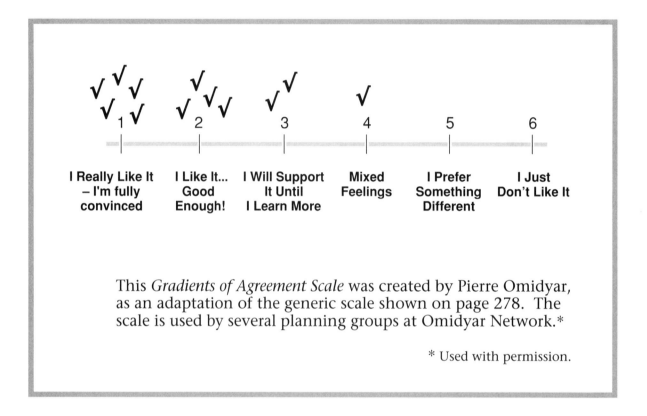

1	2	3	4	5	6
I Really Like It – I'm fully convinced	I Like It... Good Enough!	I Will Support It Until I Learn More	Mixed Feelings	I Prefer Something Different	I Just Don't Like It

This *Gradients of Agreement Scale* was created by Pierre Omidyar, as an adaptation of the generic scale shown on page 278. The scale is used by several planning groups at Omidyar Network.*

* Used with permission.

Many group leaders prefer to create their own set of gradients, whether to suit their leadership style or to fit the group's culture. To assist in this effort:

1. Explain the benefits of using *Gradients of Agreement.*

2. Show the person-in-charge the scale on page 278.

3. Ask whether s/he would like to customize the scale.

4. Once the person-in-charge has revised the scale, have him or her present the scale to the group, soliciting further revisions if desired.

Even when a group uses the generic scale for the first few decisions, it is entirely fine for the leader (or the participants) to propose modifications at a later time.

METHODS OF POLLING THE GROUP

Say, "Please raise your hands if you endorse this proposal." Count the raised hands. Record the data on a flipchart. Now say, "Please raise your hands if you agree with minor reservations." Count hands and record. Repeat for all gradients.

Go around the room, one person at a time, and ask each person to state which gradient s/he prefers and why. No discussion is allowed. As everyone declares his or her preference, record the data on a flipchart.

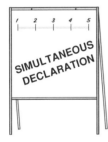

Have each person write the gradient (word or number) of his or her preference in block letters on a large piece of paper. On cue, have everyone hold up his or her card. Record the data on a flipchart.

Have each person write his or her preference on a slip of paper. When everyone has finished, collect the ballots and tally the results. Post the data on a flipchart.

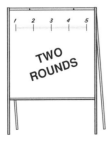

Before beginning the poll, let people know that the first poll is a preliminary round and that it will be followed by a brief discussion and then a final poll. Next, gather the data in any of the ways listed above. After a brief, time-limited discussion, poll again. This method lets a person see where others stand before registering a final preference.

19

REACHING CLOSURE STEP BY STEP

WORKING WITH THE
COMMUNITY AT WORK
PROCEDURE FOR REACHING CLOSURE

DECISION RULES: A BASIC DILEMMA

Many work groups have difficulty establishing a clear *decision rule*. Frequently, the problem is that the person-in-charge does not feel obligated to use a single decision rule. "Sometimes," said a division manager, "I want everyone in my group to agree to a plan before we act on it. At other times I don't want to waste time, so I make the decision myself."

From the point of view of the person-in-charge, it does not make sense to be tied down to a particular rule. But from the perspective of the group members, the inconsistency can be enormously confusing.

For example, a software publishing company held monthly meetings that were chaired by the chief operating officer and attended by all department managers. The managers complained that the meetings were very frustrating. "Sometimes the boss cuts off discussion after five minutes," they grumbled. "At other times he lets it run on and on. Sometimes it seems like he wants us to buy into a decision he's already made; other times he couldn't care less what we think; and then there are times when he wants us to figure out every little detail. It's driving us crazy!"

This is an intriguing example. From the perspective of the person-in-charge, his behavior was perfectly logical! He knew what the decision rule was – *the person-in-charge makes the decision after group discussion*. But in each particular case he made a judgment call to determine how much discussion the issue warranted. At times – when the stakes were low or when a solution seemed obvious – he decided it was fine to make a quick decision with very little discussion. At other times, when he wanted everyone to take ownership of the outcome, he kept the discussion going in search of better ideas.

The problem was that he did not share this reasoning with the group. He made all his judgments in his head. The group members had no idea that there was a method to his madness. To explain his apparent inconsistency, they made up all kinds of stories: He was manipulating them. He was fearful of corporate politics. He was incompetent as a leader.

This example perfectly illustrates the classic tension between the need for a flexible procedure and the need for a clarified procedure. The person-in-charge felt that clarifying his decision rule would handcuff him. He needed the flexibility to allocate time wisely. But leaving the decision rule vague didn't work, either. It prevented the group members from knowing whether and when their manager valued their participation.

REACHING CLOSURE

THE META-DECISION*

The Discussion Reaches a Stopping Point

OPTION A

OPTION B

The person-in-charge decides that the discussion has been adequate. S/he feels ready to bring the issue to closure by making a final decision.

The person-in-charge decides that important issues still need to be thought through. S/he wants the group to continue the discussion.

This diagram portrays a situation that comes up all the time in groups: at a certain point in practically every discussion, the person-in-charge has to decide whether to end the discussion and make a decision.

To most people who play the role of person-in-charge, this fact is intuitively obvious. They recognize the situation because they deal with it every day. But it is *not* so obvious to the other participants at a meeting. They often don't know *how* to interpret what's going on. As a result of such confusion, people can become frustrated, angry, and passive – exactly as happened in the example on the previous page.

Fortunately, it is easy to reduce the disparity between the perspective of the person-in-charge and the perspective of the other members. *The solution is to show everyone what the person-in-charge is doing.* Show a simple diagram like the one drawn above, and explain the options. When the choice point is made explicit, the confusion is removed.

---

* The word *meta* is Greek and means "above" or "about." Making a decision about whether to make a decision is thus called *making a meta-decision*.

THREE META-DECISIONS

THE DOYLE AND STRAUS *FALLBACK*

One of the most well-known meta-decision procedures is the Doyle and Straus *fallback*.* Here's how it works.

Whenever a new topic is introduced, the person-in-charge sets a time limit. During that period of time, the group will strive to reach a unanimous agreement. If time runs out, the person-in-charge makes the meta-decision: either s/he will now bring the discussion to closure and make a final decision, or s/he will set a new time limit and reopen the discussion.

CAROLINE ESTES' *VOTE TO VOTE*

Meta-decisions also occur in groups that have no person-in-charge. For example, the U.S. Green Party, which uses unanimous agreement as its decision rule, has a meta-decision that allows it to switch from unanimity to majority vote. This meta-decision, called *vote to vote,* was popularized by Caroline Estes, one of the nation's leading experts in the field of large-group consensus decision-making.**

The Greens have adapted this procedure: any group member can call for a vote to close discussion and switch from unanimity to majority. Immediately following this call, the vote is taken. If 80% of the voters favor switching, the discussion ends, and the group uses majority rule to reach a decision on the proposal at hand; if fewer than 80% want to switch, the unanimity rule remains in effect and the discussion continues.

SAM KANER'S *META-DECISION*

This procedure is shown on the next page. Its central premise is that *polling helps a group obtain maximum benefit from the use of a meta-decision.*

In groups with a person-in-charge, it is highly advantageous for that person to use a *Gradients of Agreement scale* to take a poll before s/he makes a decision. If s/he sees adequate support from the group, s/he can make a decision with confidence that it will be implemented. However, if s/he sees that a proposal lacks sufficient support, s/he can reopen the discussion rather than make a decision that would be difficult to implement.

---

  * M. Doyle and D. Strauss, *How to Make Meetings Work* (New York: Berkeley Books, 1993)
** Personal observation by Sam Kaner, while co-facilitating the founding conference of the U.S.A. Green Party, Eugene, Oregon, 1989.

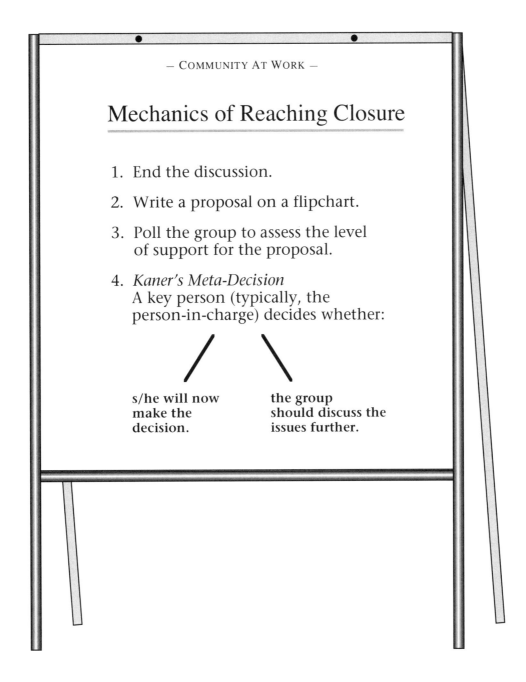

This is the *Community At Work* procedure for reaching closure at meetings. This procedure allows groups to make simple decisions quickly, and it also supports them to take as much time as necessary when the stakes are high and the impact is substantial. It provides groups with the benefits of participatory decision-making whether or not their organizations are hierarchically structured.

All groups that use this procedure are encouraged to customize it to fit their own circumstances.

KANER'S META-DECISION
REAL-LIFE EXAMPLES

The Spectrem Group
Consulting Services

1. Anyone may call for closure.

2. Someone seconds.

3. The proposal is summarized.

4. Poll, using gradients of agreement.

5. If no one vetoes the proposal,
   the person-in-charge decides:

   /   \
   she will now   the group
   make the   should continue to
   decision.   discuss the issues.

Used with permission from Amy J. Errett, chairman, Spectrem Group.

VISA International
Global Access Technologies

1. Anyone can move to close discussion.
   The group is then polled. In case of
   disagreement, the person-in-charge
   decides whether to end discussion.

2. Clarify the proposal by writing it down.

3. Poll, using gradients of agreement.

4. If no one vetoes the proposal,
   the person-in-charge decides:

   /   \
   there is enough   the group
   agreement   should discuss the
   to formalize   issues further.
   a decision.

Used with permission from Paul Weintraub, vice president.

Charles Schwab & Co.
Retail Employee Performance Support

1. Clarify the decision rule to be used. If
   using the meta-decision process, *identify
   the meta-decision maker* and proceed as
   follows:

2. Anyone can close the discussion.

3. Anyone can offer a proposal. If someone
   is not clear, clarify the proposal.

4. Poll the group. Anyone can block.

5. The meta-decision-maker decides:

   /   \
   s/he will now   the group
   make the   should continue to
   decision.   discuss the issues.

Used with permission from Janet Manchester, vice president.

KANER'S META-DECISION
MORE REAL-LIFE EXAMPLES

Marshall Medical Center

1. Anyone may call for closure. The chair decides whether to close.

2. A proposal is made by anyone in the group and written down.

3. Clarify the proposal with questions and "friendly amendments."

4. Poll, using gradients of agreement.

5. The chair decides whether:

to move forward on the proposal.

topic needs more discussion.

the proposal will be dropped.

Used with permission from James Whipple, CEO.

Hospitality Valuation Financial Services

1. Identify issues as *group issues* or *person-in-charge decisions*. For group issues, proceed as follows:

2. Clarify the proposal.

3. Poll the group.

4. The person-in-charge decides:

s/he will now make the decision.

the group should continue to discuss the issues.

5. Proceed as specified in Step 4.

6. After the person-in-charge has made the decision, feedback is welcome.

Used with permission from Harvey Christensen, vice president.

Watsonville Healthy Families Collaborative

1. Select a *Poll Assessor* at each meeting.

2. Anyone can call to close the discussion.

3. Clarify the proposal and write it down.

4. Poll the group using the polling scale. Everyone in attendance (individual or agency representative) can participate.

5. If no one vetoes, the *Poll Assessor* decides:

The poll result is good enough to be our final decision.

We need more discussion.

6. If no decision has been made after three rounds of discussion, a majority vote will take place, with one vote per agency.

Used with permission from Defensa de Mujers for the Watsonville Healthy Families Collaborative.

KANER'S META-DECISION
EVEN MORE REAL-LIFE EXAMPLES

San Lorenzo School District Facilities Planning Group

1. Anyone can call for closure to end discussion.

2. Clarify proposal.

3. Poll for preferences by holding up cards that show gradients of agreement.

4. Person-in-charge assesses: Is this enough agreement to be considered a final decision?

If yes, the decision is considered final.

If no, return to discussion. Members identify areas of nonsupport and suggest alternatives.

Used with permission from Janis Duran, superintendent.

Hollister School District Strategic Planning Team

1. Call for closure to end discussion.

2. Clarify proposal.

3. Poll for preferences.

4. Ask group, "Is this enough agreement?"

If No
Return to discussion, with purpose of revising the proposal to get higher support. (Up to 3 rounds of discussion, then it is final).

If Yes
Decision is final. A "5" is a veto and the proposal doesn't pass.

Used with permission of full membership of the Strategic Planning Team, Hollter School District.

Santa Cruz Gardens School

1. Close discussion.
   • Anyone can call for closure.
   • Needs a second and a third.
   • Make time for anyone who hasn't spoken yet to speak if they want.

2. Create or clarify the proposal.

3. Poll the group.

4. Meta-decision: The person-in-charge decides whether:

S/he will now make the decision.

The group should discuss the issue further.

Used with permission from Carl Pearson, principal.

KANER'S META-DECISION
STILL MORE REAL-LIFE EXAMPLES

Urban Strategies Council
Leadership Technical Team

1. *Call for closure,* to end discussion.

2. Clarify the proposal.

3. Check for consensus by polling.

4. The *meta-decision-maker,* a role that rotates each meeting, decides:

| there is enough agreement to formalize the decision. | there is not enough agreement to make a decision. Reopen the discussion. |

Used with permission from Maria Campbell Casey, president.

Youth Advocates
Of Marin County

1. Close discussion by unanimity.

2. Collect proposals.

3. Poll for preferences among options.

4. The person-in-charge decides:

| s/he will now make the decision. | the *Procedure Person,* a rotating role, will now make the decision. |

the group should continue discussing the issues.

5. Proceed as specified in step 4.

Used with permission from David Barkan, program director.

Larkin Street
Youth Services

1. Collect proposals.

2. Poll for preferences among alternatives.

3. Time-limited attempt to reach unanimity:
   • set time limit,
   • proceed until time expires.

4. The person-in-charge decides:

| she will now make the final decision. | the group should continue to discuss the issues. |

Used with permission from Diane Flannery, executive director.

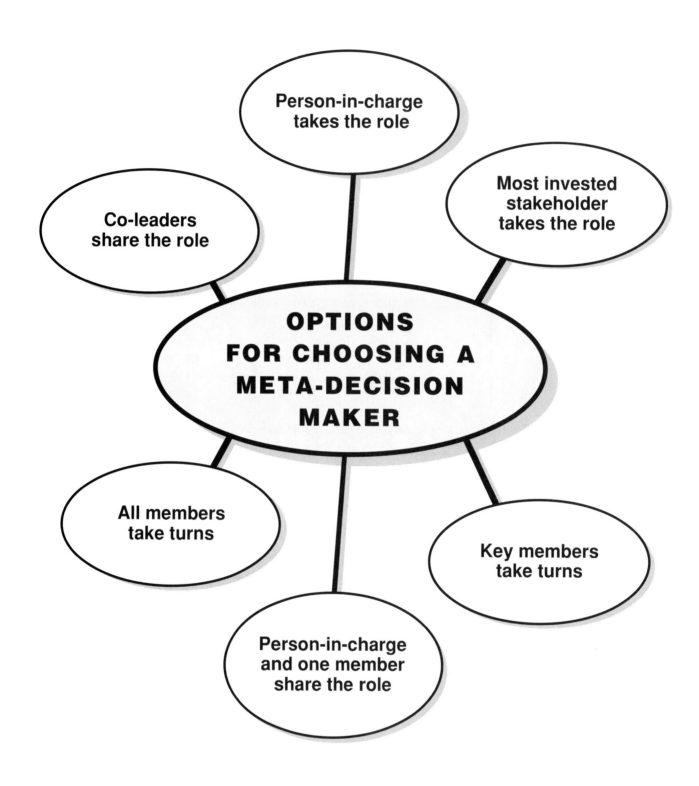

The *meta-decision maker* is the person who decides whether an issue needs further discussion. The role of the *meta-decision maker* can be assigned using any of the options shown above.

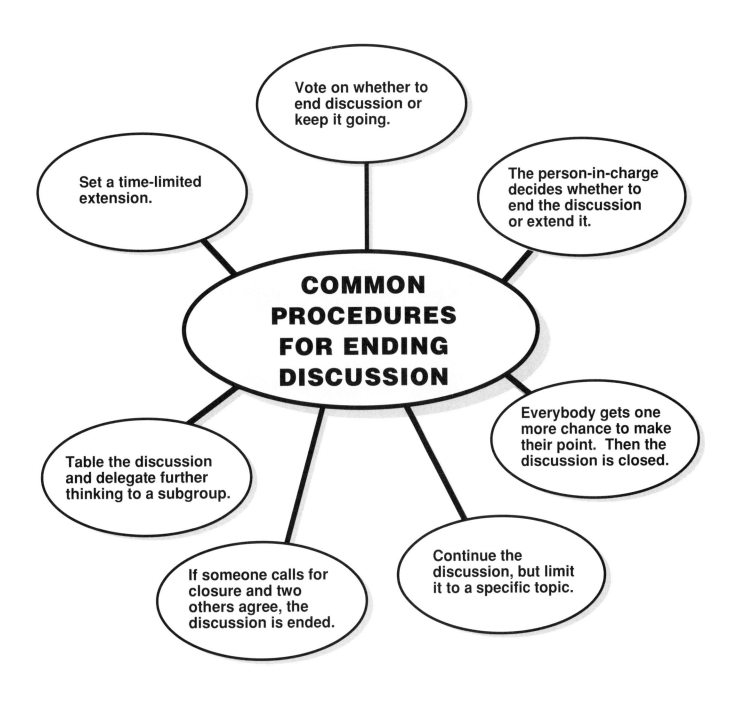

Vote on whether to end discussion or keep it going.

Set a time-limited extension.

The person-in-charge decides whether to end the discussion or extend it.

COMMON PROCEDURES FOR ENDING DISCUSSION

Table the discussion and delegate further thinking to a subgroup.

Everybody gets one more chance to make their point. Then the discussion is closed.

If someone calls for closure and two others agree, the discussion is ended.

Continue the discussion, but limit it to a specific topic.

A group can use any of these procedures to end discussion. Once selected, the procedure should be posted and followed consistently, so that everyone has the same expectations of how the group ends discussions.

HELPING THE PERSON-IN-CHARGE DESIGN A DECISION PROCEDURE

1. *Show the person-in-charge a flipchart of "The Mechanics of Reaching Closure" (see chart on page 293).* Read the text out loud. State that you will now explain the mechanics and rationale for each step, starting with Step 4: the Meta-Decision.

2. *Describe the use of the Meta-Decision.* Describe the differences between enthusiastic support and lukewarm support. Ask the person-in-charge, "Under what circumstances would you be comfortable proceeding with lukewarm support? And under what circumstances would you want to build more support, even if it meant reopening the discussion?"

3. *Show the Gradients of Agreement.* Describe how the polling process works, and demonstrate a result by placing dots on the scale. Explain that there is nothing sacred about the labels or the number of points on the scale and that most groups customize the scale to fit their own group culture.

4. *Briefly explain the need for a rule to end discussion.* Give examples of different ways a group can close discussion. (Several are shown on page 299.)

5. *Briefly explain the importance of writing a proposal on a flipchart.* Emphasize that the first draft of a proposal does not have to be perfect. People may wish to tweak it before a poll is taken.

6. *Invite and encourage the client to customize any or all steps.* Make sure the person-in-charge is 100 percent comfortable with his/her adaptation of the Meta-Decision.

7. *Make a plan for bringing the revised procedure to the whole group.* Encourage the person-in-charge to expect — and even hope — that the group will revise the procedure further to make it their own.

INSTALLING THE DECISION PROCEDURE

1.
SET THE FRAME

Person-In-Charge: Tell the group that you are about to show them a proposal for a decision-making procedure. Explain that you want them to revise this proposal as needed, until it suits the group. Then overview the ratification process (Step 4.)

2.
SHOW YOUR PROPOSAL

Person-In-Charge: Show the group your proposed decision-making procedure in its entirety. Use a flipchart so you can make changes easily.

3.
DISCUSS EACH STEP

Facilitator: Describe the *gradients of agreement* and explain how your polling process will work. Then explain the *meta-decision.* Facilitate a group discussion of each step. Record all suggested revisions on the flipchart.

4.
REVISE AND RATIFY

Facilitator: Have the group use the proposed procedure to end discussion. Then poll for support of suggested revisions, and have the person-in-charge make the meta-decision. Usually there are several suggestions to deal with. If so, take them one at a time, repeating the sequence until all revisions have been ratified or rejected. Finish by polling for support of the entire final product.

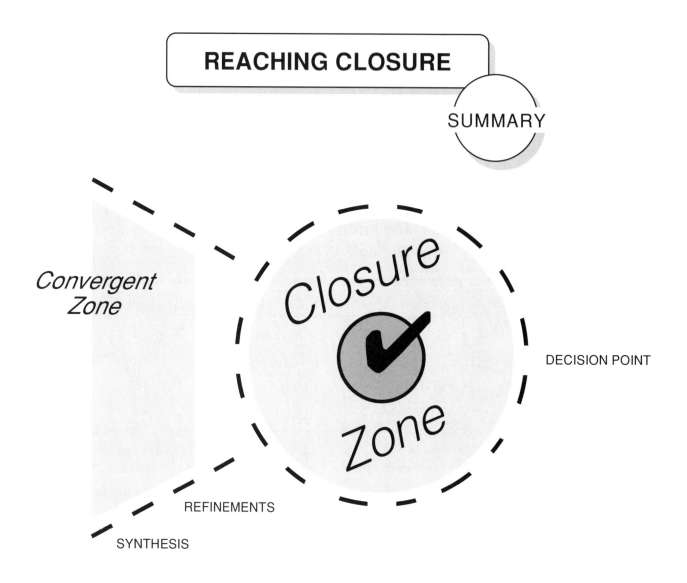

REACHING CLOSURE

SUMMARY

Convergent Zone

Closure Zone

DECISION POINT

REFINEMENTS

SYNTHESIS

The *Closure Zone* can be viewed as the final phase of decision-making. It consists of four distinct steps:

1. End the discussion.
2. Write a proposal on a flipchart.
3. Poll the group members.
4. Use the group's decision rule to reach a final decision.

Sometimes these steps can be navigated quickly and informally, without the help of explicit procedures – for example, when someone proposes a clear, compelling solution to the problem at hand and everyone gladly accepts it. But in the long run, for all the reasons discussed in this chapter, groups will benefit from establishing an explicit, formal decision rule – even if they use it only occasionally. Facilitators are advised to study carefully the principles covered in this chapter. Understanding the mechanics of reaching closure is essential for anyone who wants to help a group build sustainable agreements.

FACILITATING SUSTAINABLE AGREEMENTS

A SUMMARY AND INTEGRATION OF THE MAIN POINTS OF THIS BOOK

- ▶ Overview

- ▶ The Divergent Zone

- ▶ The Groan Zone

- ▶ The Convergent Zone

- ▶ The Closure Zone

- ▶ One Last Look at the Role of Facilitator

FACILITATING SUSTAINABLE AGREEMENTS

INTRODUCTION

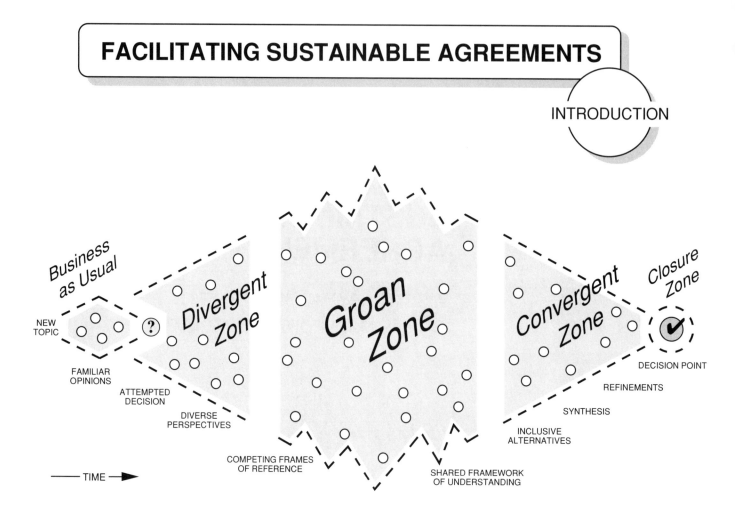

Sustainable agreements don't happen in a burst of inspiration; they develop slowly. It takes time and effort for people to build a shared framework of understanding, and groups need different types of support at different points in the process. Facilitators who understand this will vary their technique to match the group's current dynamics.

The following pages review the Diamond of Participatory Decision-Making. Each page summarizes the significance of one zone of the Diamond, with emphasis on issues that hold particular interest for facilitators.

FACILITATING SUSTAINABLE AGREEMENTS

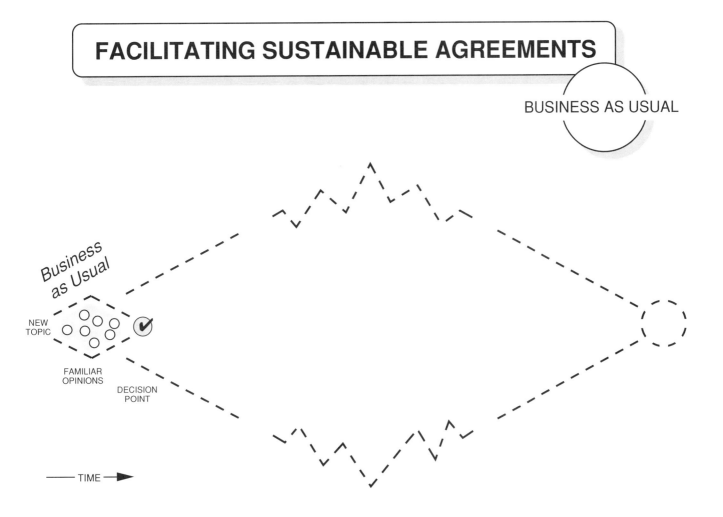

BUSINESS AS USUAL

Business
as Usual

NEW
TOPIC

FAMILIAR
OPINIONS

DECISION
POINT

TIME

When a new topic comes up for discussion in a group, people normally begin the conversation by proposing obvious solutions to obvious problems. The emotional atmosphere is usually congenial but superficial. People refrain from taking risks that would put them in vulnerable positions. If an idea seems workable, it usually leads to quick agreement. "Sounds good to me," people say. The facilitator's main task during this phase is to pay attention to the quality and quantity of each person's participation. Is everyone engaged? Does everyone seem comfortable with the discussion? If so, great! The facilitator then summarizes the proposals under consideration and helps the group reach agreement quickly.

But suppose some people in the group do not support the proposal – as indicated by statements like, "I don't think this will work, but I don't want to stand in the group's way." The facilitator can support the group to see the implication of these comments – namely, that more thinking would be useful. Then, the facilitator can help them break out of the narrow band of familiar opinions and move their discussion into the *Divergent Zone*.

FACILITATING SUSTAINABLE AGREEMENTS

THE DIVERGENT ZONE

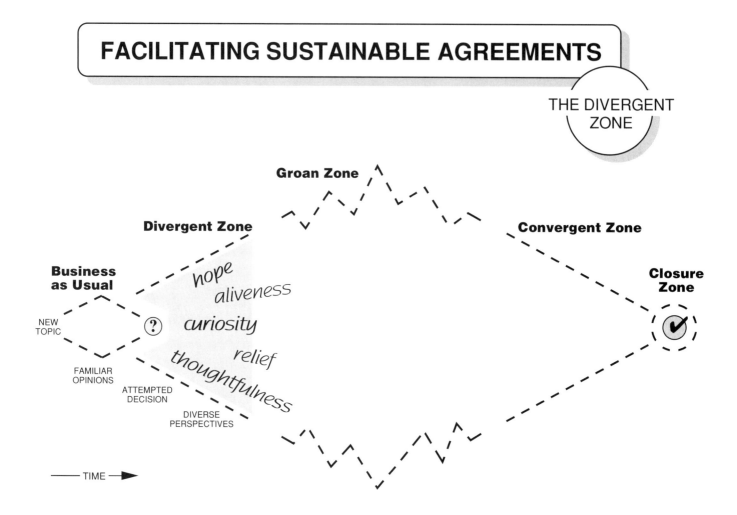

When a facilitator supports a group to move from *Business as Usual* to the *Divergent Zone,* the mood changes dramatically. *Business as Usual* discussions are tedious and stiff; people censor themselves rather than risk being embarrassed by criticism. In contrast, laughter and playfulness are common in the *Divergent Zone.* So are feelings of curiosity and discovery. ("Whoa," said one group member to another. "You mean *that's* your point of view? I had no idea!")

What creates such a difference between the two zones? To a large extent, the answer is simple: *the attitude of suspended judgment.*

Suspended judgment is one of the most important *thinking skills* facilitators can teach their groups. Facilitators can provide groups with opportunities to *experience* suspended judgment through formats like brainstorming and go-arounds. By teaching suspended judgment and by modeling it whenever possible, a respectful, supportive facilitator can create a relaxed, open atmosphere that gives people permission to speak freely – the very essence of divergent thinking.

FACILITATING SUSTAINABLE AGREEMENTS

THE AGONY OF
THE GROAN ZONE

Groan Zone

Divergent Zone

Convergent Zone

**Business
as Usual**

**Closure
Zone**

NEW
TOPIC

confusion   aggravation

frustration   disgust

perplexity   boredom

anxiety

exasperation

FAMILIAR
OPINIONS

ATTEMPTED
DECISION

DIVERSE
PERSPECTIVES

COMPETING FRAMES
OF REFERENCE

SHARED FRAMEWORK
OF UNDERSTANDING

TIME ➔

Once a group has expressed several diverging points of view, the members face a quandary. They often don't understand each other's perspectives very well, yet they may not be able to resolve the issue at hand until they do understand each other. This is one of the fundamental problems of working in groups.

Even in groups whose members get along reasonably well, the *Groan Zone* is agonizing. People have to wrestle with foreign concepts and unfamiliar biases. They have to try to understand other people's reasoning – even when that reasoning leads to a conclusion they don't agree with.

The difficulties are compounded by the fact that many people respond awkwardly to this kind of stress. Under pressure, some people lose their focus and start rambling. Others become short-tempered and rude. Some people feel misunderstood and repeat themselves endlessly. Others get so impatient they'll agree to anything: "Let's just get this over with! Now!"

FACILITATING SUSTAINABLE AGREEMENTS

THE COMMITMENT
TO STRUGGLE

Patience
Perseverance
Tolerance

confusion *aggravation* *frustration* *complexity* *boredom* *anxiety* *exasperation*

NEW
TOPIC
?

FAMILIAR
OPINIONS
ATTEMPTED
DECISION
DIVERSE
PERSPECTIVES
COMPETING FRAMES
OF REFERENCE
SHARED FRAMEWORK
OF UNDERSTANDING
DECISION POINT

TIME →

Many facilitators, especially beginners, think their task is to prevent people from experiencing the pain and frustration groups face in the *Groan Zone*. *This is a mistake.* The only way to insulate a group from the *Groan Zone* is to block them from doing the hard work necessary to build a shared framework of understanding.

What, then, *is* the facilitator's task in the *Groan Zone?* Essentially, the job is to hang in there – hang in and support people while they struggle to understand each other. Support *them* to hang in there with each other; support them not to give up and mentally check out.

The facilitator's tenacity is grounded in a *client-centered attitude* – a faith that the wisdom to solve the problems at hand *will emerge* from the group, as long as people don't give up trying. It is this attitude that allows a facilitator to tolerate the labor pains of authentic collaboration.

FACILITATING SUSTAINABLE AGREEMENTS

THE CONVERGENT ZONE

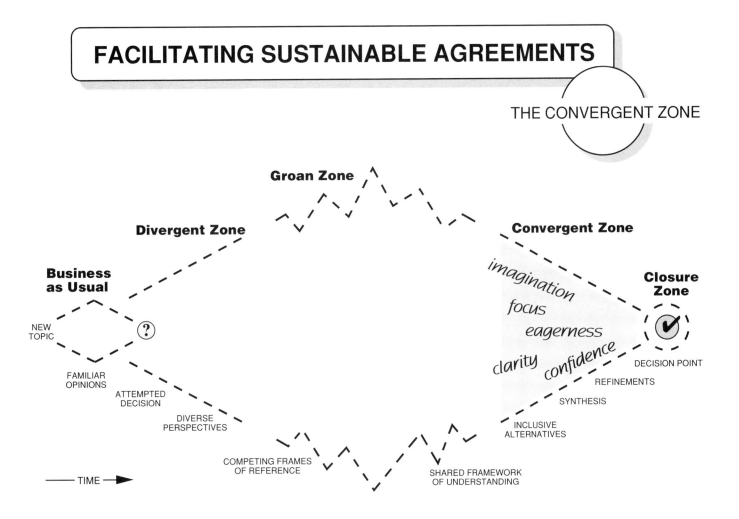

Once a group has a developed a shared framework of understanding, everything feels faster, smoother, easier. The pace of discussion accelerates. People say, "Finally, we're getting something done!" Confidence runs high during this period. People show up on time and stay until the end of the meeting. Between sessions, work that needs to be done gets done.

The experience of searching for an inclusive solution is stimulating and invigorating. People are surprised to discover how well they seem to understand one another. Members now perceive the group as a team. Years later, many people can still remember the *joyful intensity* of this phase.

Facilitators play a double role during this period of a group's work: sometimes teaching and sometimes getting out of the way. It may be crucial for a facilitator to teach participants how to turn an *Either/Or problem* into a *Both/And solution*. Often the facilitator is the only one who recognizes that *Both/And thinking* is even possible. But for much of the time, a facilitator might be reduced to chartwriting and keeping track of time. When this happens, be happy! It means the facilitation is succeeding.

FACILITATING SUSTAINABLE AGREEMENTS

THE EXPERIENCE OF
REACHING CLOSURE

Convergent Zone

truthfulness

alertness

suspense

completion

satisfaction

DECISION POINT

REFINEMENTS

SYNTHESIS

In the *Closure Zone* most people are *focused*. They pay attention to nearly every comment – and most comments are brief and to the point.

These experiences occur, of course, only when the group knows *how the decision will be made*. When a group *does not* have a clear understanding of how they are going to reach closure, the facilitator must look for the earliest opportunity to help the members clarify their decision rules.

The tools for reaching closure might be the single most important set of thinking skills a facilitator can teach a group. The *Gradients of Agreement Scale* helps members discern the *actual* degree of support for a proposal. Furthermore, a meta-decision procedure allows a group to use different decision rules for different circumstances.

Overall, when group members grasp the principles and mechanics of reaching closure, their group's capacity strengthens dramatically.

FACILITATING SUSTAINABLE AGREEMENTS

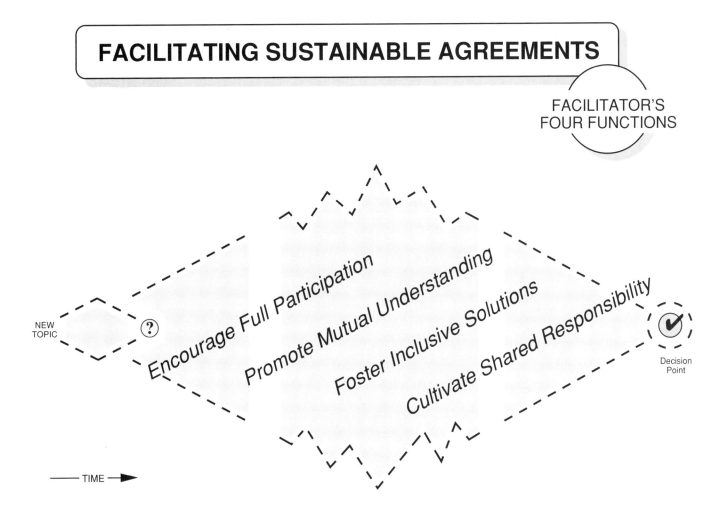

FACILITATOR'S
FOUR FUNCTIONS

NEW TOPIC

Encourage Full Participation

Promote Mutual Understanding

Foster Inclusive Solutions

Cultivate Shared Responsibility

Decision Point

TIME

The facilitator's mission is to support people to do their best thinking. The four functions shown above are the guiding principles for enacting that mission.

Embedded in the four functions are the core values of participatory decision-making. They ground the work of group facilitation. They strengthen individuals. They strengthen the whole group. And they enable groups to tap the deep collective wisdom of their membership to develop intelligent, sane, sustainable agreements.

When we facilitate, we are the "delivery system" for participatory values. We embody them, we express them, and we enact them. As such, we are keepers of the flame – we're the advocates, the teachers, and the midwives – for the emergence of inclusive solutions to the world's toughest problems.

PHOTOCOPYING POLICY

YES: Photocopying portions of this book is encouraged for the purpose of supporting a group you are facilitating.

If a group has retained you as a facilitator to help them solve problems and make decisions, and you feel that your group needs to use one or more of the tools presented in this book, feel free to photocopy and distribute the relevant page(s). We want you to be able to use this book to become as effective as possible at facilitating group decision-making.

NO: Photocopying portions of this book to conduct fee-for-service training requires our written permission.

If a group has retained you specifically to train them in the process of group facilitation, group decision-making, or a related topic, and your primary role is to serve as their trainer, you may not photocopy these pages without express written permission from *Community At Work*. Our policies are fair and supportive, but please ask first. If you are making money from our work, we will ask you to make a reasonable contribution.

BIBLIOGRAPHY

Adams, James. *Conceptual Blockbusting* (4th ed.). Cambridge, MA: Perseus Publishing, 2001.

Atlee, Tom and Rosa Zubizarreta. *The Tao of Democracy: Using Co-Intelligence to Create a World That Works for All.* Eugene, OR: Writers Collective, 2003.

Auvine, Brian et al. *A Manual for Group Facilitators.* Madison, WI: Center for Conflict Resolution, 1978.

Avery, Michel et al. *Building United Judgment.* Madison, WI: Center for Conflict Resolution, 1981.

Beer, Jennifer. *The Mediator's Handbook.* Gabriola Island, BC, Canada: New Society Publishers, 1997.

Bens, Ingrid. *Facilitating with Ease! Core Skills for Facilitators, Team Leaders and Members, Managers, Consultants, and Trainers.* San Francisco: Jossey-Bass, 2005.

Block, Peter. *Flawless Consulting: A Guide to Getting Your Expertise Used* (2nd ed.). San Francisco: Jossey-Bass/Pfeiffer, 2000.

Bray, John, Joyce Lee, Linda L. Smith and Lyle Yorks. *Collaborative Inquiry in Practice: Action Reflection and Making Meaning.* Thousand Oaks, CA: Sage Publications, 2000.

Brown, Juanita, David Isaacs and Margaret J. Wheatly. *World Café: Shaping Our Futures Though Conversations That Matter.* San Francisco: Berrett-Koehler Publishers, 2005.

Bunker, Barbara, and Billie T. Alban. *The Handbook of Large Group Methods: Creating Systemic Change in Organizations and Communities.* San Francisco: Jossey-Bass, 2006.

Butler, C.T. Lawrence and Amy Rothstein. *On Conflict and Consensus.* Cambridge, MA: Food Not Bombs Publishing, 1991.

Cameron, Esther. *Facilitation Made Easy.* London, UK: Kogan Page Limited, 2001.

Carpenter, Susan and W.J.D. Kennedy. *Managing Public Disputes.* San Francisco: Jossey-Bass, 2001.

Chambers, Robert. *Participatory Workshops: A Sourcebook of 21 Sets of Ideas & Activities.* London, UK: Earthscan, 2002.

Chrislip, David. *Collaborative Leadership: How Citizens and Civic Leaders Can Make a Difference.* San Francisco: Jossey-Bass, 1994.

Chrislip, David. *The Collaborative Leadership Fieldbook.* San Francisco: Jossey-Bass, 2002.

Cloud, Henry and John Townsend. *Making Small Groups Work: What Every Small Group Leader Needs to Know.* Grand Rapids, MI: Zondervan Publishing, 2003.

Cochran, Alice Collier. *Roberta's Rules of Order: Sail Through Meetings for Stellar Results Without the Gavel.* San Francisco: Jossey-Bass, 2004.

Conklin, Jeff. *Dialogue Mapping: Building Shared Understanding of Wicked Problems.* West Sussex, UK: John Wiley & Sons, Ltd., 2006.

de Bono, Edward. *Lateral Thinking.* New York: Harper and Row, 1970.

de Bono, Edward. *Serious Creativity.* New York: Harper Collins, 1992.

Doyle, Michael and David Straus. *How to Make Meetings Work.* New York: Berkley Books, 1993.

Estes, Caroline. "Consensus." *In Context* (Autumn 1984): 19-22.

Fisher, Roger, William Ury and Bruce Patton. *Getting to Yes* (2nd ed.). New York: Penguin Books, 1991.

Fisk, Sarah. *Psychological Effects of Involvement in Ecological Restoration.* Ann Arbor, MI: University Microfilms International, 1995.

Gastil, John. *Democracy in Small Groups.* Gabriola Island, B.C.: New Society Publishers, 1993.

Gastil, John and Peter Levine. *Deliberative Democracy Handbook: Strategies for Effective Civic Engagement in the Twenty-First Century.* San Francisco: Jossey-Bass, 2005.

Gesell, Izzy. *Playing Along: 37 Group Learning Activities Borrowed from Improvisational Theater.* Northhampton, MA: Whole Person Associates, 1997.

Gray, Barbara. *Collaborating.* San Francisco: Jossey-Bass, 1989.

Hogan, Christine. *Understanding Facilitation: Theory & Principles.* London, UK: Kogan Page Limited, 2002.

Howard, V.A. and J.H. Barton. *Thinking Together.* New York: William Morrow and Company, 1992.

Howell, Johnna L. *Tools for Facilitating Team Meetings.* Seattle, WA: Integrity Publishing, 1995.

Iacofano, Daniel. *Meeting of the Minds: A Guide to Successful Meeting Facilitation.* Berkeley, CA: MIG Communications, 2001.

Janis, Irving. *Victims of Groupthink* (2nd ed.). Boston: Houghton-Mifflin, 1982.

Janis, Irving and Leon Mann. *Decision Making.* New York: The Free Press, 1977.

Johnson, David W. and Frank P. Johnson. *Joining Together.* Englewood Cliffs, NJ: Prentice-Hall, 1975.

Kaner, Sam. "Promoting Mutual Understanding for Effective Collaboration in Cross-Funcrional Groups with Multiple Stakeholders." In Schuman, Sandy, ed. *The IAF Handbook of Group Facilitation: Best Practices from the Leading Organization in Facilitation.* San Francisco: Jossey-Bass, 2005.

Kaner, Sam. "Five Transformational Leaders Discuss What They've Learned." In Schuman, Sandy, ed. *Creating a Culture of Collaboration: The International Association of Facilitators Handbook.* San Francisco: Jossey-Bass, 2006.

Kaner, Sam, Eileen Palmer and Duane Berger. "What Can O.D. Professionals Learn From Grassroots Peace Activists?" *Vision/Action*, 9 (1989): 8 -12.

Kearny, Lynn. *The Facilitator's Toolkit*. Amherst, MA: HRD Press, 1995.

Kelsey, Dee and Pam Plumb. *Great Meetings! Great Results*. Portland, ME: Great Meetings! Inc., 2004.

Kepner, C.H. and Tregoe, B.B. *The New Rational Manager*. Princeton, NJ: Kepner-Tregoe, 1997.

Lakey, George, Berit Lakey, Rod Napier and Janice M. Robinson. *Grassroots and Nonprofit Leadership: A Guide for Organizations in Changing Times*. Gabriola Island, B.C.: New Society Publishers, 1996.

Lencioni, Patrick M. *Death by Meeting: A Leadership Fable*. San Francisco: Jossey-Bass, 2004.

Lind, Lenny with Karl Danskin and Todd Erickson. "Interactive Meeting Technologies." In Bunker, Barbara, and Billie T. Alban. *The Handbook of Large Group Methods: Creating Systemic Change in Organizations and Communities*. San Francisco: Jossey-Bass, 2006.

Means, Janet A. and Tammy Adams. *Facilitating the Project Lifecycle: The Skills & Tools to Accelerate Progress for Project Managers, Facilitators, and Six Sigma Project Teams*. San Francisco: Jossey-Bass, 2005

Michalko, Michael. *Thinkertoys*. Berkeley, CA: Ten Speed Press, 1991.

Nelson, Jo. *The Art of Focused Conversation for Schools*. Gabriola Island, BC, Canada: New Society Publishers, 2001

Nutt, Paul C. *Making Tough Decisions*. San Francisco: Jossey-Bass, 1989.

Osborne, Alex. *Applied Imagination: Principles and Procedures of Creative Problem-Solving* (3rd ed.). Hadley, MA.: Creative Education Foundation, 1993.

Owen, Harrison. *Open Space Technology: A User's Guide*. San Francisco: Berrett-Koehler Publishers, 1997.

Parker, Marjorie. *Creating Shared Vision*. Clarendon Hills, IL: Dialog International, Ltd., 1990.

Patterson, Kerry, Joseph Grenny, Ron McMillan, Al Switzler and Sephen R. Covey. *Crucial Conversations: Tools for Talking When Stakes are High*. New York: McGraw-Hill, 2002.

Phillips, Gerald M. and Julia T. Wood. *Emergent Issues in Human Decision Making*. Carbondale, IL: Southern Illinois University Press, 1984.

Roberts, Joan M. *Alliances, Coalitions and Partnerships: Building Collaborative Organizations*. Gabriola Island, BC, Canada: New Society Publishers, 2004.

Rogers, Carl R. *The Carl Rogers Reader*. Edited by Howard Kirschenbaum and Valerie Land Henderson. Boston: Houghton Mifflin, 1989.

Russo, J. Edward and Paul J.H. Shoemaker. *Decision Traps*. New York: Simon and Schuster, 1989.

Schrage, Michael. *Shared Minds: The New Technologies of Collaboration.* New York: Random House, 1990.

Schuman, Sandy. *The IAF Handbook of Group Facilitation: Best Practices from the Leading Organization in Facilitation.* San Francisco: Jossey-Bass, 2005.

Schuman, Sandy. *Creating a Culture of Collaboration: The International Association of Facilitators Handbook.* San Francisco: Jossey-Bass, 2006.

Schwarz, Roger. *The Skilled Facilitator.* San Francisco: Jossey-Bass, 2002.

Senge, Peter M., Art Kleiner, Charlotte Roberts, Rick Ross and Bryan Smith. *The Fifth Discipline Fieldbook.* New York: Currency, 1994.

Sheeran, Michael J. *Beyond Majority Rule.* Philadelphia: Philadelphia Yearly Meeting of the Religious Society of Friends, Book Services Committee, 1983.

Shields, Katrina. *In the Tiger's Mouth: An Empowerment Guide for Social Action.* Philadelphia and Gabriola Island, B.C.: New Society Publishers, 1994.

Sibbet, David. *I See What You Mean.* San Francisco: Sibbet and Associates, 1981.

Sibbet, David. *Principles of Facilitation: The Purpose and Potential of Leading Group Process.* San Francisco: The Grove Consultants, 2002.

Spencer, Laura J. *Winning through Participation.* Dubuque, IA: Kendall/Hunt Publishing Co., 1989.

Stanfield, R. Brian. *The Workshop Book: From Individual Creativity to Group Action.* Gabriola Isalnd, BC, Canada: New Society Publishers, 2002.

Stone, Douglas, Bruce Patton, Sheila Heen, and Roger Fisher. *Difficult Conversations: How to Discuss What Matters Most.* New York: Penguin Books, 2000.

Strachan, Dorothy. *Making Questions Work: A Guide to How and What to Ask for Facilitators, Consultants, Managers, Coaches, and Educators.* San Francisco: Jossey-Bass, 2006.

Strauss, David. *How to Make Collaboration Work: Powerful Ways to Build Consensus, Solve Problems, and Make Decisions.* San Francisco: Berrett-Koehler Publishers, 2002.

Toldi, Catherine. *Collaborative Thinking: Becoming a Community That Learns.* Ann Arbor, MI: University Microfilms International, 1993.

Troxel, James P. *Participation Works: Business Cases from Around the World.* Alexandra, VA: Miles River Press, 1993.

VanGundy, Jr., Arthur B. *Techniques of Structured Problem-Solving* (2nd ed.). New York: John Wiley and Sons, Inc.,1998.

Weisbord, Marvin. *Productive Workplaces, Revisited: Organizing and Managing for Dignity, Meaning and Community in the 21st Century.* San Francisco: Jossey-Bass/Pfeiffer, 2004.

Williams, R. Bruce. *More Than Fifty Ways to Build Team Consensus.* Palatine, IL: IRI/Skylight Publishing, 1993.

Wilson, Priscilla H. *The Facilitative Way: Leadership That Makes the Difference.* Shawnee Mission, KS: Team Tech Press, 2003.

ACKNOWLEDGMENTS

The ideas contained in this book are the result of contributions from many people whose names do not appear on the cover.

The first and most important acknowledgment goes to our editor, Barbara Hirshkowitz, whose vision and commitment to this project is the reason this book exists. In early 1988 Barbara took Sam and Duane on a retreat and convinced us to write a serious theoretical book on participatory decision-making. Over the next four years, with help from an ever-changing team of co-thinkers, we wrote countless drafts and felt dissatisfied with them all. Barbara patiently encouraged us to keep going. In late 1993, Barbara saw that we had produced about a hundred pages of facilitation tools, and she persuaded us to publish the book you are now reading. So Barbara shepherded us through two years more of revising and adding and reorganizing and ambivalating . . . And finally, thanks to Barbara's unwavering faith and persistence, you have in hand the results of her labor.

Second recognition goes to Kathe Sweeney, our editor at Jossey-Bass. Kathe was instrumental in bringing the second edition into existence. For four patient years, she encouraged us to update this book and make it available to the vast audience of Jossey-Bass readers. Without her perseverance we would not have this created this edition. Beyond her editorial relationship to Community At Work, we are also deeply grateful to Kathe for her vision and stewardship in promoting group facilitation, both as a profession and as a calling. She has been midwife to many important books on collaboration, facilitation, and participatory values – books that may never have been written without her support and gentle guidance. In the true sense of the word, Kathe Sweeney is a leader in our field.

Many colleagues and friends contributed to the development of the second edition. We are particularly indebted to Libby Bachhuber, who joined the staff of Community At Work in 1999, and who worked diligently for the next six years to help us improve the logic of our most frequently used pages. Libby's insights into the application of those tools led to numerous upgrades. She was the person who kept track of all revisions that found their way into this edition. Her determination to get the details right inspired us to keep working to clarify our reasoning and strengthen our writing.

Susan Lubeck and Sunny Sabbini also joined the staff of Community At Work in 1999, and both contributed in many ways to the development of material for this edition. Susan Lubeck, now a senior associate at Community At Work, put much effort into strengthening our tools for reaching closure. Many of the revisions in our chapters on decision-making were occasioned by her suggestions. Susan has been facilitating and teaching from *Facilitator's Guide* since the book's inception, and she drew from her broad experience to give us many ideas for other improvements. Sunny Sabbini is now a collaboration specialist at Community At Work. For five years until 2004 she served as client relations coordinator. In that role she collected feedback from countless readers on the book's strengths and improvables. She thus provided us with a steady stream of suggestions for making the book more useful to our audience.

Many other people deserve to be mentioned for their suggestions or their help in preparing the manuscript for the second edition. Evi Kahle was a constant source of assistance and advice in 1995-2000. Diane Dohm assisted with the editing of our materials in 2002-03. Buffy Balderston assisted with editing and production in 2004-06. Karen Jovin gave us many useful ideas for improving Chapter 3. Roxane White provided incredibly helpful editorial assistance during the final stage of editing. Thanks to each of you for the many ways your support made this book a better product.

We also heard from several people who pointed us to books and articles worth including in the bibliography. Thanks to Miriam Abrams, Carmen Acton, Muriel Adcock, Teresa Archaga, Kate Armstrong, Emmanuel Asomba, Susan Auerbach, Vicky Baugh, Candee Basford, Lisa Behrendt, Leslie Boies, Tree Bressen, Trish Cypher, Shoshanna Cogan, Lisa DeGroot, Stacey Duccini, Anne Forbes, Scott Gassman, Gayle Gifford, Michael Hailu, Gloria Hargrove, Doug Horton, Cynthia Josayma, Julie King, Eliska Meyers, Jady Dederich Montgomery, Kathryn Moran, Cookie Murphy/Pettee, Wayne Nelson, Evan Paul, Laura Peck, Jim Roscoe, Cathy Stones, Mady Shumofsky, and Odin Zackman. Thank you each for your thoughtfulness and your generosity.

Many colleagues and friends influenced the development of the first edition of this book. Herman Gyr and Eileen Palmer deserve to be singled out for first honors. They each made deeply significant contributions over several years time. We hold them both in gratitude and high esteem.

We would also like to thank several others who contributed to the first edition. Marianne Laruffa gave her wholehearted support and encouragement to this project in its earliest forms, from 1988–1990. Rick Peterson helped refine the organization and logic of early drafts in 1990–91. David Barkan in 1990 was the first "road-tester" of the meta-decision-making procedures described in Chapter 19. Pat Morris in 1990-91 co-authored the second draft of our collection of structured thinking activities. Gene Bush, who since 1992 has given us countless hours of perceptive editorial advice, also provided the insightful critique which led us to discover the Groan Zone. Jim MacQueen co-authored a 1992 draft of the decision-making chapters. David Kirkpatrick co-authored early drafts of two structured thinking activities. Amaran Tarnoff co-authored early drafts of many pages for Chapter 7. Nancy Feinstein drafted an introduction to Chapter 7. Julie King copyedited a draft of the full manuscript. Ritch Davidson co-authored two structured thinking activities. Michael Tertes co-authored drafts of six case studies for Chapter 16. He also co-authored early drafts of four structured thinking activities. Ritch Davidson, Rob Lawrence, Mitch Glanz, Nancy Feinstein, and Melanie Burnett were readers for the final draft. Sam Fisk was the behind-the-scenes maestro who kept everything running smoothly. Evi Kahle edited and contributed to the logic of Chapters 6, 14, 15, 16 and 20, and her dedication and enthusiasm sustained us through our last year of writing.

We would like to extend our appreciation to the proprietors of the cafes where much of this book was actually written. In San Francisco thanks to *Farley's, Cup O' Blues, The Daily Scoop, Thinker's Cafe, La Boheme, Radio Valencia,* and *Sally's.* In Aptos, a nod to the *Red Apple Cafe.* Also, a special thank you to a special host. Desideriamo ringraziare i proprietari della Nave in Sperlonga, per le affabili ed affettuose attenzioni elargite a Sam mentre scriveva le revisioni di questo libro. Il calore umano ed un illimitato senso di ospitalità di tutta la famiglia hanno lasciato un profondo segno che può ancora essere sentito tra le righe di ogni pagina. We want to express our gratitude to the proprietors of La Nave in Sperlonga, Italy, who treated Sam so graciously while he wrote the first revisions of this book. The whole family's warmth and their boundless hospitality left an afterglow that can still be felt between the lines on every page.

Last, our deep appreciation goes to Gene Bush, Monika Steger and Paul Blakely. You opened your homes and your hearts to us, and loaned us your partners – often at personal sacrifice. You share our success as your own.

THE AUTHORS

SAM KANER, Ph.D.

Sam Kaner is the founder of *Community At Work*. His first full-time job as a facilitator was in 1978. In the decades since, he has dedicated his career to studying and teaching collaborative processes, and to consulting with innovative organizations that seek sustainable solutions to the world's toughest problems.

LENNY LIND

Lenny Lind is president of the organization development firm CoVision. He is a pioneer in the field of computer-assisted meetings and he is a codeveloper of WebCouncil - a fast feedback system designed for facilitators. Lenny is the creative force who crafted the design of this book.

CATHERINE TOLDI, M.A.

Catherine Toldi is a collaboration specialist and Zen Buddhist priest. She specializes in working with educators, non-profit managers and community organizations. For 30 years, she has supported her clients and students to bring both structure and heart to their planning and problem-solving efforts.

SARAH FISK, Ph.D.

Sarah Fisk is an organization development consultant specializing in collaborative systems change and participatory decision-making. As a senior associate at *Community at Work,* she devotes her consulting practice to helping groups and individuals develop their ability to be authentic in pursuit of sustainable solutions to complex situations.

DUANE BERGER, M.A.

Duane Berger is director of Insights & Applications at *Community At Work.* He has studied group dynamics and participatory decision-making for 30 years, and he has been a co-thinker and co-developer of virtually all of the *Community At Work* models and methods for putting participatory values into practice.

INDEX

Conventional groups vs. participatory groups, xvi

Conventional wisdom, discussion reflecting, 8, 10. *See also* Business-as-usual discussion

Convergence and alignment, level of involvement in, 175

Convergent thinking: divergent thinking vs., 6; and the Groan Zone, 19; in an idealized model, 13, 17; prematurely promoting, 201; problem-solving model based on divergent thinking and, questions about, 7; in a realistic model, 18; teaching about, 145; types of, 239–262

Convergent Zone: discussion in the, 262; facilitator's main task in the, 238, 309; ingenuity of the, 262; model reflecting the, 20, 21, 145, 197, 200, 204, 222, 302, 304. *See also specific elements of the Convergent Zone*

Core competency, indispensable, 21

Core values, 24, 25, 26, 27, 28, 29, 165, 311

Costs: reducing, 258; sorting by, 126, 129

Creative problem solving, promoting, 239, 240

Creative reframing, 239, 249–255, 262

Creative thinking: activities for, 213, 215; allowing for, 119. *See also* Brainstorming

Creativity, prelude to, 5

Crisis, making a decision in the midst of a, 273

Critical reasoning, emphasis on, 239, 256

Critical success factors, identifying, 165

Criticism: overcoming the tendency for, 12; of the person-in-charge, 148; premature, cost of, 118; questioning perceived as, 225

Crowded pages, avoiding, 70

Culture change, profound, steward of, 36

D

de Bono, E., 119, 213, 215

Dead ends, reaching, 11

Debriefing, 115, 124, 215

Decision point: confusion over the, 267; early, 9, 192, 193, 196; following divergent and convergent thinking, 6, 7, 13, 17; hypothetical, 4; meaning of the, 266; at mid-point, announcing, 16; as part of the Closure Zone, 20, 21, 197, 204, 302; progress up to the, 200; in a realistic model, 18, 19; in relation to gathering diverse perspectives, 206, 213, 216, 220

Decision procedures: designing, 300; installing, 301

Decision rules, clear: establishing, benefiting from, 302; importance of, 266–274, 310; need for flexibility vs., 290

Decision-makers, providing input to, that are not in attendance, 106

Decision-making capabilities, improving, 168

Decision-making dynamics, group, 4–21, 196, 197

Decisions: confusion over reaching, 267; by delegation, 268; high-stakes and low-stakes, 270, 271, 272, 273, 282, 283, 293; impact of, duration of, level of support based on, 282; ineffective, making, 193, 196; making, as a meeting goal, 162, 166, 184; poor timing of, 16; pseudo-, avoiding

temptation to make, 222; quickly reaching, 9, 25, 192, 196, 198, 238, 270, 290, 293; sabotaging, 273. *See also* Meta-decisions

Deference to the person-in-charge, overcoming group's tendency toward, 148

Delegation, making decisions by, 268

Desirability, sorting by, 126, 129

Desired outcomes: clarifying, 184; defining, 158, 171; producing, 177; two types of, 160, 161; viewing, as goals, 157. *See also* Meeting goals; Overall goals

Devil's advocate: playing, 51; thinking as a, 272

Diamond of Participatory Decision-Making, 20–21, 197, 304. *See also* Business as Usual; Closure Zone; Convergent Zone; Divergent Zone; Groan Zone

Difficult decisions, 166

Difficult dynamics, dealing with, 136–154

Difficult issues, raising, 205, 216–219, 220

Difficult people, difficult dynamics producing, 139

Difficult problems: acknowledging, and creating a structure to solve, 197; attempting to solve, as if they were routine, 9, 10, 193, 194; level of support needed for, 282, 283

Discussion: after brainstorming, 124; back-and-forth, discouraging, 218; and confusion over whether a decision has been made, 267; decision rules that encourage, 272; of decision-making procedure, 301; early rounds of, dynamics of, 8, 50; ending, common procedures for, 299; extensive, and involvement level, 174, 175; flow of, organizing the, 77–78; focusing a, 76, 82–86; frequent chartwriting during, 148; getting bogged down during, dealing with, 143; goofing around in the midst of, problem of, responding to, 149; having the person-in-charge leave during, 148; inviting groups to resume, 49; jump-starting a, 96; over categories, 128; period of, behavior during, 266; philosophical, issue with, 127; rules to end, explaining the need for, 300; stimulating, using case studies for, 242; stopping point in, reaching, 291; as a whole, taking time to reflect on, 115. *See also* Business-as-usual discussion; Open discussion

Disillusionment, 21

Disputing participants, problem of, responding to, 152

Disrespect, problem of, responding to, 150

Distractions, outside, acknowledging, 142, 144

Distrust, 16, 201

Divergent perspectives. *See* Diverse/divergent perspectives

Divergent thinking: attempted step-backs in, 15; convergent thinking vs., 6; decisions in, 9; discussion in, 8; eliciting, 98; encouraging, 25; essence of, 306; exploring possibilities in, 12; and the Groan Zone, 19; in an idealized model, 13, 17; and no obvious solution, 10; problem-solving model based on convergent thinking and, questions about, 7; reaching a dead end in, 11; in a

ple to, 235; of participants, preserving, 94; on the process, not content, 143; shifting, helping members with, 147

Follow-through, poor, problem of, responding to, 151, 261

Format, in chartwriting, 68–69

Frame, the, setting, 114, 301

Frames of reference, multiple. *See* Diverse/divergent perspectives

Framework of understanding, sharing a. *See* Shared framework of understanding

Framing, 86

Full participation: benefit of, 29; as a core value, described, 24; effect of, 25; encouraging, 24, 32, 33, 37, 62, 121, 142, 149, 151, 311; strengthening, 62

Full responsibility, person-in-charge assuming, 273

G

Gallery tour, the, 105

Genuinely liked items, all, voting for, 131

Geschka, H., 214

Global Access Technologies, 294

Goals: asking a person-in-charge about, questions for, 171; new, listing, and listing obstacles, 122; shared, underlying, searching for, 241; viewing desired outcomes as, 157. *See also* Meeting goals; Overall goals

Go-arounds. *See* Structured go-arounds

Good ideas, strengthening, 239, 256–261, 262

Goofing around, problem of, responding to, 149

Gradients of Agreement Scale: adapting the, 286; benefit of, 310; describing, to the group, 301; description of, 278; reading the, 280, 281, 284, 285; showing the, 300; using the, 279, 292

Gray, B., 245

Green Party, chapters of the, 276, 292

Griggs, R. E., 215

Groan Zone: agony of the, 307; existence of, acknowledging the, 19; facilitator's main objective in the, 222, 308; guiding a group through the, demonstrating ability in, 83; idealized sequence lacking in the, 192; inevitability of the, 197; knee-jerk reaction plunging groups into the, 124; levels of involvement that push groups into the, 175; major cause of frustration and confusion of the, 231; model reflecting the, 20, 21, 197, 200, 204, 304; needing relief from the, 232; philosophical discussion putting groups into the, 127; pressure felt by the person-in-charge in the, 277; and pseudo-solutions, 193; struggle of the, 262; surviving the, and the need for facilitation, 32; synonym for the, 76; teaching about the, 145; temptation to make a pseudo-decision in the, 222; types of thinking in the, 223, 224–234, 235. *See also specific elements of the Groan Zone*

Ground rules: for brainstorming, 120; in building a list, 92, 97, 154; clear, establishing, importance of, 119; and group behavior, 92; proposing, to deal with disrespectful behavior, 150; reviewing, 213, 215; for small groups, 103; in structured go-arounds, 100, 101

Group behavior: different domains of, 266; effect of decision rules on, 274; following a misunderstanding, 223; patterns of, discussing, 145; shifting, 92

Group cohesion, building, 147

Group decision-making dynamics, 3–21, 196, 197

Group dynamics, educating members about, 142, 145

Group integrity, restoring, 115

Group members: as human, 5; as meta-decision makers, 298

Group memory, power of, 62

Group norms, 33, 51, 138, 167

Group voice, writing with a, 72

Groups: participatory vs. conventional, xvi; stronger, 24, 29, 37, 311. *See also* Small groups; Whole groups

H

Habits of thought, breaking, 252

Hammond-Landau, J., 64

Helpful people/resources, listing, 122

Hidden beliefs or assumptions, listing, 122

Hierarchy, speaking in a, 148

High autonomy, level of support necessary for, 283

High investment, level of support necessary for, 283

Highlighting, use of colors for, 65

High-priority items, selecting, 124, 131, 132, 165

High-stakes decisions: level of support needed for, 282, 283; major decision rules for, uses and implications of, 270, 271, 272, 273; and reaching closure, 293

Hog Farm, the, 276

Hollister School District Strategic Planning Team, 296

Honest advice, group members giving, 272

Hope, instilling, 58

Hospitality Valuation Financial Services, 295

Hot colors, using, 65

Hypothetical model, 4

I

Idealized models, 13, 17, 192

Ideas: attachment to, 5; calling out, suggestions for, 97; emphasis on, 205, 213; fairly treating all, 121; gathering, 47, 213; good, strengthening, 239, 256–261, 262; ignoring, 42; posting, on sticky notes, 210; testing out, 110; volume of, generated by divergent thinking, feeling overwhelmed by, 124; world of, operating in the, 266. *See also* Listing ideas

Imagination, use of, encouraging, 119, 238

Impact, duration of, level of support needed based on, 282, 283

330

Themes: asking for, 86; grouping ideas into, 130; identifying, 113; informal discussion of, 104; losing track of, 5; meaningful, assessing, activity for, 228; restating, 60; sorting ideas into, 165

Thick-lined letters, using, 64

Thinking: advancing the, as a meeting goal, 162, 163, 165, 166, 177; fast-paced, 238; and feeling together, 276; including "devil's advocate" form of, 272; new, prompting, 210; point that separates, from action, 266; in public, injunctions against, 136, 138; refinement in, 238, 239, 262; rough-draft, 65, 95, 118, 138; under stress, symptoms exhibited in, 139; structured, opportunity for, offering an, 204, 206, 224, 249, 256, 262; whole new way of, doorway into a, 153. *See also* Convergent thinking; Divergent thinking

Thoughts and learnings, asking people to share, 103, 207

Three complaints activity, 219

Time: dividing, by group members, 185; expected, setting the, 114; more, negotiating for, 241; most efficient use of, 119; remaining, announcing the, 97, 103, 107, 121; for training, scheduling in, 168

Time estimates: giving, before beginning an activity, 97, 100, 103, 107; making, for activities, 158, 174, 178; realistic, reporting, 179; typical, for small group variations, 104

Time investment: in agenda planning, 187; in creative reframing, initial resistance to, overcoming, 251; in determining who else needs to be consulted, 260; for solving problems, mindsets and, 199

Time limits: clear, establishing, 119, 121; maximum, for processes calling for suspended judgment, 119

Time needed, sorting by, 129

Time requirements, for meetings, 181, 182, 183, 184, 185, 186

Timing, poor, 16, 118

Titling pages, 72, 73, 154, 208, 209, 210, 231

Toldi, C., 20

Tolerance, 119, 175, 235, 308

Tone of voice, communicating feelings through, 53

Topics: as a component of meetings, 157, 158, 174; deepening understanding of, 102; defining and distilling, 113; different, discussing, at the same time, problem of, responding to, 150; goals for, defining, 160; identifying, 158, 170, 179; major, as part of the agenda, 181; overview of, providing, 100; possible, identifying and listing, 187; reducing complexity of, 96; restating, 100; sequence of, belief about meeting process and, 90

Toss the beanbag method, 101

Tour groups, 105

Tracking, 49, 85, 150

Tradeshow, 95, 109

Tradition, breaking with, case study of, 243

Training time, scheduling, 168

Transitioning to meetings, 146, 147

Trends, major, increasing knowledge of, 168

Triads, working in, benefit of, 93

Trigger method, the, 214

Trivial procedures, quibbling over, problem of, responding to, 153

Troublemakers, including, in the solution, case study of, 246

Trust-building: and check-ins, 147; and mirroring, 46; tool for, 225

Trust-levels, 235

Truth, the: courage required for speaking, 148; holders of, saying about, 24; supporting expression of, 54

2–4–2 approach, 104

2–4–8 approach, 104

"Two rounds or more" approach, 104

"Two rounds" polling method, 287

Two Truths and a Lie activity, 233

U

Unacceptable communication styles, 42, 43

Unanimity: power of, 276; striving for, 276–287; switching from, to majority vote, 292; using, as the decision rule, 148, 268, 270, 272, 274, 276, 292

Unanimous, meaning of, 276

Unconventional solutions, generating a list of, 96

Underlining, 70

Understanding: deeper, simplest way to gain, 224; emphasis on, 223; of a problem, searching for, 96; of a topic, deepening, 102. *See also* Mutual understanding; Shared framework of understanding

Unexpressed concerns, listing, 122

Unfinished business, 142, 182

Unrepresented perspectives, determining, activity for, 212

Unsustainable agreements, case study of, 194

Urban Strategies Council Leadership Technical Team, 297

Urgency, sorting by, 129

Ury, W., 244

V

Validating, 43, 54, 55, 57, 58, 62, 83, 207, 218

Value systems, contrasting, 199

Values, core, 24, 25, 26, 27, 28, 29, 165, 311

VanGundy, A. B., Jr., 209, 214

Verbs, priority of, 72

Veto capacity, 276

VISA International, 294

"Vote to vote" procedure, 292

Voting: on high-priority items, 131; making decisions by, 267, 271, 272, 274, 292

W

Watsonville Healthy Families Collaborative, 295

Weisbord, M., 36

Welcoming activity, beginning with a, 179

CoVISION

CoVision is an organization development firm that supports clients in their best efforts to achieve *extensive discussion* and *alignment,* especially in large and important meetings. (See page 175.)

CoVision's primary methodology, called WebCouncil, uses software running on a network of laptop computers distributed to participants throughout a meeting. This "groupware" system makes it possible for participants to give feedback quickly in response to presentations and discussions. This, in turn, allows for themes to be distilled from the feedback, and responded to by presenters, persons-in-charge, or participants. In this manner, even large groups have a solid chance to build shared understanding and alignment in time frames commonly spent on *presenting and reporting* only.

Over 15 years, CoVision has supported hundreds of facilitators and consultants in the use of the WebCouncil method. In the client cases of many of these facilitators, situations arise where an upcoming meeting is seen as critical to the organization. In those cases, extra attention and resources are given to ensure sucessful outcomes. It is in these situations where CoVision adds the most value, supporting facilitators as they provide fast-feedback capabilities to their clients. CoVision gives advice about, for example, planning the agenda, selecting various fast-feedback processes, making transitions, managing difficult dynamics, or coaching the persons-in-charge.

This methodology has proven effective in groups of 15 to 5,000 participants. In the first Clinton Global Initiative conference in New York, 800 world leaders spent two days in interactive panel discussions enabled by WebCouncil. The mayor of Washington, DC, held four Citizen Summits, each engaging 3,000 citizens with fast-feedback processes. CoVision has supported the World Economic Forum as well as scores of Fortune 500 companies – often in alignment meetings of 80 to 300 executives.

For further information, contact Lenny Lind at 1-800-318-3521.

COMMUNITY AT WORK

Since its founding in 1987, Community At Work has been both a think tank and a consulting firm. Our motto is "building models of collaboration and putting them into practice."

AS A THINK TANK Our purpose is to study the actual dynamics of collaboraton and group decision-making – and to build more accurate models – in order to support people to find sustainable solutions to the world's toughest problems.

We intend our models to combine insights from psychology and the other human sciences with the practical ingenuity of the business community, grounded in a philosophy of social responsibility.

AS A CONSULTING FIRM We are organization development professionals. We specialize in providing collaborative approaches that enable our clients to address their most perplexing, system-level challenges.

Community At Work's consulting services have been put to good use in many different work-settings, from high tech to health care. Over time we have developed content-expertise in social entrepreneurship, community-based planning, and social enterprise. We also have numerous clients in education, human services, environmental health and international development.

To support our clients in their work we employ a variety of consulting competencies: we assess and diagnose; we facilitate; we coach; we create, test and produce relevant models; we project-manage; we advise; we conduct training to build capacity – all this and more, as dictated by the needs at hand.

A distinctive feature of our work is a determination to support our clients to think *intelligently* about the challenges they face. We are committed to helping people learn skills for putting participatory values into practice. To this end we provide clients with training in the concepts and skills of collaboration.

TRAINING FROM COMMUNITY AT WORK

Over the past 20 years, thousands of people have strengthened their facilitation skills at workshops offered by *Community At Work*.

GROUP FACILITATION SKILLS
PUTTING PARTICIPATORY VALUES INTO PRACTICE

This acclaimed 3-day workshop provides experiential training in the methods described in *Facilitator's Guide to Participatory Decision-Making*. The program gives participants numerous opportunities to practice new skills and receive feedback. This workshop is internationally recognized as one of the best available trainings in the essentials of collaboration. It has been delivered under the sponsorship of organizations as diverse as United Nations, World Bank, VISA International, Annie E. Casey Foundation, City of Edmonton, University of California, Girl Scouts, Lexis Nexis, Denver Human Services and more than 300 other businesses, foundations, NGOs, schools, CBOs, and government agencies.

LEADER AS FACILITATOR
GROUP FACILITATION SKILLS FOR MANAGERS

This workshop is specifically tailored for project managers, unit supervisors, and others who are responsible for heading up work-teams. The course emphasizes methods for balancing the responsibilities of leadership with the goal of reaching decisions that everyone owns and supports. Participants have ample opportunity to practice and receive feedback. At the request of our clients, this program has often been customized to meet specialized objectives. The course has been taught at many large organizations including Symantec, Schwab, Hewlett-Packard, Kaiser-Permanente, PricewaterhouseCoopers, Mercer, and many other Fortune 1000 companies and government departments.

For more information

Community At Work
1 Tubbs Street
San Francisco, CA 94107

Phone: (415) 282-9876
Fax: (415) 282-9878
www.CommunityAtWork.com